REPORTING CHILD ABUSE AND NEGLECT

ASPECTS AND SUMMARIES OF STATE LAWS

CHILDREN'S ISSUES, LAWS AND PROGRAMS

Additional books in this series can be found on Nova's website
under the Series tab.

Additional E-books in this series can be found on Nova's website
under the E-books tab.

CHILDREN'S ISSUES, LAWS AND PROGRAMS

REPORTING CHILD ABUSE AND NEGLECT

ASPECTS AND SUMMARIES OF STATE LAWS

HENRY J. PERVALL
EDITOR

Nova Science Publishers, Inc.

New York

For permission to use material from this book please contact us:
Telephone 631-231-7269; Fax 631-231-8175
Web Site: http://www.novapublishers.com

NOTICE TO THE READER

The Publisher has taken reasonable care in the preparation of this book, but makes no expressed or implied warranty of any kind and assumes no responsibility for any errors or omissions. No liability is assumed for incidental or consequential damages in connection with or arising out of information contained in this book. The Publisher shall not be liable for any special, consequential, or exemplary damages resulting, in whole or in part, from the readers' use of, or reliance upon, this material. Any parts of this book based on government reports are so indicated and copyright is claimed for those parts to the extent applicable to compilations of such works.

Independent verification should be sought for any data, advice or recommendations contained in this book. In addition, no responsibility is assumed by the publisher for any injury and/or damage to persons or property arising from any methods, products, instructions, ideas or otherwise contained in this publication.

This publication is designed to provide accurate and authoritative information with regard to the subject matter covered herein. It is sold with the clear understanding that the Publisher is not engaged in rendering legal or any other professional services. If legal or any other expert assistance is required, the services of a competent person should be sought. FROM A DECLARATION OF PARTICIPANTS JOINTLY ADOPTED BY A COMMITTEE OF THE AMERICAN BAR ASSOCIATION AND A COMMITTEE OF PUBLISHERS.

Additional color graphics may be available in the e-book version of this book.

Library of Congress Cataloging-in-Publication Data

Reporting Child abuse and neglect : aspects and summaries of state laws / editors, Henry J. Pervall.
  p. cm.
  Includes index.
  ISBN 978-1-62100-157-7 (hardcover)
  1. Child abuse--Law and legislation--United States--States. I. Pervall, Henry J.
  KF9323.C56 2011
  344.7303'276--dc23

                                                                          2011031031

Published by Nova Science Publishers, Inc. † New York

CONTENTS

PREFACE

All fifty States, the District of Columbia, American Samoa, Guam, the Northern Mariana Islands, Puerto Rico and the U.S. Virgin Islands have statutes specifying procedures that State agencies must follow in handling reports of suspected child abuse or neglect. This book presents aspects and summaries of state laws in regards to reporting child abuse and neglect. Some of the aspects discussed are the mandatory reporters of child abuse and neglect; cross-reporting among responders; making and screening reports of child abuse and neglect; penalties for failure to report and false reporting and immunity for reporters of child abuse and neglect.

Chapter 1- All States, the District of Columbia, American Samoa, Guam, the Northern Mariana Islands, Puerto Rico, and the U.S. Virgin Islands have statutes identifying persons who are required to report child maltreatment under specific circumstances.

Chapter 2- All 50 States, the District of Columbia, American Samoa, Guam, the Northern Mariana Islands, Puerto Rico, and the U.S. Virgin Islands have statutes specifying procedures that State agencies must follow in handling reports of suspected child abuse or neglect. In most States, these procedures include requirements for cross-system reporting and/or information sharing among professional entities. Typically, reports are shared among social services agencies, law enforcement departments, and prosecutors' offices.

Chapter 3- Every State, the District of Columbia, American Samoa, Guam, the Northern Mariana Islands, Puerto Rico, and the U.S. Virgin Islands have statutes that identify persons who are required to report child maltreatment under specific circumstances. Approximately 26 States currently include members of the clergy among those professionals specifically mandated by law to report known or suspected instances of child abuse or neglect. In approximately 18 States and Puerto Rico, any person who suspects child abuse or neglect is required to report. This inclusive language appears to include clergy but may be interpreted otherwise.

Chapter 4- All 50 States, the District of Columbia, American Samoa, Guam, the Northern Mariana Islands, Puerto Rico, and the U.S. Virgin Islands have laws and policies that specify procedures for making and responding to reports of suspected child abuse or neglect. Mandated reporters are required by States to make an immediate report when they suspect or know of abusive or neglectful situations. In all jurisdictions, the initial report may be made orally to either the child protective services (CPS) agency or a law enforcement agency. In 20 States, American Samoa, Guam, and Puerto Rico, a mandated reporter is required to submit a written report after he or she has made an oral report. In eight States, the District of

Columbia, and the U.S. Virgin Islands, a written report is required only when requested by the department or agency that received the initial report.

Chapter 5- Many cases of child abuse and neglect are not reported, even when mandated by law. Therefore, nearly every State and U.S. territory imposes penalties, often in the form of a fine or imprisonment, on mandatory reporters who fail to report suspected child abuse or neglect as required by law. In addition, to prevent malicious or intentional reporting of cases that are not founded, many States and the U.S. Virgin Islands impose penalties against any person who files a report known to be false.

Chapter 6- To be eligible to receive Federal grants under the Child Abuse Prevention and Treatment Act (CAPTA), States are required to establish provisions for immunity from liability for individuals making good faith reports of suspected or known instances of child abuse or neglect.[1]

In: Reporting Child Abuse and Neglect
Editor: Henry J. Pervall

ISBN: 978-1-62100-157-7
© 2012 Nova Science Publishers, Inc.

Chapter 1

MANDATORY REPORTERS OF CHILD ABUSE AND NEGLECT: SUMMARY OF STATE LAWS[*][1]

United States Department of Health and Human Services

All States, the District of Columbia, American Samoa, Guam, the Northern Mariana Islands, Puerto Rico, and the U.S. Virgin Islands have statutes identifying persons who are required to report child maltreatment under specific circumstances.

PROFESSIONALS REQUIRED TO REPORT

Approximately 48 States, the District of Columbia, American Samoa, Guam, the Northern Mariana Islands, Puerto Rico, and the Virgin Islands designate professions whose members are mandated by law to report child maltreatment.[1] Individuals designated as mandatory reporters typically have frequent contact with children. Such individuals may include:

- Social workers
- Teachers and other school personnel
- Physicians and other health-care workers
- Mental health professionals
- Child care providers
- Medical examiners or coroners
- Law enforcement officers

Some other professions frequently mandated across the States include commercial film or photograph processors (in 11 States, Guam, and Puerto Rico), substance abuse counselors (in

---

[*] This is an edited, reformatted and augmented version of the United States Department of Health and Human Services publication, dated April 2010.

[1] This material may be freely reproduced and distributed. However, when doing so, please credit Child Welfare Information Gateway.

14 States), and probation or parole officers (in 17 States).[2] Seven States and the District of Columbia include domestic violence workers on the list of mandated reporters, while seven States and the District of Columbia include animal control or humane officers.[3] Court-appointed special advocates are mandatory reporters in nine States.[4] Members of the clergy now are required to report in 26 States.[5]

REPORTING BY OTHER PERSONS

In approximately 18 States and Puerto Rico, any person who suspects child abuse or neglect is required to report. Of these 18 States, 16 States and Puerto Rico specify certain professionals who must report but also require all persons to report suspected abuse or neglect, regardless of profession.[6]

New Jersey and Wyoming require all persons to report without specifying any professions. In all other States, territories, and the District of Columbia, any person is permitted to report. These voluntary reporters of abuse are often referred to as "permissive reporters."

STANDARDS FOR MAKING A REPORT

The circumstances under which a mandatory reporter must make a report vary from State to State. Typically, a report must be made when the reporter, in his or her official capacity, *suspects* or *has reasons to believe* that a child has been abused or neglected. Another standard frequently used is when the reporter has knowledge of, or observes a child being subjected to, conditions that would reasonably result in harm to the child. Permissive reporters follow the same standards when electing to make a report.

PRIVILEGED COMMUNICATIONS

Mandatory reporting statutes also may specify when a communication is privileged. "Privileged communications" is the statutory recognition of the right to maintain confidential communications between professionals and their clients, patients, or congregants. To enable States to provide protection to maltreated children, the reporting laws in most States and territories restrict this privilege for mandated reporters. All but three States and Puerto Rico currently address the issue of privileged communications within their reporting laws, either affirming the privilege or denying it (i.e., not allowing privilege to be grounds for failing to report).[7] For instance:

- The physician-patient and husband-wife privileges are the most common to be denied by States.
- The attorney-client privilege is most commonly affirmed.
- The clergy-penitent privilege is also widely affirmed, although that privilege usually is limited to confessional communications and, in some States, denied altogether.[8]

INCLUSION OF THE REPORTER'S NAME IN THE REPORT

Most States maintain toll-free telephone numbers for receiving reports of abuse or neglect.[9] Reports may be made anonymously to most of these reporting numbers, but States find it helpful to their investigations to know the identity of reporters. Approximately 18 States, the District of Columbia, American Samoa, Guam, and the Virgin Islands currently require mandatory reporters to provide their names and contact information, either at the time of the initial oral report or as part of a written report.[10] The laws in Connecticut, Delaware, and Washington allow child protection workers to request the name of the reporter. In Wyoming, the reporter does not have to provide his or her identity as part of the written report, but if the person takes and submits photographs or x rays of the child, his or her name must be provided.

DISCLOSURE OF THE REPORTER'S IDENTITY

All jurisdictions have provisions in statute to maintain the confidentiality of abuse and neglect records. The identity of the reporter is specifically protected from disclosure to the alleged perpetrator in 39 States, the District of Columbia, Puerto Rico, American Samoa, Guam, Puerto Rico, and the Northern Mariana Islands.[11] This protection is maintained even when other information from the report may be disclosed.

Release of the reporter's identity is allowed in some jurisdictions under specific circumstances or to specific departments or officials. For example, disclosure of the reporter's identity can be ordered by the court when there is a compelling reason to disclose (in California, Mississippi, Tennessee, Texas, and Guam) or upon a finding that the reporter knowingly made a false report (in Alabama, Arkansas, Connecticut, Kentucky, Louisiana, Minnesota, South Dakota, Vermont, and Virginia). In some jurisdictions (California, Florida, Minnesota, Tennessee, Texas, Vermont, the District of Columbia, and Guam), the reporter can waive confidentiality and give consent to the release of his or her name.

> This publication is a product of the State Statutes Series prepared by Child Welfare Information Gateway. While every attempt has been made to be as complete as possible, additional information on these topics may be in other sections of a State's code as well as agency regulations, case law, and informal practices and procedures.

Alabama
Professionals Required to Report
Ala. Code § 26-14-3
Reports are required from all of the following:
- Hospitals, clinics, sanitariums, doctors, physicians, surgeons, medical examiners, coroners, dentists, osteopaths, optometrists, chiropractors, podiatrists, pharmacists, and nurses

- Teachers and school officials
- Peace officers and law enforcement officials
- Social workers
- Daycare workers or employees
- Mental health professionals
- Members of the clergy
- Any other person called upon to render aid or medical assistance to a child

Reporting by Other Persons
Ala. Code § 26-14-4

Any other person who has reasonable cause to suspect that a child is being abused or neglected may report.

Standards for Making a Report
Ala. Code § 26-14-3

A report must be made when the child is known or suspected of being a victim of abuse or neglect.

Privileged Communications
Ala. Code §§ 26-14-3; 26-14-10

Only clergy-penitent and attorney-client privileges are permitted.

Inclusion of Reporter's Name in Report

The reporter is not specifically required by statute to provide his or her name in the report.

Disclosure of Reporter Identity
Ala. Code § 26-14-8

The department will not release the identity of the reporter except under court order when the court has determined that the reporter knowingly made a false report.

Alaska

Professionals Required to Report
Alaska Stat. §§ 47.17.020; 47.17.023

The following persons are required to report:

- Health practitioners or administrative officers of institutions
- Teachers and school administrators
- Child care providers
- Paid employees of domestic violence and sexual assault programs, crisis intervention and prevention programs, or organizations that provide counseling or treatment to individuals seeking to control their use of drugs or alcohol
- Peace officers or officers of the Department of Corrections
- Persons who process or produce visual or printed matter, either privately or commercially
- Members of a child fatality review team or the multidisciplinary child protection team

Reporting by Other Persons
Alaska Stat. § 47.17.020

Mandated reporters may report cases that come to their attention in their nonoccupational capacities. Any other person who has reasonable cause to suspect that a child has been harmed may report.

Standards for Making a Report
Alaska Stat. §§ 47.17.020; 47.17.023

A report must be made when in the performance of his or her occupational duties, a reporter has reasonable cause to suspect that a child has suffered harm as a result of abuse or neglect.

A person providing, either privately or commercially, film, photo, or visual or printed matter processing, production, or finishing services, or computer installation, repair, or other services, or Internet or cellular telephone services who, in the process of providing those services, observes a film, photo, picture, computer file, image, or other matter and has reasonable cause to suspect that the film, photo, picture, computer file, image, or other matter visually depicts a child engaged in conduct described in § 11.41.455(a) [sexual exploitation of a minor or child pornography], shall immediately report the observation to the nearest law enforcement agency.

Privileged Communications
Alaska Stat. § 47.17.060

Neither the physician-patient nor the husband-wife privilege is recognized.

Inclusion of Reporter's Name in Report

The reporter is not specifically required by statute to provide his or her name in the report.

Disclosure of Reporter Identity

This issue is not addressed in the statutes reviewed.

American Samoa
Professionals Required to Report
Ann. Code § 45.2002

The following persons are required to report:
- Physicians or surgeons, including physicians in training, osteopaths, optometrists, chiropodists, podiatrists, child health associates, medical examiners or coroners, dentists, nurses, or hospital personnel
- Christian Science practitioners
- School officials or employees
- Social workers or workers in family care homes or child care centers
- Mental health professionals

Reporting by Other Persons
Ann. Code § 45.2002

All other persons are urged and authorized to report.

Standards for Making a Report
Ann. Code § 45.2002

A report is required when:
- A reporter has reasonable cause to know or suspect that a child has been subjected to abuse or neglect.

- A reporter has observed the child being subjected to circumstances or conditions that would result in abuse or neglect.

Privileged Communications
Ann. Code § 45.2016
The physician-patient privilege and the husband-wife privilege are not recognized as grounds for excluding evidence.

Inclusion of Reporter's Name in Report
Ann. Code § 45.2010
The name, address, and occupation of the person making the report must be included in the report.

Disclosure of Reporter Identity
Ann. Code § 45.2027
The identity of the reporter is not released to the subject of the report if that release would be detrimental to the safety or interests of the reporter.

Arizona

Professionals Required to Report
Rev. Stat. § 13-3620
The following persons are required to report:
- Physicians, physician's assistants, optometrists, dentists, behavioral health professionals, nurses, psychologists, counselors, or social workers
- Peace officers, members of the clergy, priests, or Christian Science practitioners
- Parents, stepparents, or guardians
- School personnel or domestic violence victim advocates
- Any other person who has responsibility for the care or treatment of minors

Reporting by Other Persons
Rev. Stat. § 13-3620
Any other person who reasonably believes that a minor is a victim of abuse or neglect may report.

Standards for Making a Report
Rev. Stat. § 13-3620
A report is required when the reporter reasonably believes that a minor is a victim of abuse or neglect.

Privileged Communications
Rev. Stat. § 13-3620
Only the attorney-client and the clergy-penitent privileges are recognized.

Inclusion of Reporter's Name in Report
The reporter is not specifically required by statute to provide his/ her name in the report.

Disclosure of Reporter Identity
This issue is not addressed in the statutes reviewed.

Arkansas

Professionals Required to Report
Ann. Code § 12-18-402

The following individuals are mandated reporters:

- Child care, daycare, or foster care workers
- Coroners
- Dentists, dental hygienists
- Domestic abuse advocates and domestic violence shelter employees or volunteers
- Employees of the Department of Human Services
- Employees working under contract for the Division of Youth Services of the Department of Human Services
- Foster parents
- Judges, law enforcement officials, peace officers, and prosecuting attorneys
- Licensed nurses, physicians, mental health professionals, surgeons, resident interns, osteopaths, and medical personnel who may be engaged in the admission, examination, care, or treatment of persons
- School counselors, officials, and teachers
- Social workers and juvenile intake or probation officers
- Court-appointed special advocate program staff members or volunteers
- Attorneys *ad litem*
- Clergy members
- Employees of a child advocacy center or a child safety center
- Sexual abuse advocates or volunteers who work with victims of sexual abuse as employees of a community-based victim service or mental health agency such as Safe Places, United Family Services, or Centers for Youth and Families
- Rape crisis advocates or volunteers
- Child abuse advocates or volunteers who work with child victims of abuse or maltreatment as employees of a community-based victim service or a mental health agency
- Victim/witness coordinators
- Victim assistance professionals or volunteers

Reporting by Other Persons
Ann. Code § 12-18-401
Any person who has reasonable cause to suspect child maltreatment may report.

Standards for Making a Report
Ann. Code § 12-18-402
An individual listed as a mandatory reporter shall immediately notify the Child Abuse Hotline if he or she:

- Has reasonable cause to suspect that a child has been subjected to maltreatment or died as a result of maltreatment
- Observes a child being subjected to conditions or circumstances that would reasonably result in maltreatment

Privileged Communications
Ann. Code §§ 12-18-402(c); 12-18-803
A privilege or contract shall not prevent a person from reporting child maltreatment when he or she is a mandated reporter and required to report under this section.

No privilege, except that between a lawyer and a client and between a minister, including a Christian Science practitioner, and a person confessing to or being counseled by a minister, shall prevent anyone from testifying concerning child maltreatment.

When a physician, psychologist, psychiatrist, counselor, or therapist conducts interviews with or provides therapy to a subject of a report of suspected child maltreatment for purposes related to child maltreatment, the physician, psychologist, psychiatrist, licensed counselor, or therapist is deemed to be performing services on behalf of the child.

An adult subject of a report of suspected child maltreatment cannot invoke privilege on the child's behalf.

Inclusion of Reporter's Name in Report
Ann. Code § 12-18-302

A mandated reporter may report child maltreatment or suspected child maltreatment by telephone call, facsimile transmission, or online reporting.

Facsimile transmission and online reporting may be used in nonemergency situations by an identified mandated reporter who provides the following contact information:

- Name and phone number
- In the case of online reporting, his or her email address

A mandated reporter who wishes to remain anonymous shall make a report through the toll-free Child Abuse Hotline telephone system.

Disclosure of Reporter Identity
Ann. Code § 12-18-909

The identity of the reporter shall not be disclosed unless a court determines that the reporter knowingly made a false report.

California
Professionals Required to Report
Penal Code § 11165.7

Mandated reporters include any of the following:

- Teachers, teacher's aides, administrators, and classified employees of any public or private school
- Administrators or employees of day camps, youth centers, or youth recreation programs
- Employees of a county office of education or the State Department of Education
- Licensees, administrators, or employees of licensed community care or child daycare facilities
- Head Start program teachers
- Workers or evaluators employed by a licensing agency
- Public assistance workers
- Foster parents, group home personnel, and personnel of residential care facilities
- Social workers, probation officers, and parole officers
- Employees of school district police or security departments
- Administrators, presenters, or counselors for child abuse prevention programs
- District attorney investigators, inspectors, or local child support agency caseworkers
- Peace officers and firefighters, except for volunteer firefighters
- Physicians, surgeons, psychiatrists, psychologists, dentists, residents, interns, podiatrists, chiropractors, licensed nurses, dental hygienists, optometrists, marriage, family, and child counselors, and clinical social workers
- Emergency medical technicians and paramedics

- Psychological assistants
- Marriage, family, and child therapist trainees and interns
- State or county public health employees who treat minors for venereal diseases or other conditions
- Coroners and medical examiners
- Commercial film and photographic print processors
- Child visitation monitors
- Animal control or humane society officers
- Clergy members and custodians of records of clergy members
- Employees of police departments, county sheriff's departments, county probation departments, or county welfare departments
- Employees or volunteers of a Court-Appointed Special Advocate program
- Individuals providing services to minor children
- Alcohol and drug counselors

Reporting by Other Persons
Penal Code § 11166

Any other person who reasonably suspects that a child is a victim of abuse or neglect may report.

For the purposes of this section, 'any other person' includes a mandated reporter who acts in his or her private capacity and not in his or her professional capacity or within the scope of his or her employment.

Standards for Making a Report
Penal Code §§ 11166; 11165.7

A report is required when:

- A mandated reporter, in his or her professional capacity, or within the scope of his or her employment, has knowledge of or observes a child whom the reporter knows or reasonably suspects is the victim of abuse or neglect.
- Commercial film and photographic print processors have knowledge of or observe any film, photograph, videotape, negative, or slide depicting a child under age 16 engaged in an act of sexual conduct.

Privileged Communications
Penal Code § 11166

The clergy-penitent privilege is permitted for penitential communications. This does not modify or limit a clergy member's duty to report known or suspected child abuse or neglect when the clergy member is acting in some other capacity that would otherwise make the clergy member a mandated reporter.

Inclusion of Reporter's Name in Report
Penal Code § 11167

Reports of mandated reporters shall include:

- The name, business address, and telephone number of the mandated reporter
- The capacity that makes the person a mandated reporter

Reports of other persons do not require the reporter's name.

Disclosure of Reporter Identity
Penal Code § 11167

The identity of the reporter shall be confidential and shall be disclosed only:
- To agencies investigating the report
- When the person waives confidentiality
- By court order

Colorado

Professionals Required to Report
Rev. Stat. § 19-3-304

Persons required to report include:
- Physicians, surgeons, physicians in training, child health associates, medical examiners, coroners, dentists, osteopaths, optometrists, chiropractors, podiatrists, nurses, hospital personnel, dental hygienists, physical therapists, pharmacists, registered dieticians
- Public or private school officials or employees
- Social workers, Christian Science practitioners, mental health professionals, psychologists, professional counselors, marriage and family therapists
- Veterinarians, peace officers, firefighters, or victim's advocates
- Commercial film and photographic print processors
- Counselors, marriage and family therapists, or psychotherapists
- Clergy members, including priests, rabbis, duly ordained, commissioned, or licensed ministers of a church, members of religious orders, or recognized leaders of any religious bodies
- Workers in the State Department of Human Services
- Juvenile parole and probation officers
- Child and family investigators
- Officers and agents of the State Bureau of Animal Protection and animal control officers

Reporting by Other Persons
Rev. Stat. § 19-3-304

Any other person may report known or suspected child abuse or neglect.

Standards for Making a Report
Rev. Stat. § 19-3-304

A report is required when:
- A mandated reporter has reasonable cause to know or suspect child abuse or neglect.
- A reporter has observed a child being subjected to circumstances or conditions that would reasonably result in abuse or neglect.
- Commercial film and photographic print processors have knowledge of or observe any film, photograph, videotape, negative, or slide depicting a child engaged in an act of sexual conduct.

Privileged Communications
Rev. Stat. §§ 19-3-304; 19-3-311

The clergy-penitent privilege is permitted. The physician-patient, psychologist-client, and husband-wife privileges are not allowed as grounds for failing to report.

Inclusion of Reporter's Name in Report
Rev. Stat. § 19-3-307
The report shall include the name, address, and occupation of the person making the report.
Disclosure of Reporter Identity
Rev. Stat. § 19-1-307
The identity of the reporter shall be protected.

Connecticut
Professionals Required to Report
Gen. Stat. § 17a-101
The following persons are required to report:
- Physicians, surgeons, residents, interns, nurses, medical examiners, dentists, dental hygienists, optometrists, chiropractors, podiatrists, physician assistants, pharmacists, or physical therapists
- Psychologists or other mental health professionals
- School superintendents, teachers, principals, guidance counselors, paraprofessionals, or coaches
- Social workers
- Police officers, juvenile or adult probation officers, or parole officers
- Members of the clergy
- Alcohol and drug counselors, marital and family therapists, professional counselors, sexual assault counselors, or battered women's counselors
- Licensed foster parents
- Emergency medical services providers
- Any person paid to care for a child in any public or private facility, child daycare center, group daycare home, or family daycare home that is licensed by the State
- Employees of the Department of Children and Families and the Department of Public Health who are responsible for the licensing of child daycare centers, group daycare homes, family daycare homes, or youth camps
- The Child Advocate and any employee of the Office of Child Advocate

Reporting by Other Persons
Gen. Stat. § 17a-103
Any mandated reporter acting outside his or her professional capacity, or any other person having reasonable cause to suspect that a child is being abused or neglected, may report.
Standards for Making a Report
Gen. Stat. § 17a-101a
A report is required when, in the ordinary course of his or her employment or profession, a reporter has reasonable cause to suspect or believe that a child has been abused or neglected.
Privileged Communications
This issue is not addressed in the statutes reviewed.
Inclusion of Reporter's Name in Report
Gen. Stat. §§ 17a-101d; 17a-103

The reporter is not specifically required by statute to include his or her name in the report. The Commissioner of Children and Families shall use his or her best efforts to obtain the name and address of the reporter.

Disclosure of Reporter Identity
Gen. Stat. § 17a-28(13)(i), (m)

The name of an individual reporting child abuse or neglect shall not be disclosed to anyone without his or her written consent except to:

- An employee of the department responsible for child protective services or the abuse registry
- A law enforcement officer
- An appropriate State's attorney
- An appropriate assistant attorney general
- A judge of the Superior Court and all necessary parties in a court proceeding pursuant to § 46b-129 or a criminal prosecution involving child abuse or neglect
- A State child care licensing agency; an executive director of any institution, school, or facility; or a superintendent of schools

Information identifying an individual who reported abuse or neglect of a person, including any tape recording of an oral report, shall not be released to the subject of the report unless, upon application to the Superior Court by such person and served on the Commissioner of Children and Families, a judge determines, after *in camera* inspection of relevant records and a hearing, that there is reasonable cause to believe the reporter knowingly made a false report or that other interests of justice require such release.

Delaware

Professionals Required to Report
Ann. Code Tit. 16, § 903

The following persons are required to report:

- Physicians, dentists, interns, residents, osteopaths, nurses, or medical examiners
- School employees
- Social workers or psychologists

Reporting by Other Persons
Ann. Code Tit. 16, § 903

Any person who knows or in good faith suspects child abuse- neglect shall make a report.

Standards for Making a Report
Ann. Code Tit. 16, § 903

A report is required when reporter knows or in good faith suspects child abuse or neglect.

Privileged Communications
Ann. Code Tit. 16, § 909

Only attorney-client and clergy-penitent privileges are recognized.

Inclusion of Reporter's Name in Report
Ann. Code Tit. 16, § 905

Although reports may be made anonymously, the Division of Family Services shall request the name and address of any person making a report.

Disclosure of Reporter Identity

This issue is not addressed in the statutes reviewed.

District of Columbia

Professionals Required to Report
Ann. Code § 4-1321.02

Persons required to report include:

- Child and Family Services Agency employees, agents, and contractors
- Physicians, psychologists, medical examiners, dentists, chiropractors, registered nurses, licensed practical nurses, or persons involved in the care and treatment of patients
- Law enforcement officers or humane officer of any agency charged with the enforcement of animal cruelty laws
- School officials, teachers, or athletic coaches
- Department of Parks and Recreation employees, public housing resident managers, social service workers, or daycare workers
- Domestic violence counselors or mental health professionals

Reporting by Other Persons
Ann. Code § 4-1321.02

Any other person who knows or has reason to suspect that a child is being abused or neglected may report.

Standards for Making a Report
Ann. Code § 4-1321.02

A report is required when:

- A mandated reporter knows or has reasonable cause to suspect that a child known to him or her in his or her professional or official capacity has been or is in immediate danger of being a mentally or physically abused or neglected child.
- A health professional, law enforcement officer, or humane officer, except an undercover officer whose identity or investigation might be jeopardized, has reasonable cause to believe that a child is abused as a result of inadequate care, control, or subsistence in the home environment due to exposure to drug-related activity.
- A mandated reporter knows or has reasonable cause to suspect that a child known to him or her in his or her professional or official capacity has been, or is in immediate danger of being, the victim of sexual abuse or attempted sexual abuse; the child was assisted, supported, caused, encouraged, commanded, enabled, induced, facilitated, or permitted to become a prostitute; the child has an injury caused by a bullet; or the child has an injury caused by a knife or other sharp object that was caused by other than accidental means.

Privileged Communications
Ann. Code §§ 4-1321.02(b); 4-1321.05

A mandated reporter is not required to report when employed by a lawyer who is providing representation in a criminal, civil, including family law, or delinquency matter, and the basis for the suspicion arises solely in the course of that representation.

Neither the husband-wife nor the physician-patient privilege is permitted.

Inclusion of Reporter's Name in Report
Ann. Code § 4-1321.03

Mandated reporters are required to provide their names, occupations, and contact information.

Disclosure of Reporter Identity

Ann. Code § 4-1302.03

The Child Protection Register staff shall not release any information that identifies the source of a report or the witnesses to the incident referred to in a report to the alleged perpetrator of the abuse, the child's parent or guardian, or a child-placing agency investigating a foster or adoptive placement, unless said staff first obtains permission from the source of the report or from the witnesses named in the report.

Florida

Professionals Required to Report

Ann. Stat. § 39.201

The following persons are mandated reporters:

- Physicians, osteopaths, medical examiners, chiropractors, nurses, or hospital personnel
- Other health or mental health professionals
- Practitioners who rely solely on spiritual means for healing
- Teachers or other school officials or personnel
- Social workers, daycare center workers, or other professional child care, foster care, residential, or institutional workers
- Law enforcement officers or judges

Reporting by Other Persons

Ann. Stat. § 39.201

Any person who knows or has reasonable cause to suspect that a child is abused, abandoned, or neglected shall report.

Standards for Making a Report

Ann. Stat. § 39.201

A report is required when:

- A person knows or has reasonable cause to suspect that a child is abused, abandoned, or neglected.
- A person knows that a child is in need of supervision and care and has no parent, legal custodian, or responsible adult relative immediately known and available to provide supervision and care.

Privileged Communications

Ann. Stat. § 39.204

Only attorney-client and clergy-penitent privileges are permitted.

Inclusion of Reporter's Name in Report

Ann. Stat. § 39.201

Professionals who are mandated reporters are required to provide their names to hotline staff.

Disclosure of Reporter Identity

Ann. Stat. §§ 39.201; 39.202

The names of reporters shall be entered into the record of the report but shall be held confidential. The name of the reporter may not be released to any person other than employees of the Department of Children and Family Services responsible for child protective services, the central abuse hotline, law enforcement, the child protection team, or the appropriate State attorney, without the written consent of the person reporting.

This does not prohibit the serving of a subpoena to a person reporting child abuse, abandonment, or neglect when deemed necessary by the court, the State attorney, or the department, provided the fact that such person made the report is not disclosed.

Georgia
Professionals Required to Report
Ann. Code §§ 19-7-5; 16-12-100
The following persons are required to report:
- Physicians, residents, interns, hospital and medical personnel, podiatrists, dentists, or nurses
- Teachers, school administrators, guidance counselors, visiting teachers, school social workers, or school psychologists
- Psychologists, counselors, social workers, or marriage and family therapists
- Child welfare agency personnel (including any child-caring institution, child-placing agency, maternity home, family daycare home, group daycare home, and daycare center), child-counseling personnel, or child service organization personnel
- Law enforcement personnel
- Persons who process or produce visual or printed matter

Reporting by Other Persons
Ann. Code § 19-7-5
Any other person who has reasonable cause to believe that a child has been abused may report.

Standards for Making a Report
Ann. Code §§ 19-7-5; 16-12-100
A report is required when:
- A reporter has reasonable cause to believe that a child has been abused.
- A person who processes or produces visual or printed matter has reasonable cause to believe that the visual or printed matter submitted for processing or producing depicts a minor engaged in sexually explicit conduct.

Privileged Communications
Ann. Code § 19-7-5(g)
A mandated reporter must report regardless of whether the reasonable cause to believe that abuse has occurred or is occurring is based in whole or in part upon any communication to that person that is otherwise made privileged or confidential by law.

Inclusion of Reporter's Name in Report
The reporter is not specifically required by statute to provide his or her name in the report.

Disclosure of Reporter Identity
Ann. Code § 49-5-41
Any release of records shall protect the identity of any person reporting child abuse.

Guam

Professionals Required to Report
Ann. Code Tit. 19, § 13201

Persons required to report suspected child abuse include but are not limited to:

- Physicians, medical examiners, dentists, osteopaths, optometrists, chiropractors, podiatrists, interns, nurses, hospital personnel, or Christian Science practitioners
- School administrators, teachers, nurses, or counselors
- Social services workers, daycare center workers or any other child care or foster care workers
- Mental health professionals, peace officers, or law enforcement officials
- Commercial film and photographic print processors

Reporting by Other Persons
Ann. Code Tit. 19, § 13202

Any person may make a report if that person has reasonable cause to suspect that a child is an abused or neglected child.

Standards for Making a Report
Ann. Code Tit. 19, § 13201
A report is required when:

- A reporter, who in the course of his or her employment, occupation, or professional practice comes into contact with children, has reason to suspect on the basis of his or her medical, professional, or other training and experience that a child is an abused or neglected child.
- Any commercial film and photographic print processor has knowledge of or observes any film, photograph, videotape, negative, or slide depicting a child under age 18 engaged in an act of sexual conduct.

Privileged Communications
Ann. Code Tit. 19, § 13201

No person may claim privileged communications as a basis for his or her refusal or failure to report suspected child abuse or neglect or to provide Child Protective Services or the Guam Police Department with required information.

Inclusion of Reporter's Name in Report
Ann. Code Tit. 19, § 13203

Every report should include the name of the person making the report. Persons who are required by law to report shall be required to reveal their names.

Disclosure of Reporter Identity
Ann. Code Tit. 19, § 13203

The identity of the reporter shall be confidential and may be disclosed only:

- Among child protective agencies
- To counsel representing a child protective agency
- To the attorney general's office in a criminal prosecution or family court action
- To a licensing agency when abuse in licensed out-of-home care is reasonably suspected
- When the reporter waives confidentiality
- By court order

Hawaii
Professionals Required to Report
Rev. Stat. § 350-1.1
The following persons are required to report:
- Physicians, physicians in training, psychologists, dentists, nurses, osteopathic physicians and surgeons, optometrists, chiropractors, podiatrists, pharmacists, and other health-related professionals
- Medical examiners or coroners
- Employees or officers of any public or private school
- Child care employees or employees or officers of any licensed or registered child care facility, foster home, or similar institution
- Employees or officers of any public or private agency or institution, or other individuals, providing social, medical, hospital, or mental health services, including financial assistance
- Employees or officers of any law enforcement agency, including, but not limited to, the courts, police departments, departments of public safety, correctional institutions, and parole or probation offices
- Employees of any public or private agency providing recreational or sports activities

Reporting by Other Persons
Rev. Stat. § 350-1.3
Any other person who becomes aware of facts or circumstances that cause the person to believe that child abuse or neglect has occurred may report.

Standards for Making a Report
Rev. Stat. § 350-1.1
A report is required when, in his or her professional or official capacity, a reporter has reason to believe that child abuse or neglect has occurred or that there exists a substantial risk that child abuse or neglect may occur in the reasonably foreseeable future.

Privileged Communications
Rev. Stat. § 350-5
The physician-patient, psychologist-client, husband-wife, and victim-counselor privileges are not grounds for failing to report.

Inclusion of Reporter's Name in Report
The reporter is not specifically required by statute to provide his/ her name in the report.

Disclosure of Reporter Identity
Rev. Stat. § 350-1.4
Every reasonable good-faith effort shall be made by the department to maintain the confidentiality of the name of a reporter who requests that his or her name be confidential.

Idaho
Professionals Required to Report
Idaho Code § 16-1605
The following persons are required to report:
- Physicians, residents on hospital staffs, interns, nurses, or coroners
- Teachers or daycare personnel
- Social workers or law enforcement personnel

Reporting by Other Persons
Idaho Code § 16-1605
Any person who has reason to believe that a child has been abused, abandoned, or neglected is required to report.

Standards for Making a Report
Idaho Code § 16-1605
A report is required when:

- A person has reason to believe that a child has been abused, abandoned, or neglected.
- A person observes a child being subjected to conditions or circumstances that would reasonably result in abuse, abandonment, or neglect.

Privileged Communications
Idaho Code §§ 16-1605; 16-1606
Any privilege between a husband and wife and any professional and client, except for the clergy-penitent or attorney-client privilege, shall not be grounds for failure to report.

Inclusion of Reporter's Name in Report
The reporter is not specifically required by statute to provide his or her name in the report. Disclosure of Reporter Identity

This issue is not addressed in the statutes reviewed.

Illinois

Professionals Required to Report
Comp. Stat. Ch. 325, § 5/4; Ch. 720, § 5/11-20.2
The following persons are required to report:

- Physicians, residents, interns, hospital administrators and personnel, surgeons, dentists, dental hygienists, osteopaths, chiropractors, podiatrists, physician assistants, or substance abuse treatment personnel
- Funeral home directors or employees, coroners, or medical examiners
- Emergency medical technicians, acupuncturists, or crisis line or hotline personnel
- School administrators and employees, educational advocates, or truant officers
- Members of a school board or the Chicago Board of Education
- Members of the governing body of a private school
- Social workers, social services administrators, or domestic violence program personnel
- Nurses, genetic counselors, respiratory care practitioners, advanced practice nurses, home health aides, directors or staff assistants of nursery schools or child care centers, or recreational program or facility personnel
- Law enforcement officers or probation officers
- Licensed professional counselors, psychologists, or psychiatrists
- Field personnel of the Department of Healthcare and Family Services, Juvenile Justice, Public Health, Human Services, Corrections, Human Rights, or Children and Family Services
- Supervisors and administrators of general assistance under the Illinois Public Aid Code
- Animal control officers or Department of Agriculture Bureau of Animal Health and Welfare field investigators

- Foster parents, homemakers, or child care workers
- Members of the clergy
- Commercial film and photographic print processors or computer technicians

Reporting by Other Persons
Comp. Stat. Ch. 325, § 5/4

Any other person who has reasonable cause to believe that a child is abused or neglected may report.

Standards for Making a Report
Comp. Stat. Ch. 325, § 5/4; Ch. 720, § 5/11-20.2

A report is required when:

- A reporter has reasonable cause to believe that a child known to him or her in his or her professional capacity may be abused or neglected.
- Commercial film and photographic print processors or computer technicians have knowledge of or observe any film, photograph, videotape, negative, slide, computer hard drive, or any other magnetic or optical media that depicts a child engaged in any actual or simulated sexual conduct.

Privileged Communications
Comp. Stat. Ch. 325, § 5/4; Ch. 735, § 5/8-803

The privileged quality of communication between any professional person required to report and his or her patient or client shall not apply to situations involving abused or neglected children and shall not constitute grounds for failure to report.

A member of the clergy shall not be compelled to disclose a confession or admission made to him or her as part of the discipline of the religion.

Inclusion of Reporter's Name in Report
Comp. Stat. Ch. 325, § 5/7.9

The report shall include the name, occupation, and contact information of the person making the report.

Disclosure of Reporter Identity
Comp. Stat. Ch. 325, § 5/11.1a

Any disclosure of information shall not identify the person making the report.

Indiana
Professionals Required to Report
Ann. Code § 31-33-5-2

Mandatory reporters include any staff member of a medical or other public or private institution, school, facility, or agency.

Reporting by Other Persons
Ann. Code § 31-33-5-1

Any person who has reason to believe that a child is a victim of abuse or neglect must report.

Standards for Making a Report
Ann. Code §§ 31-33-5-1; 31-33-5-2

A report is required when any person has reason to believe that a child is a victim of abuse or neglect.

Privileged Communications
Ann. Code § 31-32-11-1

Privileged communications between any of the following shall not be grounds for failing to report:

- A husband and wife
- A health-care provider and the provider's patient
- A licensed social worker, clinical social worker, marriage and family therapist, mental health counselor, addiction counselor, or clinical addiction counselor and a client of any of these professionals
- A school counselor or psychologist and a student

Inclusion of Reporter's Name in Report
Ann. Code § 31-33-7-4

The written report must include the name and contact information for the person making the report.

Disclosure of Reporter Identity
Ann. Code § 31-33-18-2

The report shall be made available to the person about whom a report has been made, with protection for the identity of:

- Any person reporting known or suspected child abuse or neglect
- Any other person if the person or agency making the information available finds that disclosure of the information would be likely to endanger the life or safety of the person

The report may also be made available to each parent, guardian, custodian, or other person responsible for the welfare of a child named in a report, with protection for the identity of reporters and other appropriate individuals.

Iowa

Professionals Required to Report
Ann. Stat. §§ 232.69; 728.14

The following persons are required to report:

- Health practitioners
- Social workers or psychologists
- School employees, certified paraeducators, coaches, or instructors employed by community colleges
- Employees or operators of health-care facilities, child care centers, Head Start programs, family development and self-sufficiency grant programs, substance abuse programs or facilities, juvenile detention or juvenile shelter care facilities, foster care facilities, or mental health centers
- Employees of Department of Human Services institutions
- Peace officers, counselors, or mental health professionals
- Commercial film and photographic print processors

Reporting by Other Persons
Ann. Stat. § 232.69

Any other person who believes that a child has been abused may report.

Standards for Making a Report

Ann. Stat. §§ 232.69; 728.14

A report is required when:

- A reporter, in the scope of his or her professional practice or employment responsibilities, reasonably believes that a child has been abused.
- A commercial film and photographic print processor has knowledge of or observes a film, photograph, videotape, negative, or slide that depicts a minor engaged in a prohibited sexual act or in the simulation of a prohibited sexual act.

Privileged Communications

Ann. Stat. § 232.74

The husband-wife or health practitioner-patient privilege does not apply to evidence regarding abuse to a child.

Inclusion of Reporter's Name in Report

Ann. Stat. § 232.70

The report shall contain the name and address of the person making the report.

Disclosure of Reporter Identity

Ann. Stat. § 232.71B

The department shall not reveal the identity of the reporter to the subject of the report.

Kansas

Professionals Required to Report

Ann. Stat. § 38-2223

The following persons are required to report:

- Persons providing medical care or treatment, including persons licensed to practice the healing arts, dentistry, and optometry; persons engaged in postgraduate training programs approved by the State Board of Healing Arts; licensed professional or practical nurses; and chief administrative officers of medical care facilities
- Persons licensed by the State to provide mental health services, including psychologists, clinical psychotherapists, social workers, marriage and family therapists, professional counselors, and registered alcohol and drug abuse counselors
- Teachers, school administrators, or other employees of an educational institution that the child is attending
- Licensed child care providers or their employees at the place where the child care services are being provided to the child
- Firefighters, emergency medical services personnel, law enforcement officers, juvenile intake and assessment workers, court services officers, community corrections officers, case managers, and mediators

Reporting by Other Persons

Ann. Stat. § 38-2223

Any person who has reason to suspect that a child may be a child in need of care may report.

Standards for Making a Report

Ann. Stat. § 38-2223

A report is required when a reporter has reason to suspect that a child has been harmed as a result of physical, mental, or emotional abuse or neglect or sexual abuse.

Privileged Communications
Ann. Stat. § 38-2249

In all proceedings under this code, the rules of evidence of the code of civil procedure shall apply, except that no evidence relating to the condition of a child shall be excluded solely on the ground that the matter is or may be the subject of a physician-patient privilege, psychologist-client privilege, or social worker-client privilege.

Inclusion of Reporter's Name in Report

The reporter is not specifically required by statute to provide his or her name in the report.

Disclosure of Reporter Identity
Ann. Stat. § 38-2213

Information authorized to be disclosed in this subsection shall not contain information that identifies a reporter of a child alleged or adjudicated to be a child in need of care.

Kentucky

Professionals Required to Report
Rev. Stat. § 620.030

All persons are required to report, including, but not limited to:

- Physicians, osteopathic physicians, nurses, coroners, medical examiners, residents, interns, chiropractors, dentists, optometrists, emergency medical technicians, paramedics, or health professionals
- Teachers, school personnel, or child-caring personnel
- Social workers or mental health professionals
- Peace officers

Reporting by Other Persons
Rev. Stat. § 620.030

Any person who knows or has reasonable cause to believe that a child is dependent, neglected, or abused shall immediately report.

Standards for Making a Report
Rev. Stat. § 620.030

A report is required when a person knows or has reasonable cause to believe that a child is dependent, neglected, or abused.

Privileged Communications
Rev. Stat. § 620.030(3)

Neither the husband-wife nor any professional-client/patient privilege, except the attorney-client and clergy-penitent privilege, shall be a ground for refusing to report.

Inclusion of Reporter's Name in Report

The reporter is not specifically required by statute to provide his/ her name in the report.

Disclosure of Reporter Identity
Rev. Stat. § 620.050

The identity of the reporter shall not be disclosed except:

- To law enforcement officials, the agency investigating the report, or to a multidisciplinary team
- Under court order, after a court has found reason to believe the reporter knowingly made a false report

Louisiana

Professionals Required to Report
Children's Code Art. 603(15)

Mandatory reporters include any of the following individuals performing their occupational duties:

- Health practitioners, including physicians, surgeons, physical therapists, dentists, residents, interns, hospital staff members, podiatrists, chiropractors, licensed nurses, nursing aides, dental hygienists, emergency medical technicians, paramedics, optometrists, medical examiners, or coroners
- Mental health/social service practitioners including psychiatrists, psychologists, marriage or family counselors, social workers, members of the clergy, aides, or other individuals who provide counseling services to a child or his or her family
- Members of the clergy, including priests, rabbis, duly ordained clerical deacons or ministers, or Christian Science practitioners
- Teachers, child care providers, teacher's aides, instructional aides, school principals, school staff members, probation officers, foster home parents, group home or other child care institutional staff members, personnel of residential home facilities, or licensed or unlicensed daycare providers
- Police officers or law enforcement officials
- Commercial film and photographic print processors
- Mediators
- Parenting coordinators
- Court-appointed special advocates

Reporting by Other Persons
Children's Code Art. 609

Any other person who has cause to believe that a child's health is endangered as a result of abuse or neglect may report.

Standards for Making a Report
Children's Code Art. 609; 610

A report is required when:

- A reporter has cause to believe that a child's physical or mental health or welfare is endangered as a result of abuse or neglect.
- A commercial film or photographic print processor has knowledge of or observes any film, photograph, videotape, negative, or slide depicting a child, whom he or she knows or should know is under age 17, that constitutes child pornography.

Privileged Communications
Children's Code Art. 603; 609

A clergy member is not required to report a confidential communication from a person to a member of the clergy who, in the course of the discipline or practice of that church, denomination, or organization, is authorized or accustomed to hearing confidential communications, and under the discipline or tenets of the church, denomination, or organization has a duty to keep such communications confidential.

Notwithstanding any claim of privileged communication, any mandatory reporter who has cause to believe that a child's physical or mental health or welfare is endangered as a result of abuse or neglect, or that abuse or neglect was a contributing factor in a child's death, shall report.

Inclusion of Reporter's Name in Report
Children's Code Art. 610
The report must include the name and address of the reporter.

Disclosure of Reporter Identity
Rev. Stat. § 46:56(F)(8)(b)
The identity of the reporter shall not be released unless a court finds that the reporter knowingly made a false report.

Maine
Professionals Required to Report
Rev. Stat. Tit. 22, § 4011-A
The following persons, when acting in a professional capacity, are required to report:
- Allopathic or osteopathic physicians, residents, interns, emergency medical services persons, medical examiners, physician's assistants, dentists, dental hygienists, dental assistants, chiropractors, podiatrists, or registered or licensed practical nurses
- Teachers, guidance counselors, school officials, youth camp administrators or counselors, or social workers
- Court-appointed special advocates or guardians *ad litem*
- Homemakers, home-health aides, medical or social service workers, psychologists, child care personnel, or mental health professionals
- Law enforcement official, State or municipal fire inspectors, or municipal code enforcement officials
- Commercial film and photographic print processors
- Clergy members
- Chairs of professional licensing boards that have jurisdiction over mandated reporters
- Humane agents employed by the Department of Agriculture, Food and Rural Resources
- Sexual assault counselors or family or domestic violence victim advocates
- School bus drivers or attendants

Reporting by Other Persons
Rev. Stat. Tit. 22, § 4011-A
Any other person who knows or has reasonable cause to suspect that a child has been or is likely to be abused or neglected may report.

An animal control officer may report to the department when that person knows or has reasonable cause to suspect that a child has been or is likely to be abused or neglected.

Standards for Making a Report
Rev. Stat. Tit. 22, §§ 4011-A; 4011-B
A report is required when:
- The person knows or has reasonable cause to suspect that a child is or is likely to be abused or neglected.
- A health-care provider involved in the delivery or care of an infant knows or has reasonable cause to suspect the infant has been born affected by illegal substance abuse or is suffering from withdrawal symptoms resulting from prenatal drug exposure.

Privileged Communications
Rev. Stat. Tit. 22, §§ 4011-A; 4015

A member of the clergy may claim privilege when information is received during a confidential communication. The husband-wife and physician- and psychotherapist-patient privileges cannot be invoked as a reason not to report.

Inclusion of Reporter's Name in Report
Rev. Stat. Tit. 22, § 4012

The report shall include the name, occupation, and contact information for the person making the report.

Disclosure of Reporter Identity
Rev. Stat. Tit. 22, § 4008

The department will protect the identity of reporters and other persons as appropriate when disclosing information in the records to a child named in a report, the child's parent, custodian, or caregiver, or a party to a child protection proceeding.

Maryland

Professionals Required to Report
Fam. Law § 5-704

Persons required to report include:
- Health practitioners
- Educators or human service workers
- Police officers

Reporting by Other Persons
Fam. Law § 5-705

Any other person who has reason to believe that a child has been subjected to abuse or neglect must report.

Standards for Making a Report
Fam. Law §§ 5-704; 5-705

A report is required when, acting in a professional capacity, the person has reason to believe that a child has been subjected to abuse or neglect.

Privileged Communications
Fam. Law § 5-705

Only attorney-client and clergy-penitent privileges are permitted.

Inclusion of Reporter's Name in Report

The reporter is not specifically required by statute to provide his or her name in the report.

Disclosure of Reporter Identity

This issue is not addressed in the statutes reviewed.

Massachusetts

Professionals Required to Report
Gen. Laws Ch. 119, § 21

Mandatory reporters include:

- Physicians, medical interns, hospital personnel, medical examiners, psychologists, emergency medical technicians, dentists, nurses, chiropractors, podiatrists, optometrists, osteopaths, allied mental health and human services professionals, drug and alcoholism counselors, psychiatrists, or clinical social workers
- Public or private schoolteachers, educational administrators, guidance or family counselors, or child care workers
- Persons paid to care for or work with a child in any public or private facility, home, or program that provides child care or residential services to children
- Persons who provide the services of child care resource and referral agencies, voucher management agencies, family child care systems, or child care food programs
- Licensors of the Department of Early Education and Care or school attendance officers
- Probation officers, clerk-magistrates of a district court, parole officers, social workers, foster parents, firefighters, or police officers
- Priests, rabbis, clergy members, ordained or licensed ministers, leaders of any church or religious body, or accredited Christian Science practitioners
- Persons performing official duties on behalf of a church or religious body that are recognized as the duties of a priest, rabbi, clergy, ordained or licensed minister, leader of any church or religious body, accredited Christian Science practitioner
- Persons employed by a church or religious body to supervise, educate, coach, train or counsel a child on a regular basis
- Persons in charge of a medical or other public or private institution, school, or facility or that person's designated agent
- The child advocate

Reporting by Other Persons
Gen. Laws Ch. 119, § 51A

Any other person who has reasonable cause to believe that a child is suffering from or has died as a result of abuse or neglect may file a report.

Standards for Making a Report
Gen. Laws Ch. 119, § 51A

A mandated reporter must report when, in his or her professional capacity, he or she has reasonable cause to believe that a child is suffering physical or emotional injury resulting from:

- Abuse inflicted upon the child that causes harm or substantial risk of harm to the child's health or welfare, including sexual abuse
- Neglect, including malnutrition
- Physical dependence upon an addictive drug at birth

Privileged Communications
Gen. Laws Ch. 119, § 51A
Effective July 1, 2010

Any privilege relating to confidential communications, established by §§ 135 to 135B, inclusive, of chapter 112 [pertaining to social worker-client privilege] or by §§ 20A [clergy-penitent privilege] and 20B [psychotherapist-patient privilege] of chapter 233, shall not prohibit the filing of a report under this section or a care and protection petition under § 24, except that a priest, rabbi, clergy, member, ordained or licensed minister, leader of a church or religious body or accredited Christian Science practitioner need not report information solely gained in a confession or similarly confidential communication in other religious faiths. Nothing in the general laws shall modify or limit the duty of a priest, rabbi, clergy member, ordained or licensed minister, leader of a church or religious body or accredited Christian Science practitioner to report suspected child abuse or neglect under this section when the priest, rabbi, clergy member, ordained or licensed minister, leader of a church or religious body, or accredited Christian Science practitioner is acting in some other capacity that would otherwise make him or her a mandated reporter.

Inclusion of Reporter's Name in Report

Gen. Laws Ch. 119, § 51A

A report shall include the name of the person making the report.

Disclosure of Reporter Identity

This issue is not addressed in the statutes reviewed.

Michigan

Professionals Required to Report Comp. Laws § 722.623

Mandatory reporters include:

- Physicians, physician assistants, dentists, dental hygienists, medical examiners, nurses, persons licensed to provide emergency medical care, or audiologists
- School administrators, counselors, or teachers
- Regulated child care providers
- Psychologists, marriage and family therapists, licensed professional counselors, social workers, or social work technicians
- Persons employed in a professional capacity in any office of the friend of the court
- Law enforcement officers
- Members of the clergy
- Department employees, including eligibility specialists, family independence managers, family independence specialists, social services specialists, social work specialists, social work specialist managers, or welfare services specialists
- Any employee of an organization or entity that, as a result of Federal funding statutes, regulations, or contracts, would be prohibited from reporting in the absence of a State mandate or court order

Reporting by Other Persons

Comp. Laws § 722.624

Any other person, including a child, who has reasonable cause to suspect child abuse or neglect, may report.

Standards for Making a Report

Comp. Laws § 722.623

A report is required when a reporters reasonable cause to suspect child abuse or neglect.

Privileged Communications

Comp. Laws § 722.631

Only the attorney-client or clergy-penitent privilege can be grounds for not reporting.

Inclusion of Reporter's Name in Report

The reporter is not specifically required statute to provide his or her name in the report.

Disclosure of Reporter Identity

Comp. Laws §§ 722,625; 722.627

The identity of a reporting person is confidential and subject to disclosure only with the consent of that person or by judicial process.

The identity of the reporter is protected in any release of information to the subject of the report.

Minnesota

Professionals Required to Report Ann. Stat. § 626.556, Subd. 3

Mandatory reporters include:

- A professional or professional's delegate who is engaged in the practice of the healing arts, hospital administration, psychological or psychiatric treatment, child care, education, social services, correctional supervision, probation or correctional services, or law enforcement
- A member of the clergy who received the information while engaged in ministerial duties

Reporting by Other Persons

Ann. Stat. § 626.556, Subd. 3

Any other person may voluntarily report if the person knows, has reason to believe, or suspects that a child is being neglected or subjected to sexual or physical abuse

Standards for Making a Report

Ann. Stat. § 626.556, Subd. 3

A report is required when a reporter knows or has reason to believe that a child is being neglected or sexually or physically abused or has been neglected or physically or sexually abused within the preceding 3 years.

Privileged Communications

Ann. Stat. § 626.556, Subd. 3 & 8

A member of the clergy is not required by this subdivision to report information that is otherwise privileged under § 595.02, subdivision 1, paragraph (c).

No evidence relating to the neglect or abuse of a child or to any prior incidents of neglect or abuse involving any of the same persons accused of neglect or abuse shall be excluded in any proceeding on the grounds of privilege set forth in § 595.02, subdivision 1, paragraph (a) [husband-wife], (d) [medical practitioner-patient], or (g) [mental health professional-client].

Inclusion of Reporter's Name in Report

Ann. Stat. § 626.556, Subd. 7

The written report from a mandatory reporter must include the name and address of the reporter.

Disclosure of Reporter Identity

Ann. Stat. § 626.556, Subd. 11

The name of the reporter shall be kept confidential while the report is under investigation. After the investigation is complete, the subject of the report may compel disclosure of the name only upon the reporter's consent or a finding by the court that the report was false and made in bad faith.

Mississippi

Professionals Required to Report Ann. Code § 43-21-353

The following professionals are required to report:

- Physicians, dentists, interns, residents, or nurses
- Public or private school employees or child care givers
- Psychologists, social workers, family protection workers, or family protection specialists
- Attorneys, ministers, or law enforcement officers

Reporting by Other Persons

Ann. Code § 43-21-353

All other persons who have reasonable cause to suspect that a child is abused or neglected must report.

Standards for Making a Report

Ann. Code § 43-21-353

A report is required when a person has reasonable cause to suspect that a child is abused or neglected. Privileged Communications

This issue is not addressed in the statutes reviewed.

Inclusion of Reporter's Name in Report

Ann. Code § 43-21-353

The department's report shall include the name and address of all witnesses, including the reporter if he or she is a material witness to the abuse.

Disclosure of Reporter Identity

Ann. Code § 43-21-353

The identity of the reporting party shall not be disclosed to anyone other than law enforcement officers or prosecutors without an order from the appropriate youth court. The identity of the reporter shall not be disclosed to an individual under investigation.

Missouri

Professionals Required to Report

Rev. Stat. §§ 210.115; 352.400; 568.110

Professionals required to report include:

- Physicians, medical examiners, coroners, dentists, chiropractors, optometrists, podiatrists, residents, interns, nurses, hospital and clinic personnel, or other health practitioners
- Daycare center workers or other child care workers, teachers, principals, or other school officials
- Psychologists, mental health professionals, or social workers
- Ministers including clergypersons, priests, rabbis, Christian Science practitioners, or other persons serving in a similar capacity for any religious organization
- Juvenile officers, probation or parole officers, peace officers, law enforcement officials, or jail or detention center personnel
- Other persons with responsibility for the care of children
- Commercial film and photographic print processors; computer providers, installers, or repair persons; or Internet service providers

Reporting by Other Persons
Rev. Stat. § 210.115

Any other person who has reasonable cause to suspect that a child has been subjected to abuse or neglect may report.

Standards for Making a Report
Rev. Stat. §§ 210.115; 568.110

A report is required when:

- A reporter has reasonable cause to suspect that a child has been subjected to abuse or neglect.
- A reporter observes a child being subjected to conditions or circumstances that would reasonably result in abuse or neglect.
- A commercial film and photographic print processor has knowledge of or observes any film, photograph, videotape, negative, slide, or computer-generated image or picture depicting a child engaged in an act of sexual conduct.

Privileged Communications
Rev. Stat. § 210.140

Only the attorney-client or clergy-penitent privilege may be grounds for failure to report. Inclusion of Reporter's Name in Report Rev. Stat. § 210.130

The report must include the name, address, occupation, and contact information for the person making the report.

Disclosure of Reporter Identity
Rev. Stat. § 210.150

The names or other identifying information of reporters shall not be furnished to any child, parent, guardian, or alleged perpetrator named in the report.

Montana
Professionals Required to Report
Ann. Code § 41-3-201

Professionals required to report include:

- Physicians, residents, interns, members of hospital staffs, nurses, osteopaths, chiropractors, podiatrists, medical examiners, coroners, dentists, optometrists, or any other health professionals
- Teachers, school officials, or school employees who work during regular school hours
- Operators or employees of any registered or licensed daycare or substitute care facility, or operators or employees of child care facilities
- Mental health professionals or social workers
- Religious healers
- Foster care, residential, or institutional workers
- Members of the clergy
- Guardians *ad litem* or court-appointed advocates authorized to investigate a report
- Peace officers or other law enforcement officials
- The term 'clergy' means:
- An ordained minister, priest, or rabbi

- A commissioned or licensed minister of a church or church denomination that ordains ministers if the person has the authority to perform substantially all the religious duties of the church or denomination
- A member of a religious order who has taken a vow of poverty
- A Christian Science practitioner

Reporting by Other Persons
Ann. Code § 41-3-201

Any other person who knows or has reasonable cause to suspect that a child is abused or neglected may report.

Standards for Making a Report
Ann. Code § 41-3-201

A report is required when:

- A reporter knows or has reasonable cause to suspect, as a result of information received in his or her professional or official capacity, that a child is abused or neglected.
- A health-care professional involved in the delivery or care of an infant knows that the infant is affected by a dangerous drug.

Privileged Communications
Ann. Code § 41-3-201

A person listed as a mandated reporter may not refuse to make a report as required in this section on the grounds of a physician-patient or similar privilege.

A member of the clergy or a priest is not required to make a report under this section if the communication is required to be confidential by canon law, church doctrine, or established church practice.

Inclusion of Reporter's Name in Report

The reporter is not specifically required by statute to provide his or her name in the report.

Disclosure of Reporter Identity
Ann. Code § 41-3-205

The identity of the reporter shall not be disclosed in any release of information to the subject of the report.

Nebraska

Professionals Required to Report
Rev. Stat. § 28-711

Professionals required to report include:

- Physicians, medical institutions, or nurses
- School employees
- Social workers

Reporting by Other Persons
Rev. Stat. § 28-711

All other persons who have reasonable cause to believe that a child has been subjected to abuse or neglect must report.

Standards for Making a Report
Rev. Stat. § 28-711

A report is required when:

- A reporter has reasonable cause to believe that a child has been subjected to abuse or neglect.
- A reporter observes a child being subjected to conditions or circumstances that reasonably would result in abuse or neglect.

Privileged Communications
Rev. Stat. § 28-714

The physician-patient, counselor-client, and husband-wife privileges shall not be grounds for failing to report.

Inclusion of Reporter's Name in Report
Rev. Stat. § 28-711

The initial oral report shall include the reporter's name and address.

Disclosure of Reporter Identity
Rev. Stat. § 28-719

The name and address of the reporter shall not be included in any release of information.

Nevada
Professionals Required to Report
Rev. Stat. § 432B.220

Mandatory reporters include:

- Physicians, dentists, dental hygienists, chiropractors, optometrists, podiatrists, medical examiners, residents, interns, nurses, physician assistants, or perfusionists
- Emergency medical technicians, other persons providing medical services, or hospital personnel
- Coroners
- School administrators, teachers, counselors, or librarians
- Any persons who maintain or are employed by facilities or establishments that provide care for children, children's camps, or other facilities, institutions, or agencies furnishing care to children
- Psychiatrists, psychologists, marriage and family therapists, clinical professional counselors, clinical alcohol and drug abuse counselors, alcohol or drug abuse counselors, athletic trainers, or social workers
- Members of the clergy, practitioners of Christian Science, or religious healers, unless they have acquired the knowledge of the abuse or neglect from the offenders during confessions
- Persons licensed to conduct foster homes
- Officers or employees of law enforcement agencies or adult or juvenile probation officers
- Attorneys, unless they have acquired the knowledge of the abuse or neglect from clients who are, or may be, accused of the abuse or neglect
- Any person who is employed by or serves as a volunteer for an approved youth shelter
- Any adult person who is employed by an entity that provides organized activities for children

- Any person who maintains, is employed by, or serves as a volunteer for an agency or service that advises persons regarding abuse or neglect of a child and refers them to services

Reporting by Other Persons
Rev. Stat. § 432B.220
Any other person may report.

Standards for Making a Report
Rev. Stat. § 432B.220
A report is required when:

- A reporter, in his or her professional capacity, knows or has reason to believe that a child is abused or neglected.
- A reporter has reasonable cause believe that a child died as result of abuse or neglect.
- A medical services provider who delivers or provides medical services to a newborn infant and in his or her professional or occupational capacity, knows or has reasonable cause to believe that the newborn infant has been affected by prenatal illegal substance abuse or has withdrawal symptoms resulting from prenatal drug exposure.

Privileged Communications
Rev. Stat. §§ 432B.220; 432B.250
The clergy-penitent privilege applies when the knowledge is gained during religious confession. The attorney-client privilege applies when the knowledge is acquired from a client who is or may be accused of abuse.

Any other person who required to report may not invoke privilege for failure to make a report.

Inclusion of Reporter's Name in Report
The reporter is not specifically required by statute to provide his or her name in the report.

Disclosure of Reporter Identity
Rev. Stat. § 432B.290
The identity of the reporter is kept confidential.

New Hampshire
Professionals Required to Report
Rev. Stat. § 169-C:29
The following professionals are required to report:

- Physicians, surgeons, county medical examiners, psychiatrists, residents, interns, dentists, osteopaths,
- optometrists, chiropractors, nurses, hospital personnel, or Christian Science practitioners
- Teachers, school officials, nurses, or counselors
- Daycare workers or any other child or foster care workers
- Social workers
- Psychologists or therapists
- Priests, ministers, or rabbis
- Law enforcement officials

Reporting by Other Persons
Rev. Stat. § 169-C:29

All other persons who have reason to suspect that a child has been abused or neglected must report.

Standards for Making a Report
Rev. Stat. § 169-C:29

A report is required when a person has reason to suspect that a child has been abused or neglected.

Privileged Communications
Rev. Stat. § 169-C:32

Only the attorney-client privilege is permitted.

Inclusion of Reporter's Name in Report

The reporter is not specifically required by statute to provide his or her name in the report.

Disclosure of Reporter Identity

This issue is not addressed in the statutes reviewed.

New Jersey

Professionals Required to Report

No professional groups are specified in statute; all persons are required to report.

Reporting by Other Persons
Ann. Stat. § 9:6-8.10

Any person having reasonable cause to believe that a child has been subjected to child abuse or neglect or acts of child abuse shall report.

Standards for Making a Report
Ann. Stat. § 9:6-8.10

A report is required when a person has reasonable cause to believe that a child has been subjected to abuse or neglect. Privileged Communications

This issue is not addressed in the statutes reviewed.

Inclusion of Reporter's Name in Report

The reporter is not specifically required by statute to provide his or her name in the report.

Disclosure of Reporter Identity
Ann. Stat. § 9:6-8.10a

The identity of the reporter shall not be made public. Any information that could endanger any person shall not be released.

New Mexico

Professionals Required to Report
Ann. Stat. § 32A-4-3

Professionals required to report include:
- Physicians, residents, or interns
- Law enforcement officers or judges
- Nurses

- Teachers or school officials
- Social workers
- Members of the clergy

Reporting by Other Persons

Ann. Stat. § 32A-4-3

Every person who knows or has a reasonable suspicion that a child is an abused or a neglected child shall report the matter immediately.

Standards for Making a Report

Ann. Stat. § 32A-4-3

A report is required when a person knows or has a reasonable suspicion that a child is abused or neglected.

Privileged Communications

Ann. Stat. §§ 32A-4-3; 32A-4-5

A clergy member need not report any information that is privileged.

The report or its contents or any other facts related thereto or to the condition of the child who is the subject of the report shall not be excluded on the ground that the matter is or may be the subject of a physician-patient privilege or similar privilege or rule against disclosure.

Inclusion of Reporter's Name in Report

Ann. Stat. § 32A-4-5

The identify of the mandated reporter will be verified before any investigation is initiated.

Disclosure of Reporter Identity

Ann. Stat. § 32A-4-33

Any release of information to a parent, guardian, or legal custodian shall not include identifying information about the reporter.

New York

Professionals Required to Report

Soc. Serv. Law § 413

The following persons and officials are required to report:

- Physicians, physician assistants, surgeons, medical examiners, coroners, dentists, dental hygienists, osteopaths, optometrists, chiropractors, podiatrists, residents, interns, psychologists, registered nurses, social workers, or emergency medical technicians
- Licensed creative arts therapists, marriage and family therapists, mental health counselors, or psychoanalysts
- Hospital personnel or Christian Science practitioners
- School officials, including but not limited to, teachers, guidance counselors, school psychologists, school social workers, school nurses, or administrators
- Social services workers, daycare center workers, providers of family or group family daycare, or employees or volunteers in a residential care facility or any other child care or foster care worker
- Mental health professionals, substance abuse counselors, alcoholism counselors, or all persons credentialed by the Office of Alcoholism and Substance Abuse Services

- Peace officers, police officers, district attorneys or assistant district attorneys, investigators employed in the office of a district attorney, or other law enforcement officials

Reporting by Other Persons
Soc. Serv. Law § 414

Any other person who has reasonable cause to suspect that a child is abused or maltreated may report.

Standards for Making a Report
Soc. Serv. Law § 413

A report is required when the reporter has reasonable cause to suspect:

- A child coming before him or her in his or her professional or official capacity is an abused or maltreated child.
- The parent, guardian, custodian, or other person legally responsible for the child comes before the reporter and states from personal knowledge facts, conditions, or circumstances that, if correct, would render the child an abused or maltreated child.

Privileged Communications
Soc. Serv. Law § 415

Notwithstanding the privileges set forth in article 45 of the civil practice law and rules, and any other provision of law to the contrary, mandated reporters who make a report that initiates an investigation of an allegation of child abuse or maltreatment are required to comply with all requests for records made by a child protective service relating to the report.

Inclusion of Reporter's Name in Report
Soc. Serv. Law § 415

The report shall include the name and contact information for the reporter.

Disclosure of Reporter Identity
Soc. Serv. Law § 422-a

Any disclosure of information shall not identify the source of the report.

North Carolina
Professionals Required to Report
Gen. Stat. § 7B-301

Any person or institution that has cause to suspect abuse or neglect shall report.

Reporting by Other Persons
Gen. Stat. § 7B-301

All persons who have cause to suspect that any juvenile is abused, neglected, or dependent, or has died as the result of maltreatment, shall report.

Standards for Making a Report
Gen. Stat. § 7B-301

A report is required when a reporter has cause to suspect that any juvenile is abused, neglected, or dependent, or has died as the result of maltreatment.

Privileged Communications
Gen. Stat. § 7B-310

No privilege shall be grounds for failing to report, even if the knowledge or suspicion is acquired in an official professional capacity, except when the knowledge or suspicion is gained by an attorney from that attorney's client during representation only in the abuse, neglect, or dependency case. No privilege, except the attorney-client privilege, shall be grounds for excluding evidence of abuse, neglect, or dependency.

Inclusion of Reporter's Name in Report

Gen. Stat. § 7B-301

The report must include the name, address, and telephone number of the reporter.

Disclosure of Reporter Identity

Gen. Stat. § 7B-302

The Department of Social Services shall hold the identity of the reporter in strictest confidence.

North Dakota

Professionals Required to Report

Cent. Code § 50-25.1-03

The following professionals are required to report:

- Physicians, nurses, dentists, optometrists, medical examiners or coroners, or any other medical or mental health professionals
- Religious practitioners of the healing arts
- Schoolteachers, administrators, or school counselors
- Addiction counselors, social workers, child care workers, or foster parents
- Police or law enforcement officers, juvenile court personnel, probation officers, division of juvenile services
- employees
- Members of the clergy

Reporting by Other Persons

Cent. Code § 50-25.1-03

Any other person who has reasonable cause to suspect that a child is abused or neglected may report.

Standards for Making a Report

Cent. Code § 50-25.1-03

A report is required when a reporter has knowledge of or reasonable cause to suspect that a child is abused or neglected if the knowledge or suspicion is derived from information received by that person in that person's official or professional capacity.

Privileged Communications

Cent. Code §§ 50-25.1-03; 50-25.1-10

A member of the clergy is not required to report such circumstances if the knowledge or suspicion is derived from information received in the capacity of spiritual adviser.

Any privilege of communication between husband and wife or between any professional person and the person's patient or client, except between attorney and client, cannot be used as grounds for failing to report.

Inclusion of Reporter's Name in Report

The reporter is not specifically required by statute to provide his or her name in the report.

Disclosure of Reporter Identity

Cent. Code § 50-25.1-11

All reports are confidential and must be made available to a parent, the child's guardian, and any person who is the subject of a report; provided, however, that the identity of persons reporting or supplying information is protected.

Northern Mariana Islands
Professionals Required to Report
Commonwealth Code Tit. 6, § 5313
Reports are required from the following:
- Any health-care worker, including anesthesiologists, acupuncturists, chiropractors, dentists, health aides, hypnotists, massage therapists, mental health counselors, midwives, nurses, nurse practitioners, osteopaths, naturopaths, physical therapists, physicians, physician's assistants, psychiatrists, psychologists, radiologists, religious healing practitioners, surgeons, or x-ray technicians
- Teachers or other school officials
- Daycare providers, nannies, au pair workers, or any other person who is entrusted with the temporary care of a minor child in return for compensation, except babysitters who are themselves minor children
- Counselors or social workers
- Peace officers or other law enforcement officials

Reporting by Other Persons
Commonwealth Code Tit. 6, § 5313
Any other person may at any time report known or suspected instances of child abuse or neglect.

Standards for Making a Report
Commonwealth Code Tit. 6, § 5313
A report is required when a mandated reporter comes into contact in a professional capacity with a child who the person knows or has reasonable cause to suspect is abused or neglected.

Privileged Communications
Commonwealth Code Tit. 6, § 5316
Only the attorney-client privilege is permitted.

Inclusion of Reporter's Name in Report
The reporter is not specifically required by statute to provide his or her name in the report.

Disclosure of Reporter Identity
Commonwealth Code Tit. 6, § 5325
The release of the identity of the reporter is prohibited.

Ohio
Professionals Required to Report
Rev. Code § 2151.421
Mandatory reporters include:

- Attorneys
- Physicians, interns, residents, dentists, podiatrists, nurses, or other health-care professionals
- Licensed psychologists, school psychologists, or marriage and family therapists
- Speech pathologists or audiologists
- Coroners
- Administrators or employees of child daycare centers, residential camps, child day camps, certified childcare agencies, other public or private children services agencies
- Teachers, school employees, or school authorities
- Persons engaged in social work or the practice of professional counseling
- Agents of county humane societies
- Persons, other than clerics, rendering spiritual treatment through prayer in accordance with the tenets of a well-recognized religion
- Superintendents, board members, or employees of county boards of mental retardation; investigative agents contracted with by a county board of mental retardation; employees of the Department of Mental Retardation and Developmental Disabilities; employees of a facility or home that provides respite care; employees of a home health agency; employees of an entity that provides homemaker services
- Persons performing the duties of an assessor or third party employed by a public children services agency to assist in providing child or family-related services

Reporting by Other Persons
Rev. Code § 2151.421
Any other person who suspects that a child has suffered or faces a threat of suffering from abuse or neglect may report.

Standards for Making a Report
Rev. Code § 2151.421
A report is required when a mandated person is acting in an official or professional capacity and knows or suspects that a child has suffered or faces a threat of suffering any physical or mental wound, injury, disability, or condition of a nature that reasonably indicates abuse or neglect of the child.

Privileged Communications
Rev. Code § 2151.421
An attorney, physician, or cleric is not required to make a report concerning any communication the attorney, physician, or cleric receives from a client, patient, or penitent in a professional relationship, if, in accordance § 2317.02, the attorney, physician, or cleric could not testify with respect to that communication in a civil or criminal proceeding.

The client, patient, or penitent in the relationship is deemed to have waived any testimonial privilege with respect to any communication the attorney, physician, or cleric receives, and the attorney, physician, or cleric shall make a report with respect to that communication if all of the following apply:

- The client, patient, or penitent, at the time of the communication, is either a child under age 18 or a mentally retarded, developmentally disabled, or physically impaired person under age 21.
- The attorney, physician, or cleric knows, or has reasonable cause to suspect based on facts that would cause a reasonable person in similar position to suspect, as a result of the communication or any observations made during that communication, that the

client, patient, or penitent has suffered or faces a threat of suffering any physical or mental wound, injury, disability, or condition of a nature that reasonably indicates abuse or neglect of the person.

- The abuse or neglect does not arise out of the person's attempt to have an abortion without the notification of her parents, guardian, or custodian in accordance with § 2151.85.

Inclusion of Reporter's Name in Report
Rev. Code § 2151.421

The reporter is not required to provide his or her name in the report, but if he or she wants to receive information on the outcome of the investigation, he or she must provide his or her name, address, and telephone number to the person who receives the report.

Disclosure of Reporter Identity
Rev. Code § 2151.421

The information provided in a report made pursuant to this section and the name of the person who made the report shall not be released for use and shall not be used as evidence in any civil action or proceeding brought against the person who made the report.

Oklahoma

Professionals Required to Report
Ann. Stat. Tit. 10A, § 1-2-101; Tit. 21, § 1021.4

Mandatory reporters include:
- All persons
- Commercial film and photographic print processors or computer technicians

Reporting by Other Persons
Ann. Stat. Tit. 10A, § 1-2-101

Every person who has reason to believe that a child is a victim of abuse or neglect must report.

Standards for Making a Report
Ann. Stat. Tit. 10A, § 1-2-101; Tit. 21, § 1021.4

A report is required when:
- Any person has reason to believe that a child under age 18 is a victim of abuse or neglect.
- A physician, surgeon, or other health-care professional, including doctors of medicine, licensed osteopathic physicians, residents, and interns, attends the birth of a child who tests positive for alcohol or a controlled dangerous substance.
- A commercial film and photographic print processor or computer technician has knowledge of or observes any film, photograph, video-tape, negative, or slide depicting a child engaged in an act of sexual conduct.

Privileged Communications
Ann. Stat. Tit. 10A, § 1-2-101

No privilege shall relieve any person from the requirement to report.

Inclusion of Reporter's Name in Report

This issue is not addressed in the statutes reviewed.

Disclosure of Reporter Identity

This issue is not addressed in the statutes reviewed.

Oregon

Professionals Required to Report
Rev. Stat. §§ 419B.005; 419B.010

A public or private official is mandated to report. Public or private officials include:

- Physicians, osteopaths, physician assistants, naturopathic physicians, podiatrists, surgeons, interns, residents, optometrists, chiropractors, dentists, nurses, nurse practitioners, pharmacists, nurse's aides, home health aides, or employees of in-home health services
- School employees
- Employees of the Department of Human Services, Oregon Health Authority, State Commission on Children and Families, Child Care Division of the Employment Department, the Oregon Youth Authority, a county health department, a community mental health program, a community developmental disabilities program, a county juvenile department, a licensed child-caring agency, or an alcohol and drug treatment program
- Peace officers
- Members of the clergy
- Psychologists, social workers, professional counselors, marriage and family therapists
- Certified foster care or child care providers
- Attorneys or court-appointed special advocates
- Firefighters or emergency medical technicians
- Members of the Legislative Assembly
- Physical, speech, or occupational therapists
- Audiologists or speech-language pathologists
- Employees of the Teacher Standards and Practices Commission directly involved in investigations or discipline by the commission
- Operators of preschool or school-age recorded programs
- Employees or a private agency or organization facilitating the provision of respite services for parents pursuant to a properly executed power of attorney

Reporting by Other Persons
Rev. Stat. § 419B.015

Any person may voluntarily make a report.

Standards for Making a Report
Rev. Stat. § 419B.010

A report is required when any public or private official has reasonable cause to believe that any child with whom the official comes in contact has suffered abuse.

Privileged Communications
Rev. Stat. § 419B.010

A psychiatrist, psychologist, member of the clergy, or attorney shall not be required to report if such communication is privileged under law. An attorney is not required to make a report of information communicated to the attorney in the course of representing a client, if disclosure of the information would be detrimental to the client.

Inclusion of Reporter's Name in Report

The reporter is not specifically required by statute to provide his/ her name in the report.

Disclosure of Reporter Identity

Rev. Stat. § 419B.015

The name, address, and other identifying information about the person who made the report may not be disclosed.

Pennsylvania
Professionals Required to Report
Cons. Stat. Tit. 23, § 6311

Persons required to report include, but are not limited to:

- Licensed physicians, osteopaths, medical examiners, coroners, funeral directors, dentists, optometrists, chiropractors, podiatrists, interns, nurses, or hospital personnel
- Christian Science practitioners or members of the clergy
- School administrators, teachers, school nurses, social services workers, daycare center workers, or any other child care or foster care workers
- Mental health professionals
- Peace officers or law enforcement officials

Reporting by Other Persons
Cons. Stat. Tit. 23, § 6312

Any person who has reason to suspect that a child is abused or neglected may report.

Standards for Making a Report
Cons. Stat. Tit. 23, § 6311

A report is required when a person, who in the course of employment, occupation, or practice of a profession, comes into contact with children, has reasonable cause to suspect, on the basis of medical, professional, or other training and experience, that a child is a victim of child abuse.

Privileged Communications
Cons. Stat. Tit. 23, § 6311

Except with respect to confidential communications made to a member of the clergy that are protected under 42 Pa.C.S. § 5943 (relating to confidential communications to clergymen), and except with respect to confidential communications made to an attorney that are protected by 42 Pa.C.S. §§ 5916 or 5928 (relating to confidential communications to an attorney), the privileged communication between any professional person required to report and the patient or client of that person shall not apply to situations involving child abuse and shall not constitute grounds for failure to report as required by this chapter.

Inclusion of Reporter's Name in Report Cons. Stat. Tit. 23, § 6313

Mandated reporters must make a written report that includes their name and contact information.

Disclosure of Reporter Identity
Cons. Stat. Tit. 23, § 6340

The release of the identity of the mandated reporter is prohibited unless the secretary finds that the release will not be detrimental to the safety of the reporter.

Puerto Rico
Professionals Required to Report
Ann. Laws Tit. 8, § 446

The following individuals and entities are required to report:
- Professionals or public officials
- Public, private, and privatized entities
- Professionals in the fields of health, justice, education, social work, or public order
- Persons who administer or work in caregiving institutions or centers, rehabilitation institutions, centers for minors, or foster homes
- Processors of film or photographs

Reporting by Other Persons

Ann. Laws Tit. 8, § 446

Any person who has knowledge of or suspects that a minor is a victim of abuse or neglect must report.

Standards for Making a Report

Ann. Laws Tit. 8, § 446

A report is required when:
- A person, in his or her professional capacity and in the performance of his or her functions, learns or comes to suspect that a minor is, has been, or is at risk of becoming a victim of abuse.
- A film processor has knowledge of or observes any motion picture, photograph, videotape, negative, or slide that depict a minor involved in a sexual activity.

Privileged Communications

This issue is not addressed in the statutes reviewed.

Inclusion of Reporter's Name in Report

The reporter is not specifically required by statute to provide his/ her name in the report.

Disclosure of Reporter Identity

Ann. Laws Tit. 8, § 446

The identity of the person who made the report shall be kept in strict confidence.

Rhode Island

Professionals Required to Report

Gen. Laws § 40-11-6

Any physician or duly certified registered nurse practitioner is required to report.

Reporting by Other Persons

Gen. Laws § 40-11-3(a)

Any person who has reasonable cause to know or suspect that a child has been abused or neglected must report.

Standards for Making a Report

Gen. Laws §§ 40-11-3(a); 40-11-6

A report is required when:
- A person has reasonable cause to know or suspect that a child has been abused or neglected.
- A physician or nurse practitioner has cause to suspect that a child brought to them for treatment is an abused or neglected child, or he or she determines that a child under age 12 is suffering from any sexually transmitted disease.

Privileged Communications

Gen. Laws § 40-11-11

The privileged quality of communication between husband and wife and any professional person and his or her patient or client, except that between attorney and client, shall not constitute grounds for failure to report.

Inclusion of Reporter's Name in Report

The reporter is not specifically required by statute to provide his or her name in the report. Disclosure of Reporter Identity

This issue is not addressed in the statutes reviewed.

South Carolina

Professionals Required to Report
Ann. Code § 63-7-310

The following professionals are required to report:

- Physicians, nurses, dentists, optometrists, medical examiners, or coroners
- Any other medical, emergency medical services, or allied health professionals
- Teachers, school counselors, principals, or assistant principals
- Child care workers in any child care centers or foster care facilities
- Mental health professionals, social or public assistance workers, or substance abuse treatment staff
- Members of the clergy including Christian Science practitioners or religious healers
- Police or law enforcement officers, judges, undertakers, or funeral home directors or employees
- Persons responsible for processing films or computer technicians

Reporting by Other Persons
Ann. Code § 63-7-310

Any other person who has reason to believe that a child's physical or mental health or welfare has been or may be adversely affected by abuse and neglect may report.

Standards for Making a Report
Ann. Code § 63-7-310

A report is required when a reporter, in his or her professional capacity, receives information that gives him or her reason to believe that a child has been or may be abused or neglected.

Privileged Communications
Ann. Code § 63-7-420

The privileged quality of communication between husband and wife and any professional person and his patient or client, except that between attorney and client or clergy member, including a Christian Science practitioner or religious healer, and penitent, does not constitute grounds for failure to report. However, a clergy member, including a Christian Science practitioner or religious healer, must report in accordance with this subarticle except when information is received from the alleged perpetrator of the abuse and neglect during a communication that is protected by the clergy and penitent privilege as provided for in § 19-11-90.

Inclusion of Reporter's Name in Report

The reporter is not specifically required by statute to provide his or her name in the report.

Disclosure of Reporter Identity
Ann. Code § 63-7-330
The identity of the person making a report pursuant to this section must be kept confidential by the agency or department receiving the report and must not be disclosed, except as specifically provided for in statute.

South Dakota
Professionals Required to Report
Codified Laws § 26-8A-3
Mandatory reporters include:
- Physicians, dentists, osteopaths, chiropractors, optometrists, nurses, or coroners
- Teachers, school counselors or officials, or child welfare providers
- Mental health professionals or counselors, psychologists, social workers, chemical dependency counselors, employees or volunteers of domestic abuse shelters, or religious healing practitioners
- Parole or court services officers or law enforcement officers
- Any safety-sensitive position (as defined in § 23-3-64), including any law enforcement officer authorized to carry firearms and any custody staff employed by any agency responsible for the rehabilitation or treatment of any adjudicated adult or juvenile

Reporting by Other Persons
Codified Laws § 26-8A-3
Any person who knows or has reasonable cause to suspect that a child has been abused or neglected may report.

Standards for Making a Report
Codified Laws § 26-8A-3
A report is required when a reporter has reasonable cause to suspect that a child has been abused or neglected.

Privileged Communications
Codified Laws § 26-8A-15
The following privileges may not be claimed as a reason for not reporting:
- Physician-patient
- Husband-wife
- School counselor-student
- Social worker-client

Inclusion of Reporter's Name in Report
The reporter is not specifically required by statute to provide his or her name in the report.

Disclosure of Reporter
Identity Codified Laws § 26-8A-11.1
The name of the reporter is not disclosed unless:
- The report is determined to be unsubstantiated.
- Within 30 days, the subject of the report requests disclosure of the reporter's identity.

- A hearing is held to determine whether the report was made with malice and without reasonable foundation and that release of the name will not endanger the life or safety of the reporter.

Tennessee

Professionals Required to Report
Ann. Code §§ 37-1-403; 37-1-605

Persons required to report include:

- Physicians, osteopaths, medical examiners, chiropractors, nurses, hospital personnel, or other health or mental health professionals
- Teachers, other school officials or personnel, daycare center workers, or other professional child care, foster care, residential, or institutional workers
- Social workers
- Practitioners who rely solely on spiritual means for healing
- Judges or law enforcement officers
- Neighbors, relatives, or friends
- Other persons

Reporting by Other Persons
Ann. Code §§ 37-1-403; 37-1-605

Any person who has knowledge that a child has been harmed by abuse or neglect must report.

Standards for Making a Report
Ann. Code §§ 37-1-403; 37-1-605

A report is required when:

- A person has knowledge that a child has been harmed by abuse or neglect.
- A person is called upon to render aid to any child who is suffering from an injury that reasonably appears to have been caused by abuse.
- A person knows or has reasonable cause to suspect that a child has been sexually abused.
- A physician diagnoses or treats any sexually transmitted disease in a child age 13 or younger or diagnoses pregnancy in an unemancipated minor.

Privileged Communications
Ann. Code § 37-1-411

The following privileges may not be claimed:

- Husband-wife
- Psychiatrist-patient or psychologist-patient

Inclusion of Reporter's Name in Report

The reporter is not specifically required by statute to provide his or her name in the report.

Disclosure of Reporter Identity
Ann. Code § 37-1-409

Except as may be ordered by the juvenile court, the name of any person reporting child abuse or neglect shall not be released to any person, other than employees of the department or other child protection team members responsible for child protective services, the abuse registry, or the appropriate district attorney general upon subpoena of the Tennessee Bureau of Investigation, without the written consent of the person reporting.

The reporter's identity shall be irrelevant to any civil proceeding and shall, therefore, not be subject to disclosure by order of any court. This shall not prohibit the issuance of a subpoena to a person reporting child abuse when deemed necessary by the district attorney general or the department to protect a child who is the subject of a report, provided that the fact that the person made the report is not disclosed.

Texas

Professionals Required to Report
Fam. Code § 261.101
Persons required to report include:
- A professional, for purposes of the reporting laws, who is licensed or certified by the State or who is an employee of a facility licensed, certified, or operated by the State and who, in the normal course of official duties or duties for which a license or certification is required, has direct contact with children.
- Professionals include:
  o Teachers or daycare employees
  o Nurses, doctors, or employees of a clinic or health-care facility that provides reproductive services
  o Juvenile probation officers or juvenile detention or correctional officers

Reporting by Other Persons
Fam. Code § 261.101
A person who has cause to believe that a child has been adversely affected by abuse or neglect shall immediately make a report.

Standards for Making a Report
Fam. Code § 261.101
A report is required when a person has cause to believe that a child has been adversely affected by abuse or neglect.

Privileged Communications
Fam. Code §§ 261.101; 261.202
The requirement to report applies without exception to an individual whose personal communications may otherwise be privileged, including an attorney, a member of the clergy, a medical practitioner, a social worker, a mental health professional, and an employee of a clinic or health-care facility that provides reproductive services.

In a proceeding regarding the abuse or neglect of a child, evidence may not be excluded on the ground of privileged communication except in the case of communication between an attorney and client.

Inclusion of Reporter's Name in Report
The reporter is not specifically required by statute to provide his or her name in the report.

Disclosure of Reporter Identity
Fam. Code §§ 261.101; 261.201
Unless waived in writing by the person making the report, the identity of an individual making a report is confidential and may be disclosed only:
- As provided by § 261.201

- To a law enforcement officer for the purposes of conducting a criminal investigation of the report

A report of alleged or suspected abuse or neglect and the identity of the person making the report are confidential. A court may order the disclosure of such confidential information, if after a hearing and an *in camera* review of the requested information, the court determines that the disclosure is:

- Essential to the administration of justice
- Not likely to endanger the life or safety of a child who is the subject of the report, a person who made the report, or any other person who participates in an investigation of reported abuse or neglect or who provides care for the child

The Texas Youth Commission shall release a report of alleged or suspected abuse if the report relates to abuse or neglect involving a child committed to the commission. The commission shall edit any report disclosed under this section to protect the identity of:

- A child who is the subject of the report
- The person who made the report
- Any other person whose life or safety may be endangered by the disclosure

Utah

Professionals Required to Report
Ann. Code § 62A-4a-403

Any person licensed under the Medical Practice Act or the Nurse Practice Act is required to report.

Reporting by Other Persons
Ann. Code § 62A-4a-403

Any person who has reason to believe that a child has been subjected to abuse or neglect must report.

Standards for Making a Report
Ann. Code § 62A-4a-403

A report is required when:

- A person has reason to believe that a child has been subjected to abuse or neglect.
- A person observes a child being subjected to conditions or circumstances that would reasonably result in sexual abuse, physical abuse, or neglect.

Privileged Communications
Ann. Code §§ 62A-4a-403; 62A-4a-412(5)

The requirement to report does not apply to a clergy member or priest without the consent of the person making the confession, with regard to any confession made to the clergy member or priest in his or her professional character in the course of discipline enjoined by the church.

The physician-patient privilege is not a ground for excluding evidence regarding a child's injuries or the cause of those injuries in any proceeding resulting from a report made in good faith pursuant to this part.

Inclusion of Reporter's Name in Report
The reporter is not specifically required by statute to provide his/ her name in the report.

Disclosure of Reporter Identity
Ann. Code § 62A-4a-412(3)(b)

The name and contact information of the reporter shall be deleted prior to any release of records to the subject of the report.

Vermont

Professionals Required to Report
Ann. Stat. Tit. 33, § 4913

The following professionals are required to report:

- Physicians, surgeons, osteopaths, chiropractors, physician's assistants, hospital administrators, nurses, medical examiners, dentists, psychologists, or other health-care providers
- School superintendents, teachers, school librarians, child care workers, school principals, school guidance counselors, mental health professionals, or social workers
- Employees, contractors, and grantees of the agency of human services who have contact with clients
- Probation officers, police officers, camp owners, camp administrators or counselors
- Members of the clergy

Reporting by Other Persons
Ann. Stat. Tit. 33, § 4913

Any other person who has reasonable cause to believe that a child has been abused or neglected may report.

Standards for Making a Report
Ann. Stat. Tit. 33, § 4913

A report is required when a reporter has reasonable cause to believe that a child has been abused or neglected.

Privileged Communications
Ann. Stat. Tit. 33, § 4913

A person may not refuse to make a report required by this section on the grounds that making the report would violate a privilege or disclose a confidential communication, except that a member of the clergy is not required to report if the knowledge comes from a communication that is required to be kept confidential by religious doctrine.

Inclusion of Reporter's Name in Report
Ann. Stat. Tit. 33, § 4914

Reports shall contain the name and address or other contact information of the reporter.

Disclosure of Reporter Identity
Ann. Stat. Tit. 33, § 4913

The name of and any identifying information about either the person making the report or any person mentioned in the report shall be confidential unless:

- The person making the report specifically allows disclosure.
- A judicial proceeding results from the report.
- A court, after a hearing, finds probable cause to believe that the report was not made in good faith and orders the department to make the name of the reporter available.

Virgin Islands

Professionals Required to Report
Ann. Code Tit. 5, § 2533

The following professionals are required to report:

- Physicians, hospital personnel, nurses, dentists, or any other medical or mental health professionals
- Teachers or other school personnel, social service workers, daycare workers, or other child care or foster care workers
- Peace officers or law enforcement officials

Reporting by Other Persons
Ann. Code Tit. 5, § 2533
Any other person who has reasonable cause to suspect that a child has been abused or neglected may report.

Standards for Making a Report
Ann. Code Tit. 5, § 2533
A report is required when:

A reporter has reasonable cause to suspect that a child has been subjected to abuse, sexual abuse, or neglect.

A reporter observes the child being subjected to conditions or circumstances that would reasonably result in abuse or neglect.

Privileged Communications
Ann. Code Tit. 5, § 2538
The privileged quality of communications between husband and wife and between any professional person and his or her patient or client, except that between attorney and client, shall not constitute grounds for failure to report.

Inclusion of Reporter's Name in Report
Ann. Code Tit. 5, § 2534
The report shall include the name, address, and occupation of the reporter.

Disclosure of Reporter Identity
This issue is not addressed in the statutes reviewed.

Virginia
Professionals Required to Report
Ann. Code § 63.2-1509
The following professionals are required to report:
- Persons licensed to practice medicine or any of the healing arts
- Hospital residents, interns, or nurses
- Social workers or probation officers
- Teachers or other persons employed in a public or private school, kindergarten, or nursery school
- Persons providing full-time or part-time child care for pay on a regular basis
- Mental health professionals
- Law enforcement officers, animal control officers, or mediators
- All professional staff persons, not previously enumerated, employed by a private or State-operated hospital, institution, or facility to which children have been committed or where children have been placed for care and treatment
- Persons associated with or employed by any private organization responsible for the care, custody, or control of children
- Court-appointed special advocates

- Persons, over age 18, who have received training approved by the Department of Social Services for the purposes of recognizing and reporting child abuse and neglect
- Any person employed by a local department who determines eligibility for public assistance
- Emergency medical services personnel

Reporting by Other Persons
Ann. Code § 63.2-1510
Any person who suspects that a child is abused or neglected may report.

Standards for Making a Report
Ann. Code § 63.2-1509
A report is required when, in his or her professional or official capacity, a reporter has reason to suspect that a child is abused or neglected. For purposes of this section, 'reason to suspect that a child is abused or neglected' shall include:

- A finding made by an attending physician within 7 days of a child's birth that the results of a blood or urine test conducted within 48 hours of the birth of the child indicate the presence of a controlled substance not prescribed for the mother by a physician
- A finding by an attending physician made within 48 hours of a child's birth that the child was born dependent on a controlled substance that was not prescribed by a physician for the mother and has demonstrated withdrawal symptoms
- A diagnosis by an attending physician made within 7 days of a child's birth that the child has an illness, disease, or condition that, to a reasonable degree of medical certainty, is attributable to *in utero* exposure to a controlled substance that was not prescribed by a physician for the mother or the child
- A diagnosis by an attending physician made within 7 days of a child's birth that the child has fetal alcohol syndrome attributable to *in utero* exposure to alcohol

Privileged Communications
Ann. Code §§ 63.2-1509; 63.2-1519
The requirement to report shall not apply to any regular minister, priest, rabbi, imam, or duly accredited practitioner of any religious organization or denomination usually referred to as a church as it relates to information required by the doctrine of the religious organization or denomination to be kept in a confidential manner.

The physician-patient or husband-wife privilege is not permitted.

Inclusion of Reporter's Name in Report
The reporter is not specifically required by statute to provide his or her name in the report.

Disclosure of Reporter Identity
Ann. Code § 63.2-1514
Any person who is the subject of an unfounded report who believes that the report was made in bad faith or with malicious intent may petition the court for the release of the records of the investigation or family assessment. If the court determines that there is a reasonable question of fact as to whether the report was made in bad faith or with malicious intent and that disclosure of the identity of the reporter would not be likely to endanger the life or safety of the reporter, it shall provide to the petitioner a copy of the records of the investigation or family assessment.

Washington
Professionals Required to Report
Rev. Code § 26.44.030
The following persons are required to report:
- Practitioners, county coroners, or medical examiners
- Law enforcement officers
- Professional school personnel
- Registered or licensed nurses, social service counselors, psychologists, or pharmacists
- Employees of the Department of Early Learning
- Licensed or certified child care providers or their employees
- Employees of the Department of Social and Health Services
- Juvenile probation officers
- Placement and liaison specialists, responsible living skills program staff, or HOPE center staff
- State family and children's ombudsman or any volunteer in the ombudsman's office
- Persons who supervise employees or volunteers who train, educate, coach, or counsel children or have regular unsupervised access to children
- Department of Corrections personnel
- Any adult with whom a child resides
- Guardians *ad litem* and court-appointed special advocates

Reporting by Other Persons
Rev. Code § 26.44.030
Any person who has reasonable cause to believe that a child has suffered abuse or neglect may report.

Standards for Making a Report
Rev. Code § 26.44.030
A report is required when:
- A reporter has reasonable cause to believe that a child has suffered abuse or neglect.
- Any person, in his or her official supervisory capacity with a nonprofit or for-profit organization, has reasonable cause to believe that a child has suffered abuse or neglect caused by a person over whom he or she regularly exercises supervisory authority.
- Department of Corrections personnel observe offenders or the children with whom the offenders are in contact, and as a result of these observations have reasonable cause to believe that a child has suffered abuse or neglect.
- Any adult has reasonable cause to believe that a child who resides with them has suffered severe abuse.

Privileged Communications
Rev. Code §§ 26.44.030; 26.44.060
A person who supervises employees or volunteers who train, educate, coach, or counsel children, or have regular unsupervised access to children, shall not be required to report when he or she obtains the information solely as a result of a privileged communication.

Information considered privileged by statute and not directly related to reports required by this section must not be divulged without a valid written waiver of the privilege.

Conduct conforming with reporting requirements shall not be deemed a violation of the confidential communication privilege of §§ 5.60.060 (3) and (4) [pertaining to clergy-penitent and physician-patient privilege], 18.53.200 [pertaining to optometrist-patient privilege], and 18.83.110 [pertaining to psychologist-client privilege].

Inclusion of Reporter's Name in Report
Rev. Code § 26.44.030
The department shall make reasonable efforts to learn the name, address, and telephone number of the reporter.

Disclosure of Reporter Identity
Rev. Code § 26.44.030
The department shall provide assurances of appropriate confidentiality of the identification of persons reporting under this section.

West Virginia
Professionals Required to Report
Ann. Code § 49-6A-2
The following professionals are required to report:
- Medical, dental, or mental health professionals
- Christian Science practitioners or religious healers
- Teachers or other school personnel
- Social service, child care, or foster care workers
- Emergency medical services personnel
- Peace officer, law enforcement officials, or humane officers
- Members of the clergy
- Circuit court judges, family court judges, employees of the Division of Juvenile Services, or magistrates

Reporting by Other Persons
Ann. Code § 49-6A-2
Any person who has reasonable cause to suspect that a child is abused or neglected may report. Standards for Making a Report

Ann. Code § 49-6A-2
A report is required when:
- A reporter has reasonable cause to suspect that a child is abused or neglected.
- A reporter observes a child being subjected to conditions that are likely to result in abuse or neglect.
- A reporter believes that a child has suffered serious physical abuse, sexual abuse, or sexual assault.

Privileged Communications
Ann. Code § 49-6A-7
The privileged quality of communications between husband and wife and between any professional person and his or her patient or client, except that between attorney and client, cannot be invoked in situations involving suspected or known child abuse or neglect.

Inclusion of Reporter's Name in Report
The reporter is not specifically required by statute to provide his/her name in the report.

Disclosure of Reporter Identity

Wisconsin
Professionals Required to Report
Ann. Stat. § 48.981
The following professionals are required to report:
- Physicians, coroners, medical examiners, nurses, dentists, chiropractors, optometrists, acupuncturists, other medical or mental health professionals, physical therapists, physical therapist assistants, dietitians, occupational therapists, speech-language pathologists, audiologists, or emergency medical technicians
- Schoolteachers, administrators, or counselors
- Child care workers in child care centers, group homes, or residential care centers, or child care providers
- Alcohol or other drug abuse counselors, marriage and family therapists, professional counselors, or members of the treatment staff employed by or working under contract with a county department or a residential care center for children and youth
- Social workers, public assistance workers, first responders, police or law enforcement officers, mediators, or court-appointed special advocates
- Members of the clergy or a religious order, including brothers, ministers, monks, nuns, priests, rabbis, or sisters

Reporting by Other Persons
Ann. Stat. § 48.981
Any person, including an attorney, who has reason to suspect that a child has been abused or neglected or who has reason to believe that a child has been threatened with abuse or neglect and that abuse or neglect of the child will occur may report.

Standards for Making a Report
Ann. Stat. § 48.981
A report is required when:
- A reporter, in the course of his or her professional duties, has reasonable cause to suspect that a child has been abused or neglected.
- A reporter, in the course of his or her professional duties, has reason to believe that a child has been threatened with abuse or neglect or that abuse or neglect will occur.

Privileged Communications
Ann. Stat. § 48.981
A member of the clergy is not required to report child abuse information that he or she receives solely through confidential communications made to him or her privately or in a confessional setting if he or she is authorized to hear or is accustomed to hearing such communications and, under the disciplines, tenets, or traditions of his or her religion, has a duty or is expected to keep those communications secret. Those disciplines, tenets, or traditions need not be in writing.

Inclusion of Reporter's Name in Report
The reporter is not specifically required by statute to provide his/ her name in the report.

Disclosure of Reporter Identity
Ann. Stat. § 48.981
The identity of the reporter shall not be disclosed to the subject of the report.

Wyoming

Professionals Required to Report

No professional groups are specified in statute; all persons are required to report.

Reporting by Other Persons

Ann. Stat. § 14-3-205

All persons must report.

Standards for Making a Report

Ann. Stat. § 14-3-205

A report is required when:

- A person knows or has reasonable cause to believe or suspect that a child has been abused or neglected.
- A person observes any child being subjected to conditions or circumstances that would reasonably result in abuse or neglect.

Privileged Communications

Ann. Stat. § 14-3-210

Only the clergy-penitent and attorney-client privileges are permitted.

Inclusion of Reporter's Name in Report

Ann. Stat. § 14-3-206

The report must include any available photographs, videos, and x rays with the identification of the person who created the evidence and the date the evidence was created.

Disclosure of Reporter Identity

This issue is not addressed in the statutes reviewed.

End Notes

[1] The word *approximately* is used to stress the fact that States frequently amend their laws. This information is current only through April 2010. At that time, New Jersey and Wyoming were the only two States that did not enumerate specific professional groups as mandated reporters but required all persons to report.

[2] Film processors are mandated reporters in Alaska, California, Colorado, Georgia, Illinois, Iowa, Louisiana, Maine, Missouri, Oklahoma, and South Carolina. Substance abuse counselors are required to report in Alaska, California, Connecticut, Illinois, Iowa, Kansas, Massachusetts, Nevada, New York, North Dakota, Oregon, South Carolina, South Dakota, and Wisconsin. Probation or parole officers are mandated reporters in Arkansas, California, Colorado, Connecticut, Hawaii, Illinois, Louisiana, Massachusetts, Minnesota, Missouri, Nevada, North Dakota, South Dakota, Texas, Vermont, Virginia, and Washington.

[3] Domestic violence workers are mandated reporters in Alaska, Arizona, Arkansas, Connecticut, Illinois, Maine, and South Dakota. Humane officers are mandated reporters in California, Colorado, Illinois, Maine, Ohio, Virginia, and West Virginia.

[4] Arkansas, California, Louisiana, Maine, Montana, Oregon, Virginia, Washington, and Wisconsin.

[5] Alabama, Arizona, Arkansas, California, Colorado, Connecticut, Illinois, Louisiana, Maine, Massachusetts, Michigan, Minnesota, Mississippi, Missouri, Montana, Nevada, New Hampshire, New Mexico, North Dakota, Ohio, Oregon, Pennsylvania, South Carolina, Vermont, West Virginia, and Wisconsin. For more information, see Child Welfare Information Gateway's *Clergy as Mandatory Reporters of Child Abuse and Neglect* at www.childwelfare.gov/systemwide/laws

[6] Delaware, Florida, Idaho, Indiana, Kentucky, Maryland, Mississippi, Nebraska, New Hampshire, New Mexico, North Carolina, Oklahoma, Rhode Island, Tennessee, Texas, and Utah.

[7] Connecticut, Mississippi, and New Jersey do not currently address the issue of privileged communications within their reporting laws. The issue of privilege may be addressed elsewhere in the statutes of these States, such as rules of evidence.

[8] New Hampshire, North Carolina, Oklahoma, Rhode Island, Texas, and West Virginia disallow the use of the clergy-penitent privilege as grounds for failing to report suspected child abuse or neglect. For a more complete discussion of the requirement for clergy to report child abuse and neglect, see the Information Gateway's Clergy as *Mandatory Reporters of Child Abuse and Neglect* at www.childwelfare.gov/systemwide/laws policies/statutes/clergymandated.cfm.

[9] For State-specific information about these hotlines, see Information Gateway's *Child Abuse Reporting Numbers* at www.childwelfare.gov/pubs/reslist/rl_dsp. cfm?rs_id=5&rate_chno=11-11172.

[10] California, Colorado, Florida, Illinois, Indiana, Iowa, Louisiana, Maine, Massachusetts, Minnesota, Mississippi, Missouri, Nebraska, New Mexico, New York, North Carolina, Pennsylvania, and Vermont have this requirement.

[11] The statutes in Alaska, Arizona, Delaware, Idaho, Maryland, Massachusetts, New Hampshire, Oklahoma, Rhode Island, West Virginia, Wyoming, and the Virgin Islands do not specifically protect reporter identity but do provide for confidentiality of records in general.

In: Reporting Child Abuse and Neglect
Editor: Henry J. Pervall

ISBN: 978-1-62100-157-7
© 2012 Nova Science Publishers, Inc.

Chapter 2

CROSS-REPORTING AMONG RESPONDERS TO CHILD ABUSE AND NEGLECT: SUMMARY AND STATE LAWS[*][1]

United States Department of Health and Human Services

All 50 States, the District of Columbia, American Samoa, Guam, the Northern Mariana Islands, Puerto Rico, and the U.S. Virgin Islands have statutes specifying procedures that State agencies must follow in handling reports of suspected child abuse or neglect. In most States, these procedures include requirements for cross-system reporting and/or information sharing among professional entities. Typically, reports are shared among social services agencies, law enforcement departments, and prosecutors' offices.

THE PURPOSE OF CROSS-REPORTING STATUTES

In most States, a mandated reporter or other person who is concerned about a child's safety and welfare can make a report of suspected child maltreatment to a reporting hotline, the child protection agency, or a law enforcement agency. State laws that require the agencies receiving the initial reports to share the reports with other specific agencies (i.e., cross-report) ensure that needed information is available to the agency that must respond to the report.

Specific models for information sharing vary from State to State. For example, child protective services agencies generally have the responsibility of responding to cases in which the suspected abuse or neglect is caused by a parent, family member, or other caregiver. In approximately 27 States, cases in which the suspected abuse is caused by someone other than a family member, or in which the abuse involves sexual abuse or severe injury to the child, are considered crimes and must be cross-reported to law enforcement agencies for investigation.[1]

---

[*] This is an edited, reformatted and augmented version of the United States Department of Health and Human Services publication, dated on January 2010.

[1] This material may be freely reproduced and distributed. However, when doing so, please credit Child Welfare Information Gateway.

In nine States, child protective and law enforcement agencies are required to coordinate investigations and share information in order to minimize the number of times individual children are interviewed.[2] Five States require information sharing among multidisciplinary teams that conduct assessments and provide services to families.[3]

This publication is a product of the State Statutes Series prepared by Child Welfare Information Gateway. While every attempt has been made to be as complete as possible, additional information on these topics may be in other sections of a State's code as well as agency regulations, case law, and informal practices and procedures.

Alabama

Ala. Code § 26-14-7(d) (LexisNexis through 2009 1st Spec. Sess.)

The county Department of Human Resources shall make a complete written report of the investigation, together with its recommendations. Such reports may be made available to the appropriate court, the district attorney, and the appropriate law enforcement agency upon request.

Ala. Code § 26-14-3(b)-(d) (LexisNexis through 2009 1st Spec. Sess.)

When an initial report is made to a law enforcement official, the official subsequently shall inform the Department of Human Resources of the report so the department can carry out its responsibility to provide protective services, when deemed appropriate to the respective child or children.

When the Department of Human Resources receives an initial report of suspected abuse or neglect involving discipline or corporal punishment committed in a public or private school or suspected abuse or neglect in a State-operated child residential facility, the Department of Human Resources shall transmit a copy of school reports to the law enforcement agency, and residential facility reports to the operating State agency, which shall conduct the investigation.

Nothing in this chapter shall preclude interagency agreements among departments of human resources, law enforcement, and other State agencies on procedures for investigating reports of suspected child abuse and neglect to provide for departments of human resources to assist law enforcement and other State agencies in these investigations.

Alaska

Alaska Stat. § 47.17.020(c), (e) (LexisNexis through 2009 1st Spec. Sess.)

If the person making a report of harm under this section cannot reasonably contact the nearest office of the Department of Health and Social Services and immediate action is necessary for the well-being of the child, the person shall make the report to a peace officer. The peace officer shall immediately take action to protect the child and shall, at the earliest opportunity, notify the nearest office of the department.

The department shall immediately notify the nearest law enforcement agency if the department:

- Concludes that the harm was caused by a person who is not responsible for the child's welfare
- Is unable to determine who caused the harm to the child or whether the person who is believed to have caused the harm has responsibility for the child's welfare
- Concludes that the report involves possible criminal conduct or abuse or neglect that results in the need for medical treatment of the child

Alaska Stat. § 47.17.025(a) (LexisNexis through 2009 1st Spec. Sess.)

A law enforcement agency shall immediately notify the Department of Health and Social Services of the receipt of a report of harm to a child from abuse. Upon receipt from any source of a report of harm to a child from abuse, the department shall notify the Department of Law and investigate the report and, within 72 hours of the receipt of the report, shall provide a written report of its investigation of the harm to a child from abuse to the Department of Law for review.

American Samoa

A.S. Code § 45.2010(a) (A.S. Bar 2003)

Reports of known or suspected child abuse or neglect made under this chapter are immediately made to the Department [of Public Safety] by a written report prepared by those persons required to report, if so requested by the receiving agency. The receiving agency forwards a copy of its own report to the central registry on forms supplied by the registry.

If at any time a report of suspected child abuse or neglect is made to the [child protection] agency, the Department [of Public Safety] must be notified. If a report of suspected child abuse or neglect is made to the department, the agency must be notified.

Arizona

Ariz. Rev. Stat. Ann. § 13-3620(H) (LexisNexis through 2009 3rd Spec. Sess.)

When telephone or in-person reports are received by a peace officer, the officer shall immediately notify child protective services in the Department of Economic Security and make the information available to them. Notwithstanding any other statute, when child protective services receives these reports by telephone or in person, it shall immediately notify a peace officer in the appropriate jurisdiction.

Arkansas

Ark. Code Ann. § 12-18-503 (LexisNexis through 2009 Reg. Sess.)

The Department of Human Services shall notify the following of any report of child maltreatment within 5 business days:

- The legal parents, legal guardians, and current foster parent of a child in foster care who is named as a victim or alleged offender

- The attorney ad litem for any child named as the victim or alleged offender
- A person appointed by the court as the court-appointed special advocate volunteer for any child named as the victim or alleged offender
- Counsel in a dependency-neglect case or family in need of services case when the child is named as a victim or alleged offender
- The attorney ad litem and court-appointed special advocate volunteer for all other children in the same foster home if the child maltreatment occurred in a foster home
- The attorney ad litem and court-appointed special advocate for any child in foster care when the alleged juvenile offender or underaged juvenile aggressor is placed in the same placement as the attorney ad litem or court-appointed special advocate's client
- The appropriate multidisciplinary team

Ark. Code Ann. § 12-18-504 (LexisNexis through 2009 Reg. Sess.)

The Department of Human Services shall immediately notify local law enforcement of all reports of severe maltreatment.

Notification of a report of child maltreatment shall be provided within 5 business days to the prosecuting attorney on an allegation of severe maltreatment.

- The prosecuting attorney may provide written notice to the department that the department does not need to provide notification of the initial child maltreatment report to the prosecuting attorney's office.
- Upon receiving the notification, the department shall not be required to provide notification of the initial child maltreatment report to the prosecuting attorney's office.

California

Cal. Penal Code § 11166(k) (LexisNexis through 2009 Reg. Sess.)

A law enforcement agency shall immediately, or as soon as practicably possible, report by telephone, fax, or electronic transmission to the agency given responsibility for investigation of cases under § 300 of the Welfare and Institutions Code and to the district attorney's office every known or suspected instance of child abuse or neglect reported to it, except acts or omissions coming within § 11165.2(b), which shall be reported only to the county welfare or probation department. A law enforcement agency shall report to the county welfare or probation department every known or suspected instance of child abuse or neglect reported to it that is alleged to have occurred as a result of the action of a person responsible for the child's welfare, or as the result of the failure of a person responsible for the child's welfare to adequately protect the minor from abuse when the person responsible for the child's welfare knew or reasonably should have known that the minor was in danger of abuse. A law enforcement agency also shall send, fax, or electronically transmit a written report thereof within 36 hours of receiving the information concerning the incident to any agency to which it makes a telephone report.

Cal. Penal Code § 11166(j) (LexisNexis through 2009 Reg. Sess.)

A county probation or welfare department shall immediately, or as soon as practicably possible, report by telephone, fax, or electronic transmission to the law enforcement agency having jurisdiction over the case, to the agency given the responsibility for investigation of cases, and to the district attorney's office every known or suspected instance of child abuse or neglect, or reports made based on risk to a child that relates solely to the inability of the parent to provide the child with regular care due to the parent's substance abuse, that shall be reported only to the county welfare or probation department. A county probation or welfare department also shall send, fax, or electronically transmit a written report thereof within 36 hours of receiving the information concerning the incident to any agency to which it is required to make a telephone report under this subdivision.

Colorado

Colo. Rev. Stat. Ann. § 19-3-308(4)(b), (5) (LexisNexis through 2009 Sess.)

Upon the receipt of a report, if the county Department of Social Services reasonably believes that an incident of intrafamilial abuse or neglect has occurred, it shall immediately offer social services to the child who is the subject of the report and his or her family and may file a petition in the juvenile court or the district court with juvenile jurisdiction on behalf of such child. If, before the investigation is completed, the opinion of the investigators is that assistance of the local law enforcement agency is necessary for the protection of the child or other children under the same care, the local law enforcement agency shall be notified. If immediate removal is necessary to protect the child or other children under the same care from further abuse, the child or children may be placed in protective custody in accordance with §§ 19-3- 401(1)(a) and 19-3-405.

If a local law enforcement agency receives a report of a known or suspected incident of intrafamilial abuse or neglect, it shall immediately attempt to contact the county department in order to refer the case for investigation. If the local law enforcement agency is unable to contact the county department, it shall immediately make a complete investigation and may institute appropriate legal proceedings on behalf of the subject child or other children under the same care. As a part of an investigation, the local law enforcement agency shall have access to the records and reports of child abuse or neglect maintained by the State department for information under the name of the child or the suspected perpetrator. The local law enforcement agency, upon the receipt of a report and upon completion of any investigation it may undertake, shall immediately forward a summary of the investigatory data plus all relevant documents to the county department.

Colo. Rev. Stat. Ann. § 19-3-307(3) (LexisNexis through 2009 Sess.)

A copy of the report of known or suspected child abuse or neglect shall be transmitted immediately by the county Department of Social Services to the district attorney's office and to the local law enforcement agency.

When the county department reasonably believes a criminal act of abuse or neglect of a child in foster care has occurred, the county department shall transmit immediately a copy of the written report prepared by the county department to the district attorney's office and to the local law enforcement agency.

Connecticut

Conn. Gen. Stat. Ann. § 17a-101h (LexisNexis through 11-6-09)

Notwithstanding any provision of the general statutes to the contrary, any person authorized to conduct an investigation of abuse or neglect shall coordinate investigatory activities in order to minimize the number of interviews of any child and share information with other persons authorized to conduct an investigation of child abuse or neglect, as appropriate.

Conn. Gen. Stat. Ann. § 17a-101b(c) (LexisNexis through 11-6-09)

If the Commissioner of Children and Families, or the commissioner's designee, receives a report alleging sexual abuse or serious physical abuse, including, but not limited to, a report that (1) a child has died; (2) a child has been sexually assaulted; (3) a child has suffered brain damage or loss or serious impairment of a bodily function or organ; (4) a child has been sexually exploited; or (5) a child has suffered serious nonaccidental physical injury, the commissioner shall, within 12 hours of receipt of such report, notify the appropriate law enforcement agency.

Delaware

Del. Code Ann. Tit. 16, § 906(b)(3)-(4), (13), (15) (LexisNexis through 9-4-07)

The Division of Family Services may investigate any report but shall conduct an investigation involving all reports, which, if true, would constitute violations against a child by a person responsible for the care, custody, and control of the child pursuant to the provisions of statute, or an attempt to commit any such crimes. The division staff shall contact the appropriate law enforcement agency upon receipt of any report and shall provide such agency with a detailed description of the report received.

The assisting law enforcement agency shall promptly conduct its own criminal investigation and keep the division regularly apprised of the status and findings of its investigation. Law enforcement agencies and the division shall develop protocols to ensure compliance with this subsection.

When a written report is made by a person required to report, the division shall contact the person who made such report within 48 hours of the receipt of the report in order to ensure that full information has been received and to obtain any additional information and/or medical records that may be pertinent.

Multidisciplinary services shall be used whenever possible in conducting the investigation or family assessment and services approach, including the services of law enforcement agencies, the medical community, and other agencies, both public and private. The division and the Attorney General's Office shall cooperate with law enforcement agencies and the family court to develop training programs to increase the ability of division personnel, court personnel, and law enforcement officers to investigate suspected cases of abuse and neglect.

District of Columbia

D.C. Code Ann. § 4-1321.02(d) (LexisNexis through 6-11-09)

In addition to the requirements in subsections (a) and (b) of this section [pertaining to reporting requirements], any health professional licensed pursuant to Chapter 12 of Title 3, law enforcement officer, or humane officer of any agency charged with the enforcement of animal cruelty laws, except an undercover officer whose identity or investigation might be jeopardized, shall report immediately in writing to the Child and Family Services Agency that the law enforcement officer or health professional has reasonable cause to believe that a child is abused as a result of inadequate care, control, or subsistence in the home environment due to exposure to drug-related activity.

Florida

Fla. Stat. Ann. § 39.301(2)(a), (c) (LexisNexis through 2009 Reg. Sess.)

The Department of Children and Family Services shall immediately forward allegations of criminal conduct to the municipal or county law enforcement agency of the municipality or county in which the alleged conduct has occurred.

Upon receiving a written report of an allegation of criminal conduct from the department, the law enforcement agency shall review the information in the written report to determine whether a criminal investigation is warranted. If the law enforcement agency accepts the case for criminal investigation, it shall coordinate its investigative activities with the department, whenever feasible. If the law enforcement agency does not accept the case for criminal investigation, the agency shall notify the department in writing.

Georgia

Ga. Code Ann. § 19-7-5(e) (LexisNexis through 2009 Reg. Sess.)

If a report of child abuse is made to the child welfare agency or independently discovered by the agency, and the agency has reasonable cause to believe such report is true or the report contains any allegation or evidence of child abuse, then the agency shall immediately notify the appropriate police authority or district attorney.

Guam

Guam Code Ann. Tit. 19, § 13203(b) (LexisNexis through 8-26-08)

Child Protective Services shall immediately or as soon as practicably possible report by telephone to the Guam Police Department and to the Attorney General's Office every known or suspected instance of child abuse, except acts or omissions coming under § 13101(t)(4) [concerning neglect]. Child Protective Services shall also send a written report within 48 hours of receiving information concerning the incident to any agency to which it is required to make a telephone report.

The Guam Police Department shall immediately or as soon as practicably possible report by telephone to Child Protective Services and to the Attorney General's office every known or suspected instance of child abuse reported to it, except acts or omissions coming under § 13101(t)(4) [concerning neglect], which shall only be reported to Child Protective Services. However, the Guam Police Department shall report to Child Protective Services every known or suspected instance of child abuse reported to it that is alleged to have occurred as a result of the inaction of a person responsible for the child's welfare to adequately protect the minor from abuse when such person knew or reasonably should have known that the minor was in danger of abuse. The Guam Police Department shall also send a written report within 48 hours of receiving the information concerning the incident to any agency to which it is required to make a telephone report.

Child Protective Services and the Guam Police Department shall immediately or as soon as practicably possible report by telephone to the appropriate Department of Defense Family Advocacy Program every known or suspected instance of child abuse reported to them when such report involves active duty military personnel or their dependents.

Hawaii

Haw. Rev. Stat. § 350-1.1(c) (LexisNexis through 2009 Spec. Sess.)

If a police department or the Department of Public Safety is the initiating agency, a written report shall be filed with the Department of Human Services for cases that the police or Department of Public Safety take further action on or for active cases in the Department of Human Services under this chapter.

Haw. Rev. Stat. § 350-2(b)-(c) (LexisNexis through 2009 Spec. Sess.)

The Department of Human Services shall inform the appropriate police department of all reports received by the department regarding a case of child abuse or neglect, including reports received under § 350-1.1, provided that the name of the person who reported the case of child abuse or neglect shall be released to the police department pursuant only to court order or the person's consent.

The department shall inform the appropriate police department or office of the prosecuting attorney of the relevant information concerning a case of child abuse or neglect when such information is required by the police department or the office of the prosecuting attorney for the investigation of that case--provided the name of the person who reported the case of child abuse or neglect shall be released only to a police department or an office of the prosecuting attorney pursuant to court order or the person's consent.

Idaho

Idaho Code § 16-1605(1) (LexisNexis through 2009 Reg. Sess.)

Any [mandated reporter] or other person having reason to believe that a child under age 18 years has been abused, abandoned, or neglected, or who observes the child being subjected to conditions or circumstances that would reasonably result in abuse, abandonment, or neglect shall report or cause to be reported within 24 hours such conditions or circumstances to the proper law enforcement agency or the Department of Health and Welfare. The department shall be informed by law enforcement of any report made directly to it.

Illinois

325 Ill. Comp. Stat. Ann. 5/7 (LexisNexis through 11-2-09)

Reports made to the central register through the statewide, toll-free telephone number shall be immediately transmitted by the Department of Children and Family Services to the appropriate Child Protective Service Unit. All such reports alleging the death of a child; serious injury to a child, including but not limited to, brain damage, skull fractures, subdural hematomas, and internal injuries; torture of a child; malnutrition of a child; and sexual abuse of a child, including but not limited to sexual intercourse, sexual exploitation, sexual molestation, and sexually transmitted disease in a child age 12 and under, shall also be immediately transmitted by the department to the appropriate local law enforcement agency.

The department shall within 24 hours orally notify local law enforcement personnel and the Office of the State's Attorney of the involved county of the receipt of any report alleging the death of a child; serious injury to a child, including but not limited to brain damage, skull fractures, subdural hematomas, and internal injuries; torture of a child; malnutrition of a child; and sexual abuse of a child, including but not limited to sexual intercourse, sexual exploitation, sexual molestation, and sexually transmitted disease in a child age 12 and under.

All oral reports made by the department to local law enforcement personnel and the Office of the State's Attorney of the involved county shall be confirmed in writing within 24 hours of the oral report.

Indiana

Ind. Code Ann. § 31-33-7-7 (LexisNexis through 2009 Spec. Sess.)

When a law enforcement agency receives an initial report under the reporting law that a child may be a victim of child abuse or neglect, the law enforcement agency shall:

- Immediately communicate the report to the Department of Child Services, whether or not the law enforcement agency has reason to believe there exists an imminent danger to the child's health or welfare
- Conduct an immediate onsite assessment of the report along with the department whenever the law enforcement agency has reason to believe that an offense has been committed

In all cases, the law enforcement agency shall forward any information, including copies of assessment reports, on incidents of cases in which a child may be a victim of child abuse or neglect, whether or not obtained under the reporting laws, to the department and the juvenile court.

Ind. Code Ann. § 31-33-7-5 (LexisNexis through 2009 Spec. Sess.)

A copy of the written report from the Department of Child Services shall immediately be made available to:

- The appropriate law enforcement agency
- The prosecuting attorney
- In a case involving death, the coroner for the coroner's consideration

Iowa

Iowa Code Ann. § 232.70(5), (7), (8) (LexisNexis through 9-10-09)

Upon receipt of a report, the Department of Human Services shall do all of the following:

- Immediately make a determination whether the report constitutes an allegation of child abuse
- Notify the appropriate county attorney of receipt of the report

If the report is made to any agency other than the Department of Human Services, such agency shall promptly refer the report to the Department of Human Services.

If a report would be determined to constitute an allegation of child abuse relating to a sexual offense with or to a child, except that the suspected abuse resulted from the acts or omissions of a person other than a person responsible for the care of the child, the department shall refer the report to the appropriate law enforcement agency having jurisdiction to investigate the allegation. The department shall refer the report orally as soon as practicable and in writing within 72 hours of receiving the report.

Kansas

Kan. Ann. Stat. § 38-2223(c) (LexisNexis through 2008 Supp.)

Reports made pursuant to this section shall be made to the secretary, except as follows:

- When the Department of Social and Rehabilitation Services is not open for business, reports shall be made to the appropriate law enforcement agency. On the next day that the department is open for business, the law enforcement agency shall report to the department any report received and any investigation initiated pursuant to § 38-2226. The reports may be made orally or, on request of the secretary, in writing.
- Reports of child abuse or neglect occurring in an institution operated by the Secretary of Social and Rehabilitation Services or the Commissioner of Juvenile Justice shall be made to the attorney general.
- All other reports of child abuse or neglect by persons employed by or of children of persons employed by the Department of Social and Rehabilitation Services shall be made to the appropriate law enforcement agency.

Kan. Ann. Stat. § 38-2226(a), (b), (f) (LexisNexis through 2008 Supp.)

The secretary and law enforcement officers shall have the duty to receive and investigate reports of child abuse or neglect for the purpose of determining whether the report is valid and whether action is required to protect a child. If the secretary and such officers determine that no action is necessary to protect the child but that a criminal prosecution should be considered, such law enforcement officers shall make a report of the case to the appropriate law enforcement agency.

When a report of child abuse or neglect indicates that there is serious physical harm to, serious deterioration of, or sexual abuse of the child, and that action may be required to protect the child, the investigation shall be conducted as a joint effort between the secretary and the appropriate law enforcement agency or agencies, with a free exchange of information between them pursuant to § 38-2210. If a statement of a suspect is obtained by either agency, a copy of the statement shall be provided to the other.

Law enforcement agencies and the secretary shall assist each other in taking action that is necessary to protect a child regardless of which agency conducted the initial investigation.

Kentucky

Ky. Rev. Stat. Ann. § 620.040(1)(c)-(d), (3) (LexisNexis through 2009 1st Ex. Sess.)

The Cabinet of Health and Family Services shall, within 72 hours, exclusive of weekends and holidays, make a written report to the Commonwealth's or county attorney and the local enforcement agency or Kentucky State Police concerning the action that has been taken on the investigation.

If the report alleges abuse or neglect by someone other than a parent, guardian, or person exercising custodial control or supervision, the cabinet shall immediately notify the Commonwealth's or county attorney and the local law enforcement agency or Kentucky State Police.

If the cabinet or its designated representative receives a report of abuse by a person other than a parent, guardian, or other person exercising custodial control or supervision of a child, it shall immediately notify the local law enforcement agency or Kentucky State Police and the Commonwealth's or county attorney of the receipt of the report and its contents, and they shall investigate the matter. The cabinet or its designated representative shall participate in an investigation of noncustodial physical abuse or neglect at the request of the local law enforcement agency or the Kentucky State Police. The cabinet shall participate in all investigations of reported or suspected sexual abuse of a child.

Ky. Rev. Stat. Ann. § 620.030(1), (4) (LexisNexis through 2009 1st Ex. Sess.)

If the cabinet receives a report of abuse or neglect allegedly committed by a person other than a parent, guardian, or person exercising custodial control or supervision, the cabinet shall refer that matter to the Commonwealth's attorney or the county attorney and the local law enforcement agency or the Kentucky State Police. Nothing in this section shall relieve individuals of their obligation to report.

The cabinet upon request shall receive from any agency of the State or any other agency, institution, or facility providing services to the child or his or her family, such cooperation, assistance, and information as will enable the cabinet to fulfill its responsibilities under the law.

Louisiana

La. Children's Code Art. 610(E) (LexisNexis through 2009 Reg. Sess.)

All reports made to any local or State law enforcement agency involving abuse or neglect in which the child's parent or caregiver, a person who maintains an interpersonal dating or engagement relationship with the parent or caregiver, or a person living in the same residence with the parent or caregiver as a spouse, whether married or not, is believed responsible shall be promptly communicated to the local child protection unit of the Department of Social Services in accordance with a written working agreement developed between the local law enforcement agency and child protection unit.

A local child protection unit shall promptly communicate abuse or neglect cases not involving a parent, caregiver, or occupant of the household to the appropriate law enforcement agency in accordance with a written working agreement developed between the local child protection unit and law enforcement agency. The local child protection unit shall also report all cases of child death that involve a suspicion of abuse or neglect as a contributing factor in the child's death to the local or State law enforcement agencies, the office of the district attorney, and the coroner.

Reports involving a felony-grade crime against a child shall be promptly communicated to the appropriate law enforcement authorities as part of the interagency protocols for multidisciplinary investigations of child abuse and neglect in each judicial district.

Maine

Me. Rev. Stat. Ann. Tit. 22, § 4011-A(1), (2) (LexisNexis through 2009 1st Reg. Sess.)

Persons [who are mandated by law to report] shall immediately report or cause a report to be made to the Department of Health and Human Services when the person knows or has reasonable cause to suspect that a child has been or is likely to be abused or neglected.

When, while acting in a professional capacity, any person required to report knows or has reasonable cause to suspect that a child has been abused or neglected by a person not responsible for the child, the person immediately shall report or cause a report to be made to the appropriate district attorney's office.

Maryland

Md. Code Ann. Fam. Law § 5-704(b) (LexisNexis through 2009 Reg. Sess.)

An individual who notifies the appropriate authorities under this section shall make:

- An oral report, by telephone or direct communication, as soon as possible, to either of the following:
  - The local department or appropriate law enforcement agency if the person has reason to believe that the child has been subjected to abuse
  - The local department if the person has reason to believe that the child has been subjected to neglect
- A written report:

- To the local department not later than 48 hours after the contact, examination, attention, or treatment that caused the individual to believe that the child had been subjected to abuse or neglect
- With a copy to the local State's attorney if the individual has reason to believe that the child has been subjected to abuse

An agency to which an oral report of suspected abuse is made shall immediately notify the other agency. This paragraph does not prohibit a local Department of Social Services and an appropriate law enforcement agency from agreeing to cooperative arrangements.

Massachusetts

Mass. Gen. Laws Ann. Ch. 119, § 51B(l) (LexisNexis through 2009 Sess.)

If the department substantiates a report alleging that abuse or neglect occurred at a facility approved, owned, operated, or funded, in whole or in part, by the Department of Elementary and Secondary Education, Department of Early Education and Care, Department of Mental Health, Department of Developmental Services, Department of Public Health, or Department of Youth Services, the department shall notify the Office of the Child Advocate and the affected department, in writing, by transmitting a copy of the report filed under § 51A and the department's written evaluation and written determination.

Mass. Gen. Laws Ann. Ch. 119, § 51B(k) (LexisNexis through 2009 Sess.)

The Department of Social Services shall notify and transmit copies of substantiated reports and its written evaluations and written determinations to the district attorney for the county in which the child resides and for the county in which the suspected abuse or neglect occurred, and to the local law enforcement authorities in the city or town in which the child resides and in which the suspected abuse or neglect occurred when the department has reasonable cause to believe that one of the conditions listed below resulted from abuse or neglect.

The department shall immediately report to the district attorney and local law enforcement authorities when early evidence indicates there is reasonable cause to believe that one of the conditions listed below resulted from abuse or neglect:

- A child has died, suffered brain damage, loss or substantial impairment of a bodily function or organ, substantial disfigurement, or serious physical injury including, but not limited to, a fracture of any bone, severe burn, impairment of any organ, or an injury requiring the child to be placed on life-support systems.
- A child has been sexually assaulted or sexually exploited.
- There is a disclosure of physical abuse involving physical evidence that may be destroyed, any current disclosure by a child of sexual assault, or the presence of physical evidence of sexual assault.

No provision of chapter 66A, §§ 135 to 135B, inclusive, chapter 112, or §§ 51E and 51F of this chapter relating to confidential data or confidential communications shall prohibit the department from making such notifications or from providing to the district attorney or local law enforcement authorities any information obtained. Nothing herein shall be construed to prevent the department from notifying a district attorney relative to any incident reported to the department under § 51A or to limit the prosecutorial power of a district attorney.

Michigan

Mich. Comp. Laws Ann. § 722.623(b)(5)-(6) (LexisNexis through 1-13-09)

Upon receipt of a written report of suspected child abuse or neglect, the Family Independence Agency (department) may provide copies to the prosecuting attorney and the probate court of the counties in which the child suspected of being abused or neglected resides and is found.

If an allegation, written report, or subsequent investigation of suspected child abuse or child neglect indicates a violation of the Michigan penal code § 333.7401c involving methamphetamine has occurred, or if the allegation, written report, or subsequent investigation indicates that the suspected child abuse or child neglect was committed by an individual who is not a person responsible for the child's health or welfare, including, but not limited to, a member of the clergy, a teacher, or a teacher's aide, the department shall transmit a copy of the allegation or written report and the results of any investigation to a law enforcement agency in the county in which the incident occurred.

If an allegation, written report, or subsequent investigation indicates that the individual who committed the suspected abuse or neglect is a child care provider and the department believes that the report has basis in fact, the department shall, within 24 hours of completion, transmit a copy of the written report or the results of the investigation to the child care regulatory agency with authority over the child care provider's child care organization or adult foster care location authorized to care for a child.

Mich. Comp. Laws Ann. § 722.623(b)(7) (LexisNexis through 1-13-09)

If a local law enforcement agency receives an allegation or written report of suspected child abuse or child neglect or discovers evidence of or receives a report of an individual allowing a child to be exposed to or to have contact with methamphetamine production, and the allegation, written report, or subsequent investigation indicates that the child abuse or child neglect or allowing a child to be exposed to or to have contact with methamphetamine production was committed by a person responsible for the child's health or welfare, the local law enforcement agency shall refer the allegation or provide a copy of the written report and the results of any investigation to the county department of the county in which the abused or neglected child is found.

If an allegation, written report, or subsequent investigation indicates that the individual who committed the suspected abuse or neglect or allowed a child to be exposed to or to have contact with methamphetamine production, is a child care provider and the local law enforcement agency believes that the report has basis in fact, the local law enforcement agency shall transmit a copy of the written report or the results of the investigation to the child care regulatory agency with authority over the child care provider's child care organization or adult foster care location authorized to care for a child. Nothing in this subsection or subsection (1) shall be construed to relieve the department of its responsibilities to investigate reports of suspected child abuse or child neglect under this act.

Minnesota

Minn. Stat. Ann. § 626.556, Subd. 3 & 7 (LexisNexis through 2009 Reg. Sess.)

The police department or the county sheriff, upon receiving a report, shall immediately notify the local welfare agency or agency responsible for assessing or investigating the report, orally and in writing. The local welfare agency, or agency responsible for assessing or investigating the report, upon receiving a report, shall immediately notify the local police department or the county sheriff orally and in writing. The county sheriff, the head of every local welfare agency or agency responsible for assessing or investigating the report, and police department shall each designate a person within that agency, department, or office to be responsible for ensuring that the notification duties of this statute are carried out.

Written reports received by a police department or the county sheriff shall be forwarded immediately to the local welfare agency or the agency responsible for assessing or investigating the report. The police department or the county sheriff may keep copies of reports received by them. Copies of written reports received by a local welfare department or the agency responsible for assessing or investigating the report shall be forwarded immediately to the local police department or the county sheriff.

Minn. Stat. Ann. § 626.556, Subd. 10(a), 10a(a)-(b) (LexisNexis through 2009 Reg. Sess.)

If the report alleges neglect, physical abuse, or sexual abuse by a parent, guardian, or individual functioning within the family unit as a person responsible for the child's care, or sexual abuse by a person with a significant relationship to the child when that person resides in the child's household or by a sibling, the local welfare agency shall immediately conduct a family assessment or investigation.

If the report alleges a violation of a criminal statute involving sexual abuse, physical abuse, neglect, or endangerment, the local law enforcement agency and local welfare agency shall coordinate the planning and execution of their respective investigation and assessment efforts to avoid a duplication of fact-finding efforts and multiple interviews.

If the report alleges neglect, physical abuse, or sexual abuse by a person who is not a parent, guardian, sibling, person responsible for the child's care functioning within the family unit, or a person who lives in the child's household and who has a significant relationship to the child, in a setting other than a facility, the local welfare agency shall immediately notify the appropriate law enforcement agency. [The law enforcement agency] shall conduct an investigation of the alleged abuse or neglect if a violation of a criminal statute is alleged.

The local agency may rely on the fact-finding efforts of the law enforcement investigation to make a determination whether or not threatened harm or other maltreatment has occurred if an alleged offender has minor children or lives with minors.

Mississippi

Miss. Code Ann. § 43-21-353(1), (8) (LexisNexis through 2009 3rd Ex. Sess.)

Upon receiving a report that a child has been sexually abused, or burned, tortured, mutilated, or otherwise physically abused in such a manner as to cause serious bodily harm, or upon receiving any report of abuse that would be a felony under State or Federal law, the Department of Human Services shall immediately notify the law enforcement agency in whose jurisdiction the abuse occurred and shall notify the appropriate prosecutor within 48 hours.

The department shall have the duty to provide the law enforcement agency all the names and facts known at the time of the report; this duty shall be of a continuing nature. The law enforcement agency and the department shall investigate the reported abuse immediately, file a preliminary report with the appropriate prosecutor's office within 24 hours, and make additional reports as new or additional information or evidence becomes available. The department shall advise the clerk of the youth court and the youth court prosecutor of all cases of abuse reported to the department within 72 hours and shall update such report as information becomes available.

If a report is made directly to the department that a child has been abused or neglected in an out-of-home setting, a referral shall be made immediately to the law enforcement agency in whose jurisdiction the abuse occurred, and the department shall the notify the district attorney's office within 48 hours of such report.

Missouri

Mo. Ann. Stat. § 210.145(4), (5), (10) (LexisNexis through 2009 1st Reg. Sess.)

The local office shall contact the appropriate law enforcement agency immediately upon receipt of a report that division personnel determine merits an investigation and provide such agency with a detailed description of the report received. In such cases, the local division office shall request the assistance of the local law enforcement agency in all aspects of the investigation of the complaint. The appropriate law enforcement agency shall either assist the division in the investigation or provide the division, within 24 hours, an explanation in writing detailing the reasons why it is unable to assist.

The local office of the division shall cause an investigation or family assessment and services approach to be initiated in accordance with the protocols established in § 210.145(2), except in cases where the sole basis for the report is educational neglect. If the report indicates the child is in danger of serious physical harm or threat to life, an investigation shall include direct observation of the subject child within 24 hours of the receipt of the report. Local law enforcement shall take all necessary steps to facilitate such direct observation.

Multidisciplinary teams shall be used whenever conducting the investigation as determined by the division in conjunction with local law enforcement. Multidisciplinary teams shall be used in providing protective or preventive social services, including the services of law enforcement, a liaison of the local public school, the juvenile officer, the juvenile court, and other agencies, both public and private.

Montana

Mont. Code Ann. § 41-3-202(1) (LexisNexis through 7-28-09)

Upon receipt of a report that a child is or has been abused or neglected, the Department of Public Health and Human Services shall promptly assess the information contained in the report and make a determination regarding the level of response required and the timeframe within which action must be initiated. If the department determines that an investigation is required, a social worker, the county attorney, or a peace officer shall promptly conduct a thorough investigation into the circumstances surrounding the allegations of abuse or neglect of the child.

Nebraska

Neb. Rev. Stat. Ann. § 28-711 (LexisNexis through 2009 1st Sess.)

Law enforcement agencies receiving any reports of child abuse or neglect under this subsection shall notify the Department of Health and Human Services the next working day by phone or mail.

The department shall establish a statewide toll-free number to be used by any person any hour of the day or night, any day of the week, to make reports of child abuse or neglect. Reports of child abuse or neglect not previously made to or by a law enforcement agency shall be made immediately to such agency by the department.

Neb. Rev. Stat. Ann. § 28-713(1), (4), (5) (LexisNexis through 2009 1st Sess.)

Upon the receipt of a call reporting child abuse and neglect, it is the duty of the law enforcement agency to investigate the report, to take immediate steps to protect the child, and to institute legal proceedings if appropriate. In situations of alleged out-of-home child abuse or neglect, if the person or persons to be notified have not already been notified and the person to be notified is not the subject of the report of child abuse or neglect, the law enforcement agency shall immediately notify the person or persons having custody of each child who has allegedly been abused or neglected that such report of alleged child abuse or neglect has been made and shall provide such person or persons with information of the nature of the alleged child abuse or neglect.

The law enforcement agency may request assistance from the department during the investigation and shall, by the next working day, notify either the hotline or the department of receipt of the report, including whether or not an investigation is being undertaken by the law enforcement agency. A copy of all reports, whether or not an investigation is being undertaken, shall be provided to the department.

The department shall, by the next working day after receiving a report of child abuse or neglect, make a written report or a summary on forms provided by the department to the proper law enforcement agency in the county and enter in the tracking system of child protection cases maintained pursuant to § 28-715 all reports of child abuse or neglect opened for investigation and any action taken.

The department shall, upon request, make available to the appropriate investigating law enforcement agency and the county attorney a copy of all reports relative to a case of suspected child abuse or neglect.

Nevada

Nev. Rev. Stat. Ann. § 432B.260(1), (9) (LexisNexis through 5-22-09)

Upon the receipt of a report concerning the possible abuse or neglect of a child, an agency that provides child welfare services or a law enforcement agency shall promptly notify the appropriate licensing authority, if any. A law enforcement agency shall promptly notify an agency that provides child welfare services of any report it receives.

An agency that provides child welfare services and a law enforcement agency shall cooperate in the investigation, if any, of a report of abuse or neglect of a child.

New Hampshire

N.H. Rev. Stat. Ann. § 169-C:38 (I)-(II) (LexisNexis through 2009 Sess.)

The Department of Health and Human Services shall immediately, by telephone or in person, refer all cases in which there is reason to believe that any person under age 18 has been sexually molested, sexually exploited, intentionally physically injured so as to cause serious bodily injury, physically injured by other than accidental means so as to cause serious bodily injury, and/or a victim of a crime to the local law enforcement agency in the community in which the acts of abuse are believed to have occurred. The department shall also make a written report to the law enforcement agency within 48 hours, Saturdays, Sundays, and holidays excluded. A copy of this report shall be sent to the office of the county attorney.

All law enforcement personnel and department employees shall cooperate in limiting the number of interviews of a child victim and, when appropriate, shall conduct joint interviews of the child. Employees of the department shall share with the investigating police officers all information in their possession which it is lawful for them to disclose to a law enforcement agency. Investigating police officers shall not use or reveal any confidential information shared with them by the department except to the extent necessary for the investigation and prosecution of the case.

N.H. Rev. Stat. Ann. § 169-C:38-a (LexisNexis through 2009 Sess.)

The Department of Health and Human Services and the Department of Justice shall jointly develop a standardized protocol for the interviewing of victims and the investigation and assessment of cases of child abuse and neglect. The protocol shall seek to minimize the impact on the victim. The protocol shall also be designed to protect the rights of all parties affected. The protocol shall specifically address the need to establish safe and appropriate places for interviewing children.

New Jersey

N.J. Stat. Ann. § 9:6-8.11 (LexisNexis through 2009 2nd Ann. Sess.)

Upon receipt of any such report, the Division of Youth and Family Services, or other such entity in the Department of Children and Families as may be designated by the Commissioner of Children and Families to investigate child abuse or neglect, shall immediately take such action as shall be necessary to ensure the safety of the child and to that end may request and shall receive appropriate assistance from local and State law enforcement officials.

A representative of the division or other designated entity shall initiate an investigation within 24 hours of receipt of the report, unless the division or other entity authorizes a delay based upon the request of a law enforcement official. The division or other entity shall also, within 72 hours, forward a report of such matter to the child abuse registry operated by the division in Trenton.

N.J. Stat. Ann. § 9:6-8.10a(e) (LexisNexis through 2009 2nd Ann. Sess.)

For incidents determined by the Department of Youth and Family Services to be substantiated, the department shall forward to the police or law enforcement agency in whose jurisdiction the child named in the report resides the identity of persons alleged to have committed child abuse or neglect, the identities of victims of child abuse or neglect, their addresses, the nature of the allegations, and other relevant information, including, but not limited to, prior reports of abuse or neglect and names of siblings obtained by the department during its investigation of a report of child abuse or neglect. The police or law enforcement agency shall keep such information confidential.

New Mexico

N.M. Stat. Ann. § 32A-4-3(B) (LexisNexis through 2009 1st Sess.)

Any law enforcement agency receiving the report shall immediately transmit the facts of the report and the name, address, and phone number of the reporter by telephone to the Children, Youth and Families Department and shall transmit the same information in writing within 48 hours.

The department shall immediately transmit the facts of the report and the name, address, and phone number of the reporter by telephone to a local law enforcement agency and shall transmit the same information in writing within 48 hours.

New York

N.Y. Soc. Serv. Law § 423(6) (LexisNexis through 12-4-09)

A social services district may establish a multidisciplinary investigative team or teams and may establish or work as part of a child advocacy center, at a local or regional level, for the purpose of investigating reports of suspected child abuse or maltreatment.

The social services district shall have discretion with regard to the category or categories of suspected child abuse or maltreatment such team or teams may investigate, provided, however, the social services district shall place particular emphasis on cases involving the abuse of a child, sexual abuse of a child, or the death of a child. Members of multidisciplinary teams shall include, but not be limited to, representatives from the following agencies:

- Child protective services
- Law enforcement
- The district attorney's office
- A physician or medical provider trained in forensic pediatrics
- Mental health professionals
- Victim advocacy personnel
- A child advocacy center, if one exists

Members of the multidisciplinary team primarily responsible for the investigation of child abuse reports, including child protective services, law enforcement, and the district attorney's office, shall participate in joint interviews and conduct investigative functions consistent with the mission of the particular agency member involved.

North Carolina

N.C. Gen. Stat. § 7B-307(a) (LexisNexis through 2009 Reg. Sess.)

If the director of the Department of Social Services finds evidence that a juvenile may have been abused, the director shall make an immediate oral and subsequent written report of the findings to the district attorney or the district attorney's designee and the appropriate local law enforcement agency within 48 hours after the receipt of the report.

The local law enforcement agency shall immediately, but no later than 48 hours after receipt of a report of abuse, initiate and coordinate a criminal investigation with the protective services assessment being conducted by the county Department of Social Services. Upon completion of the investigation, the district attorney shall determine whether criminal prosecution is appropriate and may request the director or the director's designee to appear before a magistrate.

If the director of the Department of Social Services receives information that a juvenile may have been physically harmed in violation of any criminal statute by any person other than the juvenile's parent, guardian, custodian, or caregiver, the director shall make an immediate oral report and subsequent written report of that information to the district attorney or the district attorney's designee and to the appropriate local law enforcement agency within 48 hours after receipt of the information.

The local law enforcement agency shall immediately, but no later than 48 hours after receipt of the information, initiate a criminal investigation. Upon completion of the investigation, the district attorney shall determine whether criminal prosecution is appropriate.

N.C. Gen. Stat. § 7B-301 (LexisNexis through 2009 Reg. Sess.)

Upon receipt of any report of sexual abuse of the juvenile in a child care facility, the director of the Department of Social Services shall notify the State Bureau of Investigation within 24 hours or on the next workday. If sexual abuse in a child care facility is not alleged in the initial report, but during the course of the assessment there is reason to suspect that sexual abuse has occurred, the director shall immediately notify the State Bureau of Investigation. Upon notification that sexual abuse may have occurred in a child care facility, the State Bureau of Investigation may form a task force to investigate the report.

North Dakota

N.D. Cent. Code § 50-25.1-05 (LexisNexis through 2009 Sess.)

The Department of Human Services, in accordance with rules adopted by the department, immediately shall initiate an assessment, or cause an assessment, of any report of child abuse or neglect including, when appropriate, the assessment of the home or the residence of the child, any school or child care facility attended by the child, and the circumstances surrounding the report of abuse or neglect.

If the report alleges a violation of a criminal statute involving sexual or physical abuse, the department and an appropriate law enforcement agency shall coordinate the planning and execution of their investigation efforts to avoid a duplication of factfinding efforts and multiple interviews. The department or the law enforcement agency may:

- Refer the case to a children's advocacy center for a forensic interview, forensic medical examination, and other services
- Interview, without the consent of a person responsible for the child's welfare, the alleged abused or neglected child and any other child who currently resides or who has resided with the person responsible for the child's welfare or the alleged perpetrator
- Conduct the interview at a school, child care facility, or any other place where the alleged abused or neglected child or other child is found

The department shall adopt guidelines for case referrals to a children's advocacy center. When cases are referred to a children's advocacy center, all interviews of the alleged abused or neglected child conducted at the children's advocacy center under this section shall be audio-recorded or video-recorded.

Northern Mariana Islands

N.M.I. Commonwealth Code Tit. 6, § 5313(b) (9-30-09)
The Department of Public Safety shall promptly notify the Office of the Attorney General and the Division of Youth Services of all reported cases of child abuse, neglect, and sexual molestation. This notification shall be made within 24 hours.

Ohio

Ohio Rev. Code Ann. § 2151.421(D) (LexisNexis through 11-10-09)
When a municipal or county peace officer receives a report concerning the possible abuse or neglect of a child or the possible threat of abuse or neglect of a child, upon receipt of the report, the municipal or county peace officer who receives the report shall refer the report to the appropriate public children services agency.

When a public children services agency receives a report pursuant to this division or division (A) or (B) of this section, upon receipt of the report, the public children services agency shall do both of the following:

- It shall comply with § 2151.422 [concerning procedures to follow if the child is living in a domestic violence or homeless shelter].

If the county served by the agency is also served by a children's advocacy center and the report alleges sexual abuse of a child or another type of abuse of a child that is specified in the memorandum of understanding that creates the center as being within the center's jurisdiction, the agency shall comply with the protocol and procedures for referrals and investigations, with the coordinating activities, and with the authority or responsibility for performing or providing functions, activities, and services stipulated in the interagency agreement entered into under § 2151.428 relative to that center.

Ohio Rev. Code Ann, § 2151.428(F) (LexisNexis through 11-10-09)

Except as provided by statute or in an interagency agreement entered into under § 2151.428 that applies to the particular report, the public children services agency shall investigate, within 24 hours, each report of known or suspected child abuse or child neglect and of a known or suspected threat of child abuse or child neglect that is referred to it to determine the circumstances surrounding the injuries, abuse, or neglect or the threat of injury, abuse, or neglect; the cause of the injuries, abuse, neglect, or threat; and the person or persons responsible.

The investigation shall be made in cooperation with the law enforcement agency and in accordance with the memorandum of understanding prepared under § 2151.428(J). A representative of the public children services agency shall, at the time of initial contact with the person subject to the investigation, inform the person of the specific complaints or allegations made against the person. The information shall be given in a manner that is consistent with § 2151.428(H)(1) and protects the rights of the person making the report.

The public children services agency shall report each case to a central registry that the Department of Job and Family Services shall maintain in order to determine whether prior reports have been made in other counties concerning the child or other principals in the case. The public children services agency shall submit a report of its investigation, in writing, to the law enforcement agency.

The public children services agency shall make any recommendations to the county prosecuting attorney or city director of law that it considers necessary to protect any children that are brought to its attention.

Oklahoma

Okla. Stat. Ann. Tit. 10A, § 1-2-102(B) (LexisNexis through Okla. 2009 Legis. Serv., Ch. 233)

Effective May 21, 2009

If, upon receipt of a report alleging abuse or neglect or during the assessment or investigation, the Department of Human Services determines that the alleged perpetrator is someone other than a person responsible for the child's health, safety, or welfare, and the alleged abuse or neglect of the child does not appear to be attributable to failure on the part of a person responsible for the child's health, safety, or welfare to provide protection for the child, the department shall immediately make a referral, either verbally or in writing, to the appropriate local law enforcement agency for the purpose of conducting a possible criminal investigation.

After making the referral to the law enforcement agency, the department shall not be responsible for further investigation unless:

- The department has reason to believe that the alleged perpetrator is a parent of another child, not the subject of the criminal investigation, or otherwise a person responsible for the health, safety, or welfare or another child.
- Notice is received from a law enforcement agency that it has determined the alleged perpetrator is a parent or a person responsible for the health, safety, or welfare of another child not the subject of the criminal investigation.
- The appropriate law enforcement agency requests the department, in writing, to participate in the investigation. If funds and personnel are available, as determined by the director of the department or a designee, the department may assist law enforcement in interviewing children alleged to be victims of physical or sexual abuse.

Okla. Stat. Ann. Tit. 10A, § 1-2-102(C) (LexisNexis through Okla. 2009 Legis. Serv., Ch. 233) *Effective May 21, 2009*

Any law enforcement agency receiving a referral as provided in this section shall provide the Department of Human Services with a copy of the report of any investigation resulting from a referral from the department.

Whenever, in the course of any criminal investigation, a law enforcement agency determines that there is cause to believe that a child may be abused or neglected by reason of the acts, omissions, or failures on the part of a person responsible for the health, safety, or welfare of the child, the law enforcement agency shall immediately contact the department for the purpose of an investigation.

Oregon

Or. Rev. Stat. Ann. § 419B.015(1)(b), (2) (LexisNexis through 11-13-09)

When a report of child abuse is received by the Department of Human Services, the department shall notify a law enforcement agency within the county where the report was made. When a report of child abuse is received by a designee of the department, the designee shall notify, according to the contract, either the department or a law enforcement agency within the county where the report was made. When a report of child abuse is received by a law enforcement agency, the agency shall notify the local office of the department within the county where the report was made.

When a report of child abuse is received under § 419B.015(1)(A), the entity receiving the report shall make the notification required by the subsection above according to rules adopted by the department.

Pennsylvania

23 Pa. Cons. Stat. Ann. § 6365(c) (LexisNexis through 2009 Reg. Sess.)

The county agency and the district attorney shall develop a protocol for the convening of investigative teams for any case of child abuse involving crimes against children that are set forth in § 6340(a)(9) and (10) (relating to the release of information in confidential reports). The county protocol shall include standards and procedures to be used in receiving and referring reports and coordinating investigations of reported cases of child abuse and a system for sharing the information obtained as a result of any interview. The protocol shall include any other standards and procedures to avoid duplication of fact-finding efforts and interviews to minimize the trauma to the child.

The district attorney shall convene an investigative team in accordance with the protocol. The investigative team shall consist of those individuals and agencies responsible for investigating the abuse or for providing services to the child and shall, at a minimum, include a health-care provider, county caseworker, and law enforcement official.

Puerto Rico

P.R. Laws Ann. tit. 8, § 446 (LexisNexis through Dec. 2007)

Professionals or public officials, public, private, and privatized entities that, in their professional capacity and in the performance of their duties, may learn of or come to suspect that a minor is, has been, or is at risk of becoming a victim of abuse, institutional abuse, neglect, and/or institutional neglect; professionals in the fields of health, the system of justice, education, social work, public order, persons who administer or work in caregiving institutions or centers that provide care services for 24 hours a day or part thereof, or in rehabilitation institutions and centers for minors, or in foster homes; and all processors of film or photographs who have knowledge of or observe, in the performance of their professional responsibilities or employment, any motion picture, photograph, videotape, negative, or slide that depicts a minor involved in a sexual activity, shall report that fact immediately through the hotline to the Puerto Rico Police or the local office of the Department of the Family.

Any person who has knowledge of or suspects that a minor is a victim of abuse, institutional abuse, neglect, and/or institutional neglect shall report that fact through the hotline of the department, the Puerto Rico Police, or the local office of the department.

Persons bound to furnish information pursuant to this chapter, including technicians or social workers who provide protective services to minors, who have knowledge of or suspect that a minor has died as a result of abuse, institutional abuse, neglect, and/or institutional neglect, shall report the fact to the Puerto Rico Police and to the hotline of the department, so that they will undertake the appropriate investigation.

Rhode Island

R.I. Gen. Laws § 40-11-7(f) (LexisNexis through 6-10-09)

In the event that after investigation the Department of Children, Youth, and Families has reasonable cause to know or suspect that a child has been subjected to criminal abuse or neglect, the department shall forward immediately any information as it relates to that knowledge or suspicion to the law enforcement agency.

R.I. Gen. Laws § 40-11-9 (LexisNexis through 6-10-09)

Upon the receipt of a report concerning the alleged abuse or neglect of a child, it shall be the duty of the law enforcement agency to investigate further and to report the results of the investigation to the Department of Children, Youth, and Families and/or family court; provided, however, if there is reasonable cause to believe that a crime has been committed the law enforcement agency shall report the result of the investigation to the department of the attorney general.

South Carolina

S.C. Code Ann. § 63-7-320 (LexisNexis through 2008 Reg. Sess.)

Where reports are made pursuant to § 63-7-310 to a law enforcement agency, the law enforcement agency shall notify the county Department of Social Services of the law enforcement's response to the report at the earliest possible time.

Where a county or contiguous counties have established multicounty child protective services, the county Department of Social Services immediately shall transfer reports pursuant to this section to the service.

S.C. Code Ann. § 63-7-980 (LexisNexis through 2008 Reg. Sess.)

The Department of Social Services must cooperate with law enforcement agencies within the area it serves and establish procedures necessary to facilitate the referral of child protection cases to the department.

Where the facts indicating abuse or neglect also appear to indicate a violation of criminal law, the department must notify the appropriate law enforcement agency of those facts within 24 hours of the department's finding for the purposes of police investigation. The law enforcement agency must file a formal incident report at the time it is notified by the department of the finding.

When the intake report is of alleged sexual abuse, the department must notify the appropriate law enforcement agency within 24 hours of receipt of the report to determine if a joint investigation is necessary. The law enforcement agency must file a formal incident report at the time it is notified of the alleged sexual abuse.

The law enforcement agency must provide to the department copies of incident reports generated in any case reported to law enforcement by the department and in any case in which the officer responsible for the case knows the department is involved with the family or the child. The law enforcement officer must make reasonable efforts to advise the department of significant developments in the case, such as disposition in summary court, referral of a juvenile to the Department of Juvenile Justice, arrest or detention, trial date, and disposition of charges.

The department must include in its records copies of incident reports provided under this section and must record the disposition of charges.

South Dakota

S.D. Codified Laws § 26-8A-8 (LexisNexis through 2009 Sess.)

The reports required from mandated reporters by the reporting laws shall be made orally and immediately by telephone or otherwise to the State's attorney of the county in which the child resides or is present, to the Department of Social Services, or to law enforcement officers.

The State's attorney or law enforcement officers, upon receiving a report, shall immediately notify the Department of Social Services. Any person receiving a report of suspected child abuse or child neglect shall keep the report confidential as provided by statute.

Tennessee

Tenn. Code Ann. § 37-1-403(c)(1) (LexisNexis through 2009 Reg. Sess.)

If a law enforcement official or judge becomes aware of known or suspected child abuse through personal knowledge, receipt of a report, or otherwise, such information shall be reported to the Department of Children's Services immediately and, where appropriate, the child protective team shall be notified to investigate the report for the protection of the child in accordance with the provisions of this part. Further criminal investigation by such official shall be appropriately conducted in coordination with the team or department to the maximum extent possible.

Tenn. Code Ann. § 37-1-605(b)(2) (LexisNexis through 2009 Reg. Sess.)

If a law enforcement official or judge becomes aware of known or suspected child sexual abuse through personal knowledge, receipt of a report, or otherwise, such information shall be reported to the Department of Children's Services immediately, and the child protective team shall be notified to investigate the report for the protection of the child in accordance with the provisions of this part. Further criminal investigation by such official shall be appropriately conducted.

Tenn. Code Ann. § 37-1-405(a), (b)(1)-(2) (LexisNexis through 2009 Reg. Sess.)

All cases reported to the juvenile court judge or to State or local law enforcement officers shall be referred immediately to the local director of the county office of the Department of Children's Services for investigation.

If the court or law enforcement officer finds that there are reasonable grounds to believe that the child is suffering from illness or injury or is in immediate danger from the child's surroundings and that the child's removal is necessary, appropriate protective action shall be taken.

The county office of the Department of Children's Services or the office of the sheriff or the chief law enforcement official of the municipality where the child resides, upon receipt of a report of harm or sexual abuse, shall give notice of the report to the judge having juvenile jurisdiction where the child resides.

If the case appears to involve severe child abuse, including child sexual abuse, the county director of the Department of Children's Services shall immediately notify and consult with the district attorney general where the harm occurred, and the district attorney general may take such action as the district attorney general deems appropriate, including petitioning the court for removal of the child or termination of parental rights.

Texas

Tex. Fam. Code Ann. § 261.105 (LexisNexis through 2009 Sess.)

All reports received by a local or State law enforcement agency that allege abuse or neglect by a person responsible for a child's care, custody, or welfare shall be referred immediately to the Department of Family and Protective Services or the designated agency.

The department or designated agency shall immediately notify the appropriate State or local law enforcement agency of any report it receives, other than a report from a law enforcement agency, that concerns the suspected abuse or neglect of a child or death of a child from abuse or neglect.

In addition to notifying a law enforcement agency, if the report relates to a child in a facility operated, licensed, certified, or registered by a State agency, the department shall refer the report to the agency for investigation.

If a report relates to a child with mental retardation receiving services in a State-supported living center or the ICF-MR component of the Rio Grande State Center, the department shall proceed with the investigation of the report.

If the department initiates an investigation and determines that the abuse or neglect does not involve a person responsible for the child's care, custody, or welfare, the department shall refer the report to a law enforcement agency for further investigation. If the department determines that the abuse or neglect involves an employee of a public primary or secondary school, and that the child is a student at the school, the department shall orally notify the superintendent of the school district in which the employee is employed about the investigation.

In cooperation with the department, the Texas Youth Commission by rule shall adopt guidelines for identifying a report made to the commission that is appropriate to refer to the department or a law enforcement agency for investigation. Guidelines adopted under this subsection must require the commission to consider the severity and immediacy of the alleged abuse or neglect of the child victim.

Tex. Fam. Code Ann. § 261.1055 (LexisNexis through 2009 Sess.)

A district attorney may inform the Department of Family and Protective Services or designated agency that the district attorney wishes to receive notification of some or all reports of suspected abuse or neglect of children who were in the county at the time the report was made or who were in the county at the time of the alleged abuse or neglect.

If the district attorney makes the notification under this section, the department or designated agency shall, on receipt of a report of suspected abuse or neglect, immediately notify the district attorney as requested, and the department or designated agency shall forward a copy of the reports to the district attorney on request.

Utah

Utah Code Ann. § 62A-4a-403(1)(b) (LexisNexis through 2009 1st Sp. Sess.)

On receipt of the notice of suspected child abuse or neglect, the peace officer or law enforcement agency shall immediately notify the nearest office of the Division of Child and Family Services.

If an initial report of child abuse or neglect is made to the division, the division shall immediately notify the appropriate local law enforcement agency. The division shall, in addition to its own investigation, comply with and lend support to investigations by law enforcement undertaken pursuant to a report made under the reporting laws.

Vermont

Vt. Stat. Ann. Tit. 33, § 4915 (LexisNexis through 2009 Spec. Sess.)

Upon receipt of a report of abuse or neglect, the Department of Social and Rehabilitation Services shall promptly determine whether it constitutes an allegation of child abuse or neglect as defined by law.

If the report is accepted as a valid allegation of abuse or neglect, the department shall determine whether to conduct an assessment or to conduct an investigation. The department shall begin either an assessment or an investigation within 72 hours after the receipt of a report, provided that it has sufficient information to proceed.

The department shall conduct an investigation when an accepted report involves allegations indicating substantial child endangerment. ''Substantial child endangerment'' includes conduct by an adult involving or resulting in sexual abuse, and conduct by a person responsible for a child's welfare involving or resulting in abandonment, child fatality, malicious punishment, or abuse or neglect that causes serious physical injury. The department may conduct an investigation of any report.

The department shall begin an immediate investigation if, at any time during an assessment, it appears that an investigation is appropriate.

The department may collaborate with child protection, law enforcement, and other departments and agencies in Vermont and other jurisdictions to evaluate risk to a child and to determine the service needs of the child and family. The department may enter into reciprocal agreements with other jurisdictions to further the purposes of this subchapter.

Vt. Stat. Ann. Tit. 33, § 4915b(e) (LexisNexis through 2009 Spec. Sess.)

The Department of Social and Rehabilitation Services shall report to and request assistance from law enforcement in the following circumstances:

- Investigations of child sexual abuse by an alleged perpetrator age 10 or older
- Investigations of serious physical abuse or neglect likely to result in criminal charges or requiring emergency medical care
- Situations potentially dangerous to the child or department worker

Vt. Stat. Ann. Tit. 33, § 4918(a) (LexisNexis through 2009 Spec. Sess.)

Multidisciplinary teams shall assist local district offices of the Department of Social and Rehabilitation Services in identifying and treating child abuse and neglect cases. With respect to any case referred to it, the team shall assist the district office by providing:

- Case diagnosis or identification
- A comprehensive treatment plan
- Coordination of services pursuant to the treatment plan

Virgin Islands

V.I. Code Ann. Tit. 5, § 2534(a) (LexisNexis through 2009 Reg. Sess.)

Reports of child abuse, sexual abuse, or neglect made pursuant to the reporting laws shall be made immediately by telephone or otherwise to the U.S. Virgin Islands Police Department

(V.I.P.D.) or to the Department of Social Welfare. The V.I.P.D. shall relay such reports to the Department of Social Welfare immediately or, at the latest, at the commencement of the next regular office hours of the Department of Social Welfare. At the request of the Department of Social Welfare, an oral report shall be followed by a written report within 48 hours.

V.I. Code Ann. Tit. 5, § 2536(f) (LexisNexis through 2009 Reg. Sess.)

The V.I.P.D. shall, on its own initiative where appropriate or at the request of the Department of Social Welfare, investigate reports of alleged child abuse, sexual abuse, or neglect, and shall convey the results of such investigation to the Department of Social Welfare and, where a petition or complaint has been filed, to the Territorial Court. If the report of child abuse or neglect involves the acts or omissions of the Department of Social Welfare, the V.I.P.D. shall investigate such report and shall convey the results of such report to the Department of Law, which shall take appropriate action.

Virginia

Va. Code Ann. § 63.2-1507 (LexisNexis through 2009 Reg. Sess.)

All law enforcement departments and other State and local departments, agencies, authorities, and institutions shall cooperate with each child protective services coordinator of a local department and any multidiscipline teams in the detection and prevention of child abuse.

Washington

Wash. Rev. Code Ann. § 26.44.030(4), (5) (LexisNexis through 2009 Reg. Sess.)

The Department of Social and Health Services, upon receiving a report of an incident of alleged abuse or neglect involving a child who has died, has had physical injury or injuries inflicted upon him or her other than by accidental means, or who has been subjected to alleged sexual abuse shall report such incident to the proper law enforcement agency.

In emergency cases, where the child's welfare is endangered, the department shall notify the proper law enforcement agency within 24 hours after a report is received by the department. In all other cases, the department shall notify the law enforcement agency within 72 hours after a report is received by the department. If the department makes an oral report, a written report shall also be made to the proper law enforcement agency within 5 days thereafter.

Any law enforcement agency receiving a report of an incident of alleged abuse or neglect involving a child who has died, has had physical injury or injuries inflicted upon him or her other than by accidental means, or who has been subjected to alleged sexual abuse shall report such incident in writing as to the proper county prosecutor or city attorney for appropriate action whenever the law enforcement agency's investigation reveals that a crime may have been committed.

The law enforcement agency shall also notify the department of all reports received and the law enforcement agency's disposition of them. In emergency cases, where the child's welfare is endangered, the law enforcement agency shall notify the department within 24 hours. In all other cases, the law enforcement agency shall notify the department within 72 hours after a report is received by the law enforcement agency.

West Virginia

W. Va. Code Ann. § 49-6A-5 (LexisNexis through 2009 4th Ex. Sess.)

A copy of any report of serious physical abuse, sexual abuse, or assault shall be forwarded by the Department of Health and Human Resources to the appropriate law enforcement agency, the prosecuting attorney, or the coroner or medical examiner's office.

Wisconsin

Wis. Stat. Ann. § 48.981(3)(bm) (LexisNexis through Wis. 2009 Legis. Serv., Act 94)

In a county that has wholly or partially within its boundaries a federally recognized Indian reservation or a Bureau of Indian Affairs service area for the Ho-Chunk Tribe, if a county department that receives a report pertaining to a child or unborn child knows or has reason to know that the child is an Indian child who resides in the county or that the unborn child is an Indian unborn child whose expectant mother resides in the county, the county department shall provide notice, which shall consist only of the name and address of the Indian child or expectant mother and the fact that a report has been received about that Indian child or Indian unborn child, within 24 hours to one of the following:

- If the county department knows with which Indian Tribe the child is affiliated, or with which Indian Tribe the Indian unborn child, when born, may be eligible for affiliation, and the Indian Tribe is a Wisconsin Indian Tribe, the Tribal agent of that Tribe
- If the county department does not know with which Indian Tribe the child is affiliated, or with which Indian Tribe the Indian unborn child, when born, may be eligible for affiliation, or the child or expectant mother is not affiliated with a Wisconsin Indian Tribe, the Tribal agent serving the reservation or Ho-Chunk service area where the child or expectant mother resides
- If neither [of the above] applies, any Tribal agent serving a reservation or Ho-Chunk service area in the county

Wis. Stat. Ann. § 48.981(3)(a) (LexisNexis through 2009 Sess.)

The sheriff or police department shall within 12 hours, exclusive of Saturdays, Sundays, or legal holidays, refer to the county department or, in a county having a population of 500,000 or more, the department or a licensed child welfare agency under contract with the department all of the following types of cases reported to the sheriff or police department:

- Cases in which a caregiver is suspected of abuse or neglect or of threatened abuse or neglect of a child
- Cases in which a caregiver is suspected of facilitating or failing to take action to prevent the suspected or threatened abuse or neglect of a child

- Cases in which it cannot be determined who abused or neglected or threatened to abuse or neglect a child
- Cases in which there is reason to suspect that an unborn child has been abused, or there is reason to believe that an unborn child is at substantial risk of abuse

The sheriff or police department may refer to the county department, the department, or a licensed child welfare agency a case reported to the sheriff or police department in which a person who is not a caregiver is suspected of abuse or of threatened abuse of a child.

A county department, the department, or a licensed child welfare agency shall within 12 hours, exclusive of Saturdays, Sundays, or legal holidays, refer to the sheriff or police department all cases of suspected or threatened abuse, as defined in § 48.02(1)(b)-(f), reported to it. For cases of suspected or threatened abuse, as defined in § 48.02(1)(a), (am), (g), or (gm), or neglect, each county department, the department, and a licensed child welfare agency shall adopt a written policy specifying the kinds of reports it will routinely report to local law enforcement authorities.

Wyoming

Wyo. Stat. Ann. § 14-3-206(a) (LexisNexis through 9-15-09)
Reports of child abuse or neglect or of suspected child abuse or neglect made to the local child protective agency or local law enforcement agency shall be conveyed immediately by the agency receiving the report to the appropriate local child protective agency or local law enforcement agency. The agencies shall continue cooperating and coordinating with each other during the investigation.

Wyo. Stat. Ann. § 14-3-204(a)(vii)-(viii) (LexisNexis through 9-15-09)
The local child protective agency shall cooperate, coordinate, and assist with the prosecution and law enforcement agencies in investigating a report of suspected child abuse or neglect. When the best interests of the child require court actions, the agency shall contact the county and prosecuting attorney to initiate legal proceedings and assist the county and prosecuting attorney during the proceedings.

End Notes

[1] The word approximately is used to stress the fact that States frequently amend their laws. This information is current only through January 2010. The States that require child protective services agencies to cross-report specific types of abuse to law enforcement agencies include Alabama, Alaska, Arkansas, California, Colorado, Connecticut, Delaware, Florida, Georgia, Illinois, Iowa, Kentucky, Louisiana, Massachusetts, Michigan, Minnesota, Mississippi, New Hampshire, North Carolina, Oklahoma, Rhode Island, South Carolina, Texas, Vermont, Washington, West Virginia, and Wisconsin.

[2] Connecticut, Indiana, Kansas, Nevada, New Hampshire, North Dakota (in cases involving criminal abuse allegations), Ohio, Virginia, and Wyoming.

[3] Delaware, Missouri, New York, Pennsylvania, and Vermont.

In: Reporting Child Abuse and Neglect
Editor: Henry J. Pervall

ISBN: 978-1-62100-157-7
© 2012 Nova Science Publishers, Inc.

Chapter 3

CLERGY AS MANDATORY REPORTERS OF CHILD ABUSE AND NEGLECT: SUMMARY OF STATE LAWS[*][1]

United States Department of Health and Human Services

Every State, the District of Columbia, American Samoa, Guam, the Northern Mariana Islands, Puerto Rico, and the U.S. Virgin Islands have statutes that identify persons who are required to report child maltreatment under specific circumstances.[1] Approximately 26 States currently include members of the clergy among those professionals specifically mandated by law to report known or suspected instances of child abuse or neglect.[2] In approximately 18 States and Puerto Rico, any person who suspects child abuse or neglect is required to report.[3] This inclusive language appears to include clergy but may be interpreted otherwise.

PRIVILEGED COMMUNICATIONS

As a doctrine of some faiths, clergy must maintain the confidentiality of pastoral communications. Mandatory reporting statutes in some States specify the circumstances under which a communication is "privileged" or allowed to remain confidential. Privileged communications may be exempt from the requirement to report suspected abuse or neglect. The privilege of maintaining this confidentiality under State law must be provided by statute. Most States do provide the privilege, typically in rules of evidence or civil procedure.[4] If the issue of privilege is not addressed in the reporting laws, it does not mean that privilege is not granted; it may be granted in other parts of State statutes.

This privilege, however, is not absolute. While clergy-penitent privilege is frequently recognized within the reporting laws, it is typically interpreted narrowly in the context of child abuse or neglect. The circumstances under which it is allowed vary from State to State, and in some States it is denied altogether. For example, among the States that list clergy as

---

[*] This is an edited, reformatted and augmented version of the United States Department of Health and Human Services publication, dated on April 2010.

[1] This material may be freely reproduced and distributed. However, when doing so, please credit Child Welfare Information Gateway.

mandated reporters, New Hampshire and West Virginia deny the clergy-penitent privilege in cases of child abuse or neglect. Four of the States that enumerate "any person" as a mandated reporter (North Carolina, Oklahoma, Rhode Island, and Texas) also deny clergy-penitent privilege in child abuse cases.

In States where neither clergy members nor "any person" are enumerated as mandated reporters, it is less clear whether clergy are included as mandated reporters within other broad categories of professionals who work with children. For example, in Virginia and Washington, clergy are not enumerated as mandated reporters, but the clergy-penitent privilege is affirmed within the reporting laws.

Many States and territories include Christian Science practitioners or religious healers among professionals who are mandated to report suspected child maltreatment. In most instances, they appear to be regarded as a type of healthcare provider. Only nine States (Arizona, Arkansas, Louisiana, Massachusetts, Missouri, Montana, Nevada, South Carolina, and Vermont) explicitly include Christian Science practitioners among classes of clergy required to report. In those States the clergy-penitent privilege is also extended to those practitioners by statute.

The chart below summarizes how States have or have not addressed the issue of clergy as mandated reporters (either specifically or as part of a broad category) and/or clergy-penitent privilege (either limiting or denying the privilege) within their reporting laws.

	Privilege granted but limited to pastoral communications	Privilege denied in cases of suspected child abuse or neglect	Privilege not addressed in the reporting laws
Clergy enumerated as mandated reporters	Alabama, Arizona, Arkansas, California, Colorado, Illinois, Louisiana, Maine, Massachusetts, Michigan, Minnesota, Missouri, Montana, Nevada, New Mexico, North Dakota, Ohio, Oregon, Pennsylvania, South Carolina, Vermont, Wisconsin	New Hampshire, West Virginia	Connecticut, Mississippi
Clergy not enumerated as mandated reporters but may be included with "any person" designation	Delaware, Florida, Idaho, Kentucky, Maryland, Utah, Wyoming	North Carolina, Oklahoma, Rhode Island, Texas	Indiana, Nebraska, New Jersey, Tennessee, Puerto Rico
Neither clergy nor "any person" enumerated as mandated reporters	Virginia, Washington[5]	Not applicable	Alaska, American Samoa, District of Columbia, Georgia, Guam, Hawaii, Iowa, Kansas, New York, Northern Mariana Islands, South Dakota, Virgin Islands

This publication is a product of the State Statutes Series prepared by Child Welfare Information Gateway. While every attempt has been made to be as complete as possible, additional information on these topics may be in other sections of a State's code as well as agency regulations, case law, and informal practices and procedures.

Alabama

Ala. Code § 26-14-3(a), (f) (LexisNexis through 2010 Reg. Sess.)

Members of the clergy (as defined in Rule 505 of the Alabama Rules of Evidence) shall be required to report or cause a report to be made immediately when a child is known or suspected to be a victim of child abuse or neglect, either by telephone or direct communication, followed by a written report, to a duly constituted authority.

A member of the clergy shall not be required to report information gained solely in a confidential communication, privileged pursuant to Rule 505 of the Alabama Rules of Evidence, as such communications shall continue to be privileged as provided by law.

Alaska

This issue is not addressed in the statutes reviewed.

American Samoa

This issue is not addressed in the statutes reviewed.

Arizona

Ariz. Rev. Stat. Ann. § 13-3620(A)-(B) (LexisNexis through 2010 2nd Reg. Sess.)

Any member of the clergy, priest, or Christian Science practitioner who reasonably believes that a minor is or has been the victim of injury, abuse, child abuse, a reportable offense, or neglect shall immediately report or cause a report to be made.

A member of the clergy, Christian Science practitioner, or priest who has received a confidential communication or a confession in that person's role as a member of the clergy, Christian Science practitioner, or priest in the course of the discipline enjoined by the church to which the member of the clergy, Christian Science practitioner, or priest belongs may withhold reporting of the communication or confession if the member of the clergy, Christian Science practitioner, or priest determines that it is reasonable and necessary within the concepts of the religion. This exemption applies only to the communication or confession and not to the personal observations the member of the clergy, Christian Science practitioner, or priest may otherwise make of the minor.

Arkansas

Ark. Code Ann. § 12-18-402 (LexisNexis through 2009 Reg. Sess.)

A clergy member shall immediately notify the Child Abuse Hotline if he or she:

- Has reasonable cause to suspect that a child has been subjected to child maltreatment or died as a result of child maltreatment

- Observes a child being subjected to conditions or circumstances that would reasonably result in child maltreatment

A clergy member includes a minister, priest, rabbi, accredited Christian Science practitioner, or other similar functionary of a religious organization, or an individual reasonably believed to be so by the person consulting him or her, except to the extent the clergy member:

- Has acquired knowledge of suspected child maltreatment through communications required to be kept confidential pursuant to the religious discipline of the relevant denomination or faith
- Received the knowledge of the suspected child maltreatment from the alleged offender in the context of a statement of admission

A privilege or contract shall not prevent a person from reporting child maltreatment when he or she is a mandated reporter and required to report under this section.

Ark. Code Ann. § 12-18-803(b) (LexisNexis through 2009 Reg. Sess.)

No privilege, except that between a lawyer and client or between a minister, including a Christian Science practitioner, and a person confessing to or being counseled by the minister, shall prevent anyone from testifying concerning child maltreatment.

California

Cal. Penal Code § 11166(d)(1)-(2) (LexisNexis through 2010 Reg. Sess.)

A clergy member who acquires knowledge or reasonable suspicion of child abuse during a penitential communication is not required to make a report. For the purposes of this subdivision, 'penitential communication' means a communication intended to be in confidence, including, but not limited to, a sacramental confession, made to a clergy member who, in the course of the discipline or practice of his or her church, denomination, or organization, is authorized or accustomed to hear those communications, and under the discipline, tenets, customs, or practices of his or her church, denomination, or organization, has a duty to keep those communications secret.

Nothing in this subdivision shall be construed to modify or limit a clergy member's duty to report known or suspected child abuse when a clergy member is acting in some other capacity that would otherwise make the clergy member a mandated reporter.

On or before January 1, 2004, a clergy member or any custodian of records for the clergy member may report to an agency specified in § 11165.9 that the clergy member or any custodian of records for the clergy member, prior to January 1, 1997, in his or her professional capacity or within the scope of his or her employment, other than during a penitential communication, acquired knowledge or had a reasonable suspicion that a child had been the victim of sexual abuse that the clergy member or any custodian of records for the clergy member did not previously report the abuse to an agency specified in § 11165.9.

This paragraph shall apply even if the victim of the known or suspected abuse has reached the age of majority by the time the required report is made.

The local law enforcement agency shall have jurisdiction to investigate any report of child abuse made pursuant to this paragraph even if the report is made after the victim has reached the age of majority.

Cal. Penal Code § 11165.7(a)(32)-(33) (LexisNexis through 2010 Reg. Sess.)

A mandated reporter is defined as any of the following:

- A clergy member, as specified in § 11166(c)
- Any custodian of records of a clergy member, as specified in this section and § 11166(c).

As used in this article, 'clergy member' means a priest, minister, rabbi, religious practitioner, or similar functionary of a church, temple, or recognized denomination or organization.

Colorado

Colo. Rev. Stat. Ann. § 13-90-107(1)(c) (LexisNexis through 2009 Sess.)

A clergy member, minister, priest, or rabbi shall not be examined without both his or her consent and also the consent of the person making the confidential communication as to any confidential communication made to him or her in his or her professional capacity in the course of discipline expected by the religious body to which he or she belongs.

Colo. Stat. Ann. § 19-3-304(2)(aa) (LexisNexis through 2009 Sess.)

Persons required to report abuse or neglect or circumstances or conditions shall include any clergy member.

The provisions of this paragraph shall not apply to a person who acquires reasonable cause to know or suspect that a child has been subjected to abuse or neglect during a communication about which the person may not be examined as a witness pursuant to § 13-90-107(1)(c), unless the person also acquires such reasonable cause from a source other than such communication.

For purposes of this paragraph, unless the context otherwise requires, 'clergy member' means a priest; rabbi; duly ordained, commissioned, or licensed minister of a church; member of a religious order; or recognized leader of any religious body.

Connecticut

Conn. Gen. Stat. Ann. § 17a-101(b) (LexisNexis through 2009 Reg. Sess.)

The following persons shall be mandated reporters: members of the clergy.

Delaware

Del. Code Ann. Tit. 16, § 903 (LexisNexis through 2/12/10)

Any other person who knows or in good faith suspects child abuse or neglect shall make a report in accordance with § 904 of this title.

Del. Code Ann. Tit. 16, § 909 (LexisNexis through 2/12/10)

No legally recognized privilege, except that between attorney and client and that between priest and penitent in a sacramental confession, shall apply to situations involving known or suspected child abuse, neglect, exploitation, or abandonment and shall not constitute grounds for failure to report as required or to give or accept evidence in any judicial proceeding relating to child abuse or neglect.

District of Columbia

This issue is not addressed in the statutes reviewed.

Florida

Fla. Stat. Ann. § 39.201(1) (LexisNexis through 2010 Reg. Sess.)

Any person who knows, or has reasonable cause to suspect, that a child is abused, abandoned, or neglected by a parent, legal custodian, caregiver, or other person responsible for the child's welfare, or that a child is in need of supervision and care and has no parent, legal custodian, or responsible adult relative immediately known and available to provide supervision and care, shall report such knowledge or suspicion to the department.

Fla. Stat. Ann. § 39.204 (LexisNexis through 2010 Reg. Sess.)

The privileged quality of communications between husband and wife and between any professional person and his or her patient or client, or any other privileged communications except that between attorney and client or the privilege provided by § 90.505 [providing for the confidentiality of communications made to a clergy member for the purpose of spiritual counsel], as such communication relates both to the competency of the witness and to the exclusion of confidential communications, shall not apply to any communication involving the perpetrator or alleged perpetrator in any situation involving known or suspected child abuse, abandonment or neglect, and shall not constitute grounds for failure to report as required by the reporting laws regardless of the source of information requiring the report, failure to cooperate with law enforcement or the department in its activities pursuant to this chapter, or failure to give evidence in any judicial proceeding relating to child abuse, abandonment, or neglect.

Georgia

This issue is not addressed in the statutes reviewed.

Guam

This issue is not addressed in the statutes reviewed.

Hawaii

This issue is not addressed in the statutes reviewed.

Idaho

Idaho Code § 16-1605 (LexisNexis through 2009 Reg. Sess.)

Any other person having reason to believe that a child has been abused, abandoned, or neglected shall report or cause a report to be made within 24 hours.

The term 'duly ordained minister of religion' means a person who has been ordained or set apart, in accordance with the ceremony, ritual, or discipline of a church or religious organization that has been established on the basis of a community of religious faith, belief, doctrines, and practices, to hear confessions and confidential communications in accordance with the bona fide doctrines or discipline of that church or religious organization.

The notification requirements do not apply to a duly ordained minister of religion, with regard to any confession or confidential communication made to him or her in his or her ecclesiastical capacity in the course of discipline enjoined by the church to which he or she belongs if:

- The church qualifies as tax-exempt under Federal law.
- The confession or confidential communication was made directly to the duly ordained minister of religion.
- The confession or confidential communication was made in the manner and context that places the duly ordained minister specifically and strictly under a level of confidentiality that is considered inviolate by canon law or church doctrine.

A confession or confidential communication made under any other circumstances does not fall under this exemption.

Illinois

325 Ill. Comp. Stat. Ann. § 5/4 (LexisNexis through 2010 Reg. Sess.)

Any member of the clergy having reasonable cause to believe that a child known to that member of the clergy in his or her professional capacity may be an abused child as defined by law shall immediately report or cause a report to be made to the Department of Children and Family Services.

Whenever such person is required to report under this act in his or her capacity as a member of the clergy, he or she shall make a report immediately to the department in accordance with the provisions of this act and may also notify the person in charge of the church, synagogue, temple, mosque, or other religious institution, or his or her designated agent, that such a report has been made. Under no circumstances shall any person in charge of the church, synagogue, temple, mosque, or other religious institution, or his or her designated agent to whom such notification is made, exercise any control, restraint, modification or other change in the report or the forwarding of such report to the department.

The privileged quality of communication between any professional person required to report and his or her patient or client shall not apply to situations involving abused or neglected children and shall not constitute grounds for failure to report.

A member of the clergy may claim the privilege under § 8-803 of the Code of Civil Procedure.

735 Ill. Comp. Stat. Ann. § 5/8-803 (LexisNexis through 2010 Reg. Sess.)

A member of the clergy or practitioner of any religious denomination accredited by the religious body to which he or she belongs shall not be compelled to disclose in any court, or to any administrative body or agency, or to any public officer, a confession or admission made to him or her in his or her professional character or as a spiritual advisor in the course of the discipline enjoined by the rules or practice of such religious body or of the religion that he or she professes, nor be compelled to divulge any information that has been obtained by him or her in such professional character or such spiritual advisor.

Indiana

Ind. Code Ann. § 31-33-5-1 (LexisNexis through 2007 Sess.)

In addition to any other duty to report arising under this article, an individual who has reason to believe that a child is a victim of child abuse or neglect shall make a report as required by this article.

Iowa

This issue is not addressed in the statutes reviewed.

Kansas

This issue is not addressed in the statutes reviewed.

Kentucky

Ky. Rev. Stat. Ann. § 620.030(1), (3) (LexisNexis through 2009 1st Ex. Sess.)

Any person who knows or has reasonable cause to believe that a child is dependent, neglected, or abused shall immediately cause an oral or written report to be made.

Neither the husband-wife nor any professional-client/patient privilege, except the attorney-client and clergy-penitent privilege, shall be ground for refusing to report or for excluding evidence regarding a dependent, neglected, or abused child or the cause thereof, in any judicial proceedings resulting from a report. This subsection shall also apply in any criminal proceeding in district or circuit court regarding a dependent, neglected, or abused child.

Louisiana

La. Children's Code Art. 603(15)(b)-(c) (LexisNexis through 2009 Reg. Sess.)

'Mental health/social service practitioner' is any individual who provides mental health or social service diagnosis, assessment, counseling, or treatment, including a psychiatrist, psychologist, marriage or family counselor, social worker, member of the clergy, aide, or other individual who provides counseling services to a child or his or her family.

'Member of the clergy' is any priest, rabbi, duly ordained deacon or minister, Christian Science practitioner, or other similarly situated functionary of a religious organization.

A member of the clergy is not required to report a confidential communication, as defined in Code of Evidence article 511(A)(2), from a person to a member of the clergy who in the course of the discipline or practice of that church, denomination, or organization is authorized and accustomed to hearing confidential communication and, under the discipline or tenets of that church, denomination, or organization, has a duty to keep such communication confidential. In that instance, the member of the clergy shall encourage that person to report the allegations to the appropriate authorities.

Maine

Me. Rev. Stat. Ann. Tit. 22, § 4011-A(1)(A)(27) (LexisNexis through 2009 2nd Reg. Sess.)

The following adult persons shall immediately report or cause a report to be made to the department when the person knows or has reasonable cause to suspect that a child has been or is likely to be abused or neglected: clergy members acquiring the information as a result of clerical professional work, except for information received during confidential communications.

Maryland
Md. Code Ann. Fam. Law § 5-705(a)(1), (a)(3) (LexisNexis through 2009 Reg. Sess.)

Except as provided below, notwithstanding any other provision of law, including a law on privileged communications, a person other than a health practitioner, police officer, or educator or human service worker who has reason to believe that a child has been subjected to abuse or neglect shall notify the local department or the appropriate law enforcement agency.

A minister of the gospel, clergy member, or priest of an established church of any denomination is not required to provide notice [when they have reason to believe that a child has been subjected to abuse or neglect] if the notice would disclose matter in relation to any communication that is protected by the clergy-penitent privilege and:

- The communication was made to the minister, clergy member, or priest in a professional character in the course of discipline enjoined by the church to which the minister, clergy member, or priest belongs.
- The minister, clergy member, or priest is bound to maintain the confidentiality of that communication under canon law, church doctrine, or practice.

Massachusetts
Mass. Gen. Laws Ann. Ch. 119, § 21 (LexisNexis through 2010 Sess.)

Mandatory reporters include:

- Priests, rabbis, clergy members, ordained or licensed ministers, leaders of any church or religious body, or accredited Christian Science practitioners
- Persons performing official duties on behalf of a church or religious body that are recognized as the duties of a priest, rabbi, clergy, ordained or licensed minister, leader of any church or religious body, accredited Christian Science practitioner
- Persons employed by a church or religious body to supervise, educate, coach, train, or counsel a child on a regular basis

Mass. Gen. Laws Ann. Ch. 119, § 51A(j) (LexisNexis through 2010 Sess.)
Effective July 1, 2010

Any privilege relating to confidential communications, established by §§ 135 to 135B, inclusive, of chapter 112 [pertaining to social worker-client privilege] or by §§ 20A [clergy-penitent privilege] and 20B [psychotherapist-patient privilege] of chapter 233, shall not prohibit the filing of a report under this section or a care and protection petition under § 24, except that a priest, rabbi, clergy member, ordained or licensed minister, leader of a church or religious body, or accredited Christian Science practitioner need not report information solely gained in a confession or similarly confidential communication in other religious faiths. Nothing in the general laws shall modify or limit the duty of a priest, rabbi, clergy member, ordained or licensed minister, leader of a church or religious body, or accredited Christian

Science practitioner to report suspected child abuse or neglect under this section when the priest, rabbi, clergy member, ordained or licensed minister, leader of a church or religious body, or accredited Christian Science practitioner is acting in some other capacity that would otherwise make him or her a mandated reporter.

Michigan

Mich. Comp. Laws Ann. § 722.623 (LexisNexis through 2010 Sess.)

A member of the clergy who has reasonable cause to suspect child abuse or neglect shall make immediately, by telephone or otherwise, an oral report, or cause on oral report to be made, of the suspected child abuse or neglect to the Family Independence Agency (department).

Mich. Comp. Laws Ann. § 722.631 (LexisNexis through 2010 Sess.)

Any legally recognized privileged communication except that between attorney and client or that made to a member of the clergy in his or her professional character in a confession or similarly confidential communication is abrogated and shall not constitute grounds for excusing a report otherwise required to be made or for excluding evidence in a civil protective proceeding resulting from a report made pursuant to this act. This section does not relieve a member of the clergy from reporting suspected child abuse or child neglect if that member of the clergy receives information concerning suspected child abuse or child neglect while acting in any other capacity listed under § 722.623.

Minnesota

Minn. Stat. Ann. § 626.556, Subd. 3(a) (LexisNexis through 2009 Reg. Sess.)

A person who knows or has reason to believe a child is being neglected or physically or sexually abused shall immediately report the information to the local welfare agency, agency responsible for assessing or investigating the report, police department, or the county sheriff if the person is employed as a member of the clergy and received the information while engaged in ministerial duties, provided that a member of clergy is not required to report information that is otherwise privileged under § 595.02(1)(c) [pertaining to clergy-penitent privilege].

Mississippi

Miss. Code Ann. § 43-21-353(1) (LexisNexis through 2009 3rd Ex. Sess.)

Any minister who has reasonable cause to suspect that a child is a neglected child or an abused child shall cause an oral report to be made immediately by telephone or otherwise to be followed as soon thereafter as possible by a report in writing to the Department of Human Services.

Missouri

Mo. Ann. Stat. § 210.140 (LexisNexis through 2009 1st Reg. Sess.)

Any legally recognized privileged communication, except that between attorney and client, or involving communications made to a minister or clergy member, shall not apply to situations involving known or suspected child abuse or neglect and shall not constitute grounds for failure to report as required or permitted, to cooperate with the division in any of its activities, or to give or accept evidence in any judicial proceeding relating to child abuse or neglect.

Mo. Ann. Stat. § 352.400 (LexisNexis through 2009 1st Reg. Sess.)

'Minister' means any person while practicing as a minister of the gospel, clergy member, priest, rabbi, Christian Science practitioner, or other person serving in a similar capacity for any religious organization who is responsible for or who has supervisory authority over one who is responsible for the care, custody, and control of a child or who has access to a child.

When a minister or designated agent has reasonable cause to suspect that a child has been or may be subjected to abuse or neglect under circumstances required to be reported, the minister or designated agent shall immediately report or cause a report to be made.

Notwithstanding any other provision of this section or any section of the reporting laws, a minister shall not be required to report concerning a privileged communication made to him or her in his or her professional capacity.

Mo. Ann. Stat. § 210.115 (LexisNexis through 2009 1st Reg. Sess.)

When any minister, as provided by § 352.400, has reasonable cause to suspect that a child has been or may be subjected to abuse or neglect or observes a child being subjected to conditions or circumstances that would reasonably result in abuse or neglect, that person shall immediately report or cause a report to be made to the division.

Montana

Mont. Code Ann. § 15-6-201(2)(a) (LexisNexis through 2009 Spec. Sess.)

The term 'clergy' means:

- An ordained minister, priest, or rabbi
- A commissioned or licensed minister of a church or church denomination that ordains ministers if the person has the authority to perform substantially all the religious duties of the church or denomination
- A member of a religious order who has taken a vow of poverty
- A Christian Science practitioner

Mont. Code Ann. § 41-3-201(2)(h), (4)(b) (LexisNexis through 2009 Spec. Sess.)

Professionals and officials required to report include members of the clergy.

A member of the clergy or priest is not required to report under this section if:

- The knowledge or suspicion of the abuse or neglect came from a statement or confession made to the member of the clergy or priest in that person's capacity as a member of the clergy or priest.
- The statement was intended to be a part of a confidential communication between the member of the clergy or the priest and a member of the church or congregation.
- The person who made the statement or confession does not consent to the disclosure by the member of the clergy or priest.

A member of the clergy or priest is not required to make a report under this section if the communication is required to be confidential by canon law, church doctrine, or established church practice.

Nebraska

Neb. Rev. Stat. Ann. § 28-711 (LexisNexis through 9 1st Spec. Sess.)

When any person has reasonable cause to believe that a child has been subjected to child abuse or neglect or observes that child being subjected to conditions or circumstances that reasonably would result in child abuse or neglect, he or she shall report such incident or cause a report of child abuse or neglect to be made to the proper law enforcement agency or to the Department of Social Services.

Nevada

Nev. Rev. Stat. Ann. § 432B.220(3)(d) (LexisNexis through Nev. 2009 Legis. Serv., Ch. 494)

A report must be made by a clergy member, practitioner of Christian Science, or religious healer, unless he or she has acquired the knowledge of the abuse or neglect from the offender during a confession.

New Hampshire

N.H. Rev. Stat. Ann. § 169-C:29 (LexisNexis through 2010 Sess.)

A priest, minister, or rabbi having reason to suspect that a child has been abused or neglected shall report the same in accordance with this chapter.

N.H. Rev. Stat. Ann. § 169-C:32 (LexisNexis through 2010 Sess.)

The privileged quality of communication between husband and wife and any professional person [including a priest, minister, or rabbi] and his patient or client, except that between attorney and client, shall not apply to proceedings instituted pursuant to this chapter and shall not constitute grounds for failure to report as required by this chapter.

New Jersey

N.J. Ann. Stat. § 9:6-8.10 (LexisNexis through 2010 Sess.)

Any person having reasonable cause to believe that a child has been subjected to child abuse or acts of child abuse shall report the same immediately to the Division of Youth and Family Services by telephone or otherwise.

New Mexico

N.M. Stat. Ann. § 32A-4-3(A) (LexisNexis through 2009 1st Spec. Sess.)

Every person, including a member of the clergy who has information that is not privileged as a matter of law, who knows or has a reasonable suspicion that a child is an abused or a neglected child shall report the matter immediately.

New York

This issue is not addressed in the statutes reviewed.

North Carolina

N.C. Gen. Stat. § 7B-310 (LexisNexis through 2009 Reg. Sess.)

No privilege shall be grounds for any person or institution failing to report that a juvenile may have been abused, neglected, or dependent, even if the knowledge or suspicion is acquired in an official professional capacity, except when the knowledge is gained by an attorney from that attorney's client during representation only in the abuse, neglect, or dependency case.

No privilege, except the attorney-client privilege, shall be grounds for excluding evidence of abuse, neglect, or dependency in any judicial proceeding (civil, criminal, or juvenile) in which a juvenile's abuse, neglect, or dependency is in issue nor in any judicial proceeding resulting from a report submitted under this article, both as the privilege relates to the competency of the witness and to the exclusion of confidential communications.

N.C. Gen. Stat. § 7B-301 (LexisNexis through 2009 Reg. Sess.)

Any person or institution that has cause to suspect that any juvenile is abused, neglected, or dependent, or has died as the result of maltreatment, shall report the case of that juvenile to the director of the Department of Social Services in the county where the juvenile resides or is found.

North Dakota

N.D. Cent. Code § 50-25.1-03(1) (LexisNexis through 2009 Sess.)

Any member of the clergy having knowledge of or reasonable cause to suspect that a child is abused or neglected, or has died as a result of abuse or neglect, shall report the circumstances to the department if the knowledge or suspicion is derived from information received by that person in that person's official or professional capacity. A member of the clergy, however, is not required to report such circumstances if the knowledge or suspicion is derived from information received in the capacity of a spiritual advisor.

Northern Mariana Islands

This issue is not addressed in the statutes reviewed.

Ohio

Ohio Rev. Code § 2151.421(A)(4)(a) (LexisNexis through 2010 Sess.)

No cleric and no person, other than a volunteer, designated by any church, religious society, or faith acting as a leader, official, or delegate on behalf of the church, religious society, or faith who is acting in an official or professional capacity, who knows or has reasonable cause to believe based on facts that would cause a reasonable person in a similar position to believe, that a child under age 18 or a mentally retarded, developmentally disabled, or physically impaired child under age 21 has suffered or faces a threat of suffering any physical or mental wound, injury, disability, or condition of a nature that reasonably indicates abuse or neglect of the child, and who knows, or has reasonable cause to believe based on facts that would cause a reasonable person in a similar position to believe, that another cleric or another person, other than a volunteer, designated by a church, religious society, or faith acting as a leader, official, or delegate on behalf of the church, religious society, or faith caused, or poses the threat of causing, the wound, injury, disability, or condition that reasonably indicates abuse or neglect shall fail to immediately report that knowledge or reasonable cause to believe to the entity or persons specified in this division.

Ohio Rev. Code § 2151.421(A)(4)(b)-(d) (LexisNexis through 2010 Sess.)

A cleric is not required to make a report concerning any communication the cleric receives from a penitent in a cleric-penitent relationship, if, in accordance with § 2317.02(C), the cleric could not testify with respect to that communication in a civil or criminal proceeding.

The penitent in a cleric-penitent relationship is deemed to have waived any testimonial privilege with respect to any communication the cleric receives from the penitent in that cleric-penitent relationship, and the cleric shall make a report with respect to that communication, if all of the following apply:

- The penitent, at the time of the communication, is either a child under age 18 or a mentally retarded, developmentally disabled, or physically impaired person under age 21.
- The cleric knows, or has reasonable cause to believe based on facts that would cause a reasonable person in a similar position to believe, as a result of the communication or any observations made during that communication, the penitent has suffered or faces a threat of suffering any physical or mental wound, injury, disability, or condition of a nature that reasonably indicates abuse or neglect of the penitent.
- The abuse or neglect does not arise out of the penitent's attempt to have an abortion performed upon a child under age 18 or upon a mentally retarded, developmentally disabled, or physically impaired person under age 21 without the notification of her parents, guardian, or custodian in accordance with § 2151.85.

The above sections do not apply in a cleric-penitent relationship when the disclosure of any communication the cleric receives from the penitent is in violation of the sacred trust.

Oklahoma

Okla. Stat. Ann. Tit. 10A, § 1-2-101 (LexisNexis through 2009 1st Reg. Sess.)

Every person having reason to believe that a child under age 18 is a victim of abuse or neglect shall report the matter promptly to the Department of Human Services.

No privilege or contract shall relieve any person from the requirement of reporting pursuant to this section.

Oregon

Or. Rev. Stat. Ann. § 419B.005(3)(h) (LexisNexis through Or. 2010 Legis. Serv., Ch. 60)

Public or private official [includes]: member of the clergy.

Or. Rev. Stat. Ann. § 419B.010(1) (LexisNexis through 2009 Reg. Sess.)

Any public or private official having reasonable cause to believe that any child with whom the official comes in contact has suffered abuse or that any person with whom the official comes in contact has abused a child shall immediately report or cause a report to be made.

Nothing shall affect the duty to report imposed by the reporting laws, except that a psychiatrist, psychologist, member of clergy, or attorney shall not be required to report such information communicated by a person if such communication is privileged under §§ 40.225 to 40.295.

Pennsylvania
23 Pa. Cons. Stat. Ann. § 6311(a), (b) (LexisNexis through 2010 Sess.)
Except with respect to confidential communications made to an ordained member of the clergy, which are protected under law relating to confidential communications to clergy members, the privileged communication between any professional person required to report and the patient or client of that person shall not apply to situations involving child abuse [or neglect] and shall not constitute grounds for failure to report as required by this chapter.

Enumeration of persons required to report [includes]: members of the clergy.

Puerto Rico
P.R. Laws Ann. Tit. 8, § 446(b) (LexisNexis through Dec. 2007)
Any person who has knowledge of or suspects that a minor is a victim of abuse, institutional abuse, neglect, and/or institutional neglect shall report that fact through the hotline of the department, to the Puerto Rico police, or to the local office of the department.

Rhode Island
R.I. Gen. Laws § 40-11-11 (LexisNexis through 2009 Sess.)
The privileged quality of communication between husband and wife and any professional and his or her patient or client, except that between attorney and client, is hereby abrogated in situations involving known or suspected child abuse or neglect and shall not constitute grounds for failure to report as required by this chapter, failure to cooperate with the department in its activities pursuant to this chapter, or failure to give or accept evidence in any judicial proceeding relating to child abuse or neglect. In any family court proceeding relating to child abuse or neglect, notwithstanding the provisions of other statutes, no privilege of confidentiality may be invoked with respect to any illness, trauma, incompetency, addiction to drugs, or alcoholism of any parent.
R.I. Gen. Laws § 40-11-3(a) (LexisNexis through 2009 Sess.)
Any person who has reasonable cause to know or suspect that any child has been abused or neglected or has been a victim of sexual abuse by another child shall, within 24 hours, transfer that information to the department.

South Carolina

S.C. Code Ann. § 63-7-310(A) (LexisNexis through 2009 Reg. Sess.)

Persons required to report include members of the clergy, including Christian Science practitioners or religious healers.

S.C. Code Ann. § 63-7-420 (LexisNexis through 2009 Reg. Sess.)

The privileged quality of communication between husband and wife and any professional person and his or her patient or client, except that between attorney and client or clergy member, including Christian Science practitioner or religious healer, and penitent, is abrogated and does not constitute grounds for failure to report or the exclusion of evidence in a civil protective proceeding resulting from a report pursuant to this article. However, a clergy member, including Christian Science practitioner or religious healer, must report in accordance with this subarticle, except when information is received from the alleged perpetrator of the abuse and neglect during a communication that is protected by the clergy and penitent privilege as defined in § 19-11-90.

South Dakota

This issue is not addressed in the statutes reviewed.

Tennessee

Tenn. Code § 37-1-605(a) (LexisNexis through 2009 1st Ex. Sess.)

Any person who knows or has reasonable cause to suspect that a child has been sexually abused shall report such knowledge or suspicion to the department.

Tenn. Code Ann. § 37-1-403(a) (LexisNexis through 2010 1st Ex. Sess.)

Any person who has knowledge of or is called upon to render aid to any child who is suffering from or has sustained any wound, injury, disability, or physical or mental condition shall report such harm immediately if the harm is of such a nature as to reasonably indicate that it has been caused by brutality, abuse, or neglect or that, on the basis of available information, reasonably appears to have been caused by brutality, abuse, or neglect.

Texas

Tex. Fam. Code Ann. § 261.101 (LexisNexis through 2009 1st Sess.)

A person having cause to believe that a child's physical or mental health or welfare has been adversely affected by abuse or neglect by any person shall immediately make a report as provided by this subchapter.

The requirement to report under this section applies without exception to an individual whose personal communications may otherwise be privileged, including an attorney, a member of the clergy, a medical practitioner, a social worker, a mental health professional, and an employee of a clinic or health-care facility that provides reproductive services.

Utah

Utah Code Ann. § 62A-4a-403 (LexisNexis through 2009 1st Spec. Sess.)

When any person has reason to believe that a child has been subjected to abuse or neglect, or who observes a child being subjected to conditions or circumstances that reasonably would result in abuse or neglect, he or she shall immediately notify the nearest peace officer, law enforcement agency, or office of the division.

The notification requirements do not apply to a clergy member or priest, without the consent of the person making the confession, with regard to any confession made to him or her in his or her professional character in the course of discipline enjoined by the church to which he or she belongs, if:

- The confession was made directly to the clergy member or priest by the perpetrator.
- The clergy member or priest is, under canon law or church doctrine or practice, bound to maintain the confidentiality of that confession.

When the clergy member or priest receives information about abuse or neglect from any source other than confession of the perpetrator, he or she is required to give notification on the basis of that information even though he or she may have also received a report of abuse or neglect from the confession of the perpetrator.

Exemption of notification requirements for a clergy member or priest does not exempt him or her from any other efforts required by law to prevent further abuse or neglect by the perpetrator.

Vermont

Vt. Stat. Ann. Tit. 33, § 4913(a), (f)-(h) (LexisNexis through 2009 Spec. Sess.)

Any member of the clergy who has reasonable cause to believe that any child has been abused or neglected shall report or cause a report to be made in accordance with the reporting laws.

Except as provided below, a person may not refuse to make a report required by this section on the grounds that making the report would violate privilege or disclose a confidential communication.

A member of the clergy shall not be required to make a report under this section if the report would be based upon information revealed in a communication that is:

- Made to a member of the clergy acting in his or her capacity as spiritual advisor
- Intended by the parties to be confidential at the time the communication is made
- Intended by the communicant to be an act of contrition or a matter of conscience
- Required to be confidential by religious law, doctrine, or tenet

When a member of the clergy receives information about abuse or neglect of a child in a manner other than as described above, he or she is required to report on the basis of that information even though he or she may have also received a report of abuse or neglect about the same person or incident in the manner described above.

Vt. Stat. Ann. Tit. 33, § 4912(12) (LexisNexis through 2009 Spec. Sess.)

'Member of the clergy' means a priest, rabbi, clergy member, ordained or licensed minister, leader of any church or religious body, or accredited Christian Science practitioner, person performing official duties on behalf of a church or religious body that are recognized as the duties of a priest, rabbi, clergy, nun, brother, ordained or licensed minister, leader of any church or religious body, or accredited Christian Science practitioner.

Virgin Islands

This issue is not addressed in the statutes reviewed.

Virginia

Va. Code Ann. § 63.2-1509 (LexisNexis through 2007 Reg. Sess.)

This subsection [enumerating mandated reporters] shall not apply to any regular minister, priest, rabbi, imam, or duly accredited practitioner of any religious organization or denomination usually referred to as a church as it relates to (i) information required by the doctrine of the religious organization or denomination to be kept in a confidential manner or (ii) information that would be subject to § 8.01-400 or 19.2-271.3 if offered as evidence in court.

Washington

Wash. Rev. Code Ann. § 26.44.060(3) (LexisNexis through 3/16/10)

Conduct conforming with reporting requirements shall not be deemed a violation of the confidential communication privilege of §§ 5.60.060 (3) and (4) [pertaining to clergy-penitent and physician-patient privilege], 18.53.200 [pertaining to optometrist-patient privilege], and 18.83.110 [pertaining to psychologist-client privilege].

Wash. Rev. Code Ann. § 26.44.030(7) (LexisNexis through 3/16/10)

Information considered privileged by statute and not directly related to reports required by this section must not be divulged without a valid written waiver of the privilege.

West Virginia

W. Va. Code Ann. § 49-6A-2 (LexisNexis through 2009 4th Ex. Sess.)

When any member of the clergy has reasonable cause to suspect that a child is neglected or abused or observes the child being subjected to conditions that are likely to result in abuse or neglect, such person shall immediately, and not more than 48 hours after suspecting this abuse, report the circumstances or cause a report to be made to the Department of Health and Human Resources.

W. Va. Code Ann. § 49-6A-7 (LexisNexis through 2009 4th Ex. Sess.)

The privileged quality of communications between husband and wife and between any professional person and his or her patient or client, except that between attorney and client, is hereby abrogated in situations involving suspected or known child abuse or neglect.

Wisconsin

Wis. Stat. Ann. § 48.981(2)(b) (LexisNexis through 2009 Wis. Act 185)

Except as provided below, a member of the clergy shall report if the member of the clergy has reasonable cause to suspect that a child seen by the member of the clergy in the course of his or her professional duties:

- Has been abused
- Has been threatened with abuse, and abuse of the child will likely occur

Except as provided below, a member of the clergy shall report if the member of the clergy has reasonable cause, based on observations made or information that he or she receives, to suspect that a member of the clergy has done any of the following:

- Abused a child
- Threatened a child with abuse, and abuse of the child will likely occur

A member of the clergy is not required to report child abuse information that he or she receives solely through confidential communications made to him or her privately or in a confessional setting if he or she is authorized to hear or is accustomed to hearing such communications and, under the disciplines, tenets, or traditions of his or her religion, has a duty or is expected to keep those communications secret. Those disciplines, tenets, or traditions need not be in writing.

Wyoming

Wyo. Stat. Ann. § 14-3-205(a) (LexisNexis through 2009 Sess.)

Any person who knows or has reasonable cause to believe or suspect that a child has been abused or neglected, or who observes any child being subjected to conditions or circumstances that would reasonably result in abuse or neglect, shall immediately report it to the child protective agency or local law enforcement agency or cause a report to be made.

Wyo. Stat. Ann. § 14-3-210 (LexisNexis through 2009 Sess.)

Evidence regarding a child in any judicial proceeding resulting from a report made pursuant to the reporting laws shall not be excluded on the ground it constitutes a privileged communication:

- Between husband and wife
- Claimed under any provision of law other than § 1-12-101(a)(i) [regarding attorney-client or physician-patient privilege] and § 1-12-101(a)(ii) [regarding privilege of a clergy member or priest as it relates to a confession made to him or her in his or her professional character if enjoined by the church to which he or she belongs]
- Claimed pursuant to § 1-12-116 [regarding the confidential communication between a family violence and sexual assault advocate and victim]

End Notes

[1] For more information on mandated reporters, see Child Welfare Information Gateway's Mandatory Reporters of Child Abuse and Neglect at www.childwelfare.gov/systemwide/laws

[2] The word *approximately* is used to stress the fact that States frequently amend their laws. This information is current only through April 2010; States that include clergy as mandated reporters are Alabama, Arizona, Arkansas, California, Colorado, Connecticut, Illinois, Louisiana, Maine, Massachusetts, Michigan, Minnesota, Mississippi, Missouri, Montana, Nevada, New Hampshire, New Mexico, North Dakota, Ohio, Oregon, Pennsylvania, South Carolina, Vermont, West Virginia, and Wisconsin.

[3] Delaware, Florida, Idaho, Indiana, Kentucky, Maryland, Mississippi, Nebraska, New Hampshire, New Jersey, New Mexico, North Carolina, Oklahoma, Rhode Island, Tennessee, Texas, Utah, and Wyoming. Three of these States (Mississippi, New Hampshire, and New Mexico) also enumerate clergy as mandated reporters.

[4] The issue of clergy-penitent privilege also may be addressed in case law, which this publication does not cover.

[5] Clergy are not mandated reporters in Washington, but if they elect to report, their report and any testimony are provided statutory immunity from liability.

In: Reporting Child Abuse and Neglect
Editor: Henry J. Pervall

ISBN: 978-1-62100-157-7
© 2012 Nova Science Publishers, Inc.

Chapter 4

MAKING AND SCREENING REPORTS OF CHILD ABUSE AND NEGLECT: SUMMARY AND STATE LAWS[*1]

United States Department of Health and Human Services

All 50 States, the District of Columbia, American Samoa, Guam, the Northern Mariana Islands, Puerto Rico, and the U.S. Virgin Islands have laws and policies that specify procedures for making and responding to reports of suspected child abuse or neglect. Mandated reporters are required by States to make an immediate report when they suspect or know of abusive or neglectful situations.[1] In all jurisdictions, the initial report may be made orally to either the child protective services (CPS) agency or a law enforcement agency. In 20 States, American Samoa, Guam, and Puerto Rico, a mandated reporter is required to submit a written report after he or she has made an oral report.[2] In eight States, the District of Columbia, and the U.S. Virgin Islands, a written report is required only when requested by the department or agency that received the initial report.[3]

CONTENT OF REPORTS

Most States specify in statute the types of information that should be included in a report of suspected abuse or neglect. The reporter will be asked to provide as much information about the child's situation as he or she can, including the names and addresses of the child and the child's parents or other persons responsible for the child's care, the child's age, conditions in the child's home environment, the nature and extent of the child's injuries, and information about other children in the same environment.

---

[*] This is an edited, reformatted and augmented version of the United States Department of Health and Human Services publication, dated January 2009.

[1] This material may be freely reproduced and distributed. However, when doing so, please credit Child Welfare Information Gateway.

SPECIAL REPORTING PROCEDURES

Some States also specify reporting procedures for special situations, such as the suspicious death of a child and cases of substance-exposed infants.

Specific reporting procedures to be followed in the event of a suspicious child death have been enacted in approximately 31 States, American Samoa, Guam, the Northern Mariana Islands, and Puerto Rico.[4] Typically, the statutes instruct a mandatory reporter to report a suspicious child death to a medical examiner or coroner. For States that do not have specific reporting procedures for suspicious child deaths, standard child abuse reporting procedures apply.

The Federal Child Abuse Prevention and Treatment Act (CAPTA) requires States to have policies and procedures to address the needs of substance-exposed infants.[5] Approximately 18 States and the District of Columbia have specific reporting procedures for cases of suspected substance-exposed infants.[6] In general, these statutes make drug exposure or a positive drug test alone the basis for reporting child abuse or neglect. Standard reporting procedures apply in those States that statutorily define infant drug exposure as child abuse and neglect but have no specific reporting procedures for substance-exposed infants.[7]

SCREENING REPORTS

The laws and policies in all jurisdictions specify procedures for the initial response required by the agencies receiving the reports. The ultimate purpose of the reporting system is to ensure the child's safety and well-being.[8] In most States, the agency that receives a report of suspected child abuse or neglect will first screen the report to determine whether it meets the criteria for acceptance. For acceptance, the report must concern actions that meet the statutory definition of child abuse or neglect in that State.[9] Typically, this will involve situations of harm or threatened harm to a child committed by a parent, guardian, or other person responsible for the child's care. Reports that do not meet the statutory criteria are screened out.

Reports that meet the criteria are screened in and accepted for investigation, usually by the State CPS agency. All States require CPS to initiate an investigation in a timely manner, generally within 72 hours. In addition, most States require investigations to be initiated immediately, in as little as 2 hours and no longer than 24 hours, when there is reasonable cause to believe that a child is in imminent danger.

The approaches used to screen reports vary from State to State, but nearly all States utilize a type of safety assessment to determine which reports require immediate responses.

Approximately 30 States and the District of Columbia categorize reports based on the level of risk of harm to the child and assign different response times.[10] Eleven States use differential response systems in which more serious cases are assigned to be investigated, and less serious cases are assigned to receive family assessments.[11]

Investigations may be conducted by the child protective agency (CPS), a law enforcement agency, or cooperatively by both agencies; family assessments are conducted by CPS. In approximately 15 States and the Virgin Islands, cases that involve physical or sexual abuse or possible criminal conduct may be investigated by a law enforcement agency.[12] In nine States, reports are referred to law enforcement agencies when the alleged perpetrator is a person other than the parent or other caregiver.[13] Most States also require cross-reporting among professional entities. Typically, reports are shared among social services agencies, law enforcement agencies, and prosecutors' offices.[14]

This publication is a product of the State Statutes Series prepared by Child Welfare Information Gateway. While every attempt has been made to be as complete as possible, additional information on these topics may be in other sections of a State's code as well as agency regulations, case law, and informal practices and procedures.

Alabama
Reporting Procedures
Individual Responsibility
Citation: Ala. Code § 26-14-3

All mandated reporters are required to immediately make an oral report when they know or suspect that a child is a victim of child abuse or neglect. The oral report shall be followed by a written report.

Content of Reports
Citation: Ala. Code § 26-14-5

The report shall contain, if known:
- The name and location of the child
- The names and addresses of the child's parents or caregivers
- The nature and extent of the child's injuries
- Any evidence of previous injuries
- Any other information that might establish the cause of the child's injuries
- The identity of the person alleged to be responsible for the child's injuries

Special Reporting Procedures
Suspicious Deaths

This issue is not addressed in the statutes reviewed.

Substance-Exposed Infants

The issue is not addressed in the statutes reviewed.

Screening Reports
Citation: Ala. Code §§ 26-14-6.1; 26-14-7; Ala. Admin. Code Ch. 660, §§ 5-34.03; 5-34.04; 5-34.05; 5-34.10

The duty and responsibility for the investigation of reports of suspected child abuse or neglect shall be as follows:
- Reports of suspected child abuse or neglect involving disciplinary or corporal punishment committed in a public or private school or kindergarten shall be investigated by law enforcement agencies.
- Reports of suspected child abuse or neglect committed in a State-operated child residential facility shall be investigated by law enforcement agencies.
- All other reports of suspected child abuse and neglect shall be investigated by the Department of Human Resources.

The department shall make a thorough investigation promptly upon either the oral or written report. The primary purpose of such an investigation shall be the protection of the child. The investigation, to the extent that is reasonably possible, shall include:

- The nature, extent and cause of the child abuse or neglect
- The identity of the responsible person
- The names and conditions of other children in the home
- An evaluation of the parents or person responsible for the care of the child
- The home environment and the relationship of the child or children to the parents or other persons responsible for their care
- All other data deemed pertinent

The county Department of Human Resources shall make a complete written report of the investigation, together with its recommendations.

In regulation:

Reports of child abuse or neglect are received by a duly constituted authority that may include a chief of police, sheriff, the department, or any person, organization, or agency authorized and designated by the department to receive such reports. Once a report has been received, it must be investigated, and the investigation is known by DHR as the child abuse/neglect initial assessment.

The following criteria must be considered at intake when determining which reports will be investigated first:

- The allegations in the report
- The seriousness of the incident(s)
- The child's vulnerability (i.e., capacity for self-protection) and the potential risk of serious harm to the child

DHR's response time is the timeframe within which in-person initial contact shall be made with the children who are allegedly abused or neglected (i.e., at risk of serious harm) and all other children in the home.

- Child welfare staff shall respond immediately, i.e., as soon as possible after a report is received, but no later than 12 hours from receipt of the intake information, when the intake information indicates serious harm will likely occur within 24 hours.
- For situations in which an immediate response is not required, child welfare staff shall respond as quickly as the intake information warrants but no later than 5 calendar days.
- Child welfare staff must make contact with all other children who live in the home of the reported child as soon as the intake information warrants, but not later than 15 calendar days.

All reports must be cleared through the central registry to determine whether there have been previous reports involving the children, their family members, and all persons allegedly responsible for abuse or neglect.

At the conclusion of the assessment, a decision regarding a family's need for ongoing protective services shall be made. This decision may be to discontinue DHR services as no protective services are needed, to provide ongoing casework services, to initiate court action, or to make a referral to another agency for services. The decision is to be made with the parents' or primary caregiver's participation to the extent feasible. In any event, the parents or primary caregivers are entitled to an explanation of the action taken and the reasons for the action.

Alaska

Reporting Procedures
Individual Responsibility
Citation: Alaska Stat. §§ 47.17.020; 47.17.023

Mandated reporters shall immediately report to the Department of Health and Social Services when they have reasonable cause to suspect that a child has suffered harm as a result of abuse or neglect.

A person providing, either privately or commercially, film, photo, or visual or printed matter processing, production, or finishing services or computer installation, repair, or other services, or Internet or cellular telephone services who, in the process of providing those services, observes a film, photo, picture, computer file, image, or other matter and has reasonable cause to suspect that it visually depicts a child engaged in sexual conduct described in § 11.41.455(a) shall immediately report the observation to the nearest law enforcement agency and provide the law enforcement agency with all information known about the nature and origin of the film, photo, picture, computer file, image, or other matter.

Content of Reports
Citation: Alaska Stat. § 47.17.025

The department's written report shall include:
- The names and addresses of the child and the child's parents
- The age and sex of the child
- The nature and extent of harm to the child from abuse
- The name, age, and address of the person believed to be responsible for the harm to the child
- Information that may be helpful in establishing the identity of the person responsible for the abuse

Special Reporting Procedures
Suspicious Deaths

This issue is not addressed in the statutes reviewed.

Substance-Exposed Infants

This issue is not addressed in the statutes reviewed.

Screening Reports
Citation: Alaska Stat. §§ 47.17.020; 47.17.025; 47.17.030

The department shall immediately notify the nearest law enforcement agency if the department concludes that the harm was caused by a person who is not responsible for the child's welfare, or involves possible criminal conduct or abuse or neglect that results in the need for medical treatment of the child.

A law enforcement agency shall immediately notify the department of the receipt of a report of harm to a child from abuse. Upon receipt from any source of a report of harm to a child from abuse, the department shall notify the Department of Law and investigate the report and, within 72 hours of the receipt of the report, shall provide a written report of its investigation of the harm to a child from abuse to the Department of Law for review.

The department may, upon receipt of the report, refer the matter to the appropriate health or social services agency if the child resides within the boundaries of a local government. For cases not referred to an agency of a local government, the department shall, for each report received, investigate and take action, in accordance with law, that may be necessary to prevent further harm to the child or to ensure the proper care and protection of the child.

A local government health or social services agency receiving a report of harm shall, for each report received, investigate and take action, in accordance with law, that may be necessary to prevent further harm to the child or to ensure the proper care and protection of the child. In addition, the agency receiving a report of harm shall forward a copy of its report of the investigation, including information the department requires by regulation, to the department.

American Samoa
Reporting Procedures
Individual Responsibility
Citation: Ann. Code § 45.2002(a), (c)

Mandated reporters who have reasonable cause to know or suspect that a child has been subjected to abuse or neglect shall immediately report or cause a report to be made to the child protection services (CPS)agency.

Content of Reports
Citation: Ann. Code § 45.2010

The mandated reporter shall submit a written report that contains the following:
- The name, address, age, sex, religion, and race of the child
- The name and address of the person responsible for the child
- The nature and extent of the child's injuries, including any evidence of previous abuse or neglect
- The names and addresses of the person or persons responsible for the abuse or neglect
- Family composition
- The name, address, and occupation of the person making the report
- Any action taken by the reporting source
- Any other information that might be helpful

Special Reporting Procedures
Suspicious Deaths
Citation: Ann. Code § 45.2003

A mandated reporter who knows or has reasonable cause to suspect that a child has died as a result of abuse or neglect shall report immediately to the Department of Public Safety.

The department shall investigate and report its findings to the attorney general and CPS.

Substance-Exposed Infants

This issue is not addressed in the statutes reviewed.

Screening Reports
Citation: Ann. Code §§ 45.2010; 45.2011

A report of known or suspected child abuse or neglect is immediately made to the Department of Public Safety by a written report prepared by a mandated reporter, if so requested by the receiving CPS agency. The receiving agency will forward a copy of its own report to the central registry on forms supplied by the registry. If at any time a report of suspected child abuse or neglect is made to the CPS agency, the Department of Public Safety must be notified. If a report of suspected child abuse or neglect is made to the department, the agency must be notified. Copies of the report of known or suspected child abuse or neglect are immediately transmitted by the receiving agency to the attorney general's office and to the department.

The CPS agency shall make a thorough investigation promptly upon receiving either the oral or the written report. The primary purpose of the investigation is the protection of the child. The investigation shall include the nature, extent, and cause of the child abuse, sexual abuse, or neglect; the identity of the person responsible; the names and conditions of other children in the home; an evaluation of the parents or persons responsible for the care of the child; and all other pertinent data.

If, before the evaluation is complete, the opinion of the investigators is that immediate removal is necessary to protect children from further abuse or neglect, the court, on petition by the investigators and with good cause shown, shall issue an order for temporary removal and custody.

Arizona
Reporting Procedures
Individual Responsibility
Citation: Rev. Stat. § 13-3620

Any mandated reporter who reasonably believes that a minor is the victim of abuse or neglect shall report immediately to a peace officer or child protective services in the Department of Economic Security. The report may be made by telephone or in person and must be followed by a written report within 72 hours.

Content of Reports
Citation: Rev. Stat. § 13-3620

The reports shall contain:
- The names and addresses of the minor and the minor's parents or the person having custody
- The minor's age
- The nature and extent of any injuries or neglect, including any evidence of previous injuries or neglect
- Any other information that might be helpful

Special Reporting Procedures
Suspicious Deaths

This issue is not addressed in the statutes reviewed.

Substance-Exposed Infants
Citation: Rev. Stat. § 13-3620

A health-care professional who, after a routine newborn physical assessment, believes that a newborn infant may be affected by the presence of alcohol or drugs shall immediately make a report to child protective services (CPS).

Screening Reports
Citation: Rev. Stat. § 13-3620(H); Admin. Code §§ R6-5-5502; 5504; 5505; 5506; 5507

When reports are received by a peace officer, the officer shall immediately notify CPS. When CPS receives a report, it shall immediately notify a peace officer in the appropriate jurisdiction.

In regulation: When the hotline receives a call, staff shall determine the type of alleged maltreatment, whether to classify the call as a report for investigation, and check the central registry for prior reports on the same persons.

If a call is screened in as a report, the hotline staff shall gather additional information using standardized questions, determine whether there are aggravating or mitigating factors, and assign each report a priority code. Staff shall enter the report into the central registry and immediately transmit the report to a local office.

Priority codes and initial response times are:
- Priority 1 High Risk:
  o Standard Response: 2 hours
  o Mitigated Response: 24 hours
- Priority 2 Moderate Risk:
  o Standard Response: 48 hours
  o Aggravated Response: 24 hours à Mitigated Response: 72 hours
- Priority 3 Low Risk:
  o Standard Response: 72 hours
  o Aggravated Response: 48 hours
  o Mitigated Response: 72 hours excluding weekends and Arizona State holidays
- Priority 4 Potential Risk:
  o Standard Response: 7 days
  o Aggravated Response: 72 hours excluding weekends and State holidays

To comply with the priority response time, entities other than CPS, such as law enforcement or emergency personnel, may initially respond to a report.

Upon receipt of a report, a CPS unit supervisor shall assign the case for a field investigation, alternative investigation, or alternative response, such as referral to Family Builders.

An alternative investigation consists of contact with a mandatory reporter who is currently involved with the family. The information will determine if the child and other children residing in the home are current victims of maltreatment or at risk of imminent harm. If results indicate that an alleged victim is at risk of harm, the case shall be immediately assigned for field investigation.

Arkansas
Reporting Procedures
Individual Responsibility
Citation: Ann. Code § 12-12-507

A mandated reporter who has reasonable cause to suspect a child has been maltreated shall report immediately to the child abuse hotline by telephone call, facsimile transmission, or online report.

Facsimile transmission and online reporting may be used in nonemergency situations by an identified reporter who provides the following contact information:
- Name and phone number
- In the case of online reporting, the email address of the identified reporter

A mandated reporter who wishes to remain anonymous shall make the report through the child abuse hotline toll-free telephone system.

Content of Reports
Citation: Ann. Code § 12-12-507
For an investigation to commence, the report must contain sufficient information to identify and locate the child or the family.
Special Reporting Procedures
Suspicious Deaths
Citation: Ann. Code § 12-12-507(a)
Any person with reasonable cause to suspect that a child has died as a result of maltreatment may immediately notify the child abuse hotline.
Substance-Exposed Infants
This issue is not addressed in the statutes reviewed.
Screening Reports
Citation: Ann. Code §§ 12-12-507; 12-12-509
The child abuse hotline shall accept a report when the allegations, if true, would constitute child maltreatment as defined by law, and sufficient identifying information is provided to identify and locate the child or the family. The hotline shall accept a report of physical abuse if any specified intentional or knowing acts are alleged to occur, but the report shall not be determined to be true unless the child suffered an injury as the result of the act.

The hotline shall accept a report of neglect only if the reporter is a nurse, physician, or other medical personnel, and the reporter has reasonable cause to suspect that a child has been subjected to neglect as defined by law.

The Department of Health and Human Services shall cause an investigation to be made upon receiving initial notification of suspected child maltreatment. All investigations shall begin within 72 hours, unless the report alleges severe maltreatment, then the investigation shall begin within 24 hours.

At the initial time of contact with the alleged offender, the investigator shall advise the alleged offender of the allegations made against the alleged offender in a manner that is consistent with the laws protecting the rights of the person who made the report.

California
Reporting Procedures
Individual Responsibility
Citation: Penal Code § 11166
A mandated reporter who knows or reasonably suspects that a child has been a victim of abuse or neglect shall make an initial report immediately by telephone and prepare and send, fax, or electronically transmit a follow-up written report within 36 hours.

Any commercial film and photographic print processor who has knowledge of or observes any film, photograph, videotape, negative, or slide depicting a child under age 16 engaged in an act of sexual conduct shall report the instance of suspected child abuse to the law enforcement agency immediately, or as soon as practicably possible, by telephone and shall prepare and send, fax, or electronically submit a written report of it with a copy of the film, photograph, videotape, negative, or slide attached within 36 hours.
Content of Reports
Citation: Penal Code § 11167
Reports of suspected child abuse or neglect shall include:

- The name, business address, and telephone number of the mandated reporter
- The capacity that makes the person a mandated reporter
- The information that gave rise to the reasonable suspicion of child abuse or neglect and the source or sources of that information
- If a report is made, the following information, if known, shall also be included in the report:
- The child's name, address, present location, and, if applicable, school, grade, and class
- The names, addresses, and telephone numbers of the child's parents or guardians
- The name, address, telephone number, and other relevant personal information about the person or persons who might have abused or neglected the child

The mandated reporter shall make a report even if some of this information is not known or is uncertain to him or her.

Special Reporting Procedures
Suspicious Deaths
Citation: Penal Code §§ 11166; 11166.1

The agency shall be notified and a report prepared and sent, faxed, or electronically submitted even if the child has died, regardless of whether or not the possible abuse was a contributing factor to the death, and even if suspected child abuse was discovered during an autopsy.

The agency shall notify within 24 hours the licensing office that has jurisdiction over a facility when a child has died while living at or enrolled in that facility.

Substance-Exposed Infants
Citation: Penal Code §§ 11165.13; 11166

A positive toxicology screen at the time of the delivery of an infant is not in and of itself a sufficient basis for reporting child abuse or neglect. However, any indication of maternal substance abuse shall lead to an assessment of the needs of the mother and child pursuant to § 123605 of the Health and Safety Code. If other factors are present that indicate risk to a child, then a report shall be made.

A report based on risk to a child that relates solely to the inability of the parent to provide the child with regular care due to the parent's substance abuse shall be made only to a county welfare or probation department, and not to a law enforcement agency.

Screening Reports
Citation: Penal Code § 11167; Welf. & Inst. Code § 16504; DSS Manual Ch. 31, §§ 100, 105, 110, 115

At the time of the initial contact with the individual who is subject to the investigation, the agency shall advise the individual of the complaints or allegations against him or her, in a manner that is consistent with laws protecting the identity of the reporter.

Any child reported to the county welfare department as endangered by abuse, neglect, or exploitation shall be eligible for initial intake and evaluation of risk services. Each county welfare department shall maintain and operate a 24-hour response system. An immediate in-person response shall be made by a county welfare department social worker in emergency situations. An in-person response is not required when the county welfare department, based upon an evaluation of risk, determines that an in-person response is not appropriate. An evaluation of risk includes collateral contacts, a review of previous referrals, and other relevant information.

In regulation: The social worker shall immediately initiate and complete the Emergency Response Protocol process to determine whether an in-person investigation is required. The social worker is not required to complete the protocol if he or she has already determined that an in-person investigation is required, such as in cases of obvious immediate danger or law enforcement referrals. The protocol requires gathering the following information:

- Identifying information about the abused child, each adult in the household, the alleged perpetrator, and each minor child in the family
- A description of the alleged incident, including risk factors
- Child and caregiver characteristics
- Family factors, including relationships and any history of abuse or neglect

The decision whether or not an in-person investigation is needed shall include the following:

- The social worker has been able to locate the child and/or the family.
- There exists an open case and the problem is being adequately addressed.
- The allegation meets the legal definition of abuse, neglect, or exploitation.
- The caregiver of the child is the alleged perpetrator or was negligent in allowing, or unable to prevent, access to the child.

If the social worker determines that an in-person investigation is necessary, he or she shall initiate the investigation immediately or within 10 calendar days, as appropriate. An immediate investigation is required when:

- There is evidence that the child is in imminent danger of physical pain, injury, disability, severe emotional harm, or death.
- The law enforcement agency making the referral states that the child is at immediate risk of abuse, neglect, or exploitation.
- The social worker determines that the child referred by the law enforcement agency is at immediate risk of abuse, neglect, or exploitation.

Colorado
Reporting Procedures
Individual Responsibility
Citation: Rev. Stat. §§ 19-3-304; 19-3-307

A mandated reporter who has reasonable cause to know or suspect that a child has been subjected to abuse or neglect shall report immediately to the Department of Human Services or a law enforcement agency. The reporter shall promptly follow up with a written report.

A film processor shall report any suspicion of sexual abuse to a law enforcement agency, immediately by telephone, and shall prepare and send a written report of it with a copy of the film, photograph, videotape, negative, or slide attached within 36 hours of receiving the information concerning the incident.

Content of Reports
Citation: Rev. Stat. § 19-3-307

The department's report, when possible, shall include the following information:

- The name, address, age, sex, and race of the child
- The name and address of the person alleged responsible for the suspected abuse
- The nature and extent of the child's injuries, including any evidence of previous cases of abuse or neglect of the child or the child's siblings

- Family composition
- The source of the report, including the name, address, and occupation of the person making the report
- Any action taken by the reporting source
- Any other information that might be helpful

Special Reporting Procedures
Suspicious Deaths
Citation: Rev. Stat. § 19-3-305

A mandated reporter who has reasonable cause to suspect that a child has died as a result of abuse or neglect shall report that fact immediately to a local law enforcement agency and the appropriate medical examiner.

Substance-Exposed Infants

This issue is not addressed in the statutes reviewed.

Screening Reports
Citation: Rev. Stat. §§ 19-3-307; 19-3-308

The county department shall submit a report of confirmed child abuse or neglect within 60 days of receipt of the report to the State department in a manner prescribed by the State department. A copy of the report of known or suspected child abuse or neglect shall be transmitted immediately by the county department to the district attorney's office and to the local law enforcement agency.

The county department shall respond immediately upon receipt of any report of a known or suspected incident of intrafamilial abuse or neglect to assess the abuse involved and the appropriate response to the report. The assessment shall be in accordance with rules adopted by the State board of social services (see Code of Colorado Rules, 12 CCR 2509-4) to determine the risk of harm to such child and the appropriate response to such risks.

Appropriate responses shall include, but are not limited to, screening reports that do not require further investigation, providing appropriate intervention services, pursuing reports that require further investigation, and conducting immediate investigations.

Connecticut

Reporting Procedures
Individual Responsibility
Citation: Gen. Stat. §§ 17a-101a; 17a-101b; 17a-101c

A mandated reporter who has reasonable cause to suspect that a child has been abused or neglected shall make an oral report, by telephone or in person, not later than 12 hours after the reporter has cause to suspect. The report shall be made to the Commissioner of Children and Families or a law enforcement agency.

Within 48 hours of making an oral report, a mandated reporter shall submit a written report to the Commissioner of Children and Families. When a mandated reporter is a member of the staff of a public or private institution or facility that provides care for such child, or a public or private school, he or she shall also submit a copy of the written report to the person in charge of such institution, school, or facility. In the case of a report concerning a school employee, a copy of the written report shall also be sent by the person in charge of such institution, school, or facility to the Commissioner of Education. In the case of an employee of a facility or institution that provides care for a child that is licensed by the State, a copy of the written report shall also be sent by the mandated reporter to the executive head of the State licensing agency.

Content of Reports
Citation: Gen. Stat. § 17a-101d

All oral and written reports shall contain, if known:

- The names and addresses of the child and the child's parents or other persons responsible for the child's care
- The age and gender of the child
- The nature and extent of the child's injuries, maltreatment, or neglect
- The approximate date and time of the child's injuries, maltreatment, or neglect
- Any information about previous injuries or maltreatment to the child or the child's siblings
- The circumstances in which the maltreatment came to be known to the reporter
- The name of the person suspected to be responsible for the maltreatment
- Whatever action, if any, was taken to assist the child

Special Reporting Procedures
Suspicious Deaths
Citation: Gen. Stat. § 17a-101b

If the Commissioner of Children and Families receives a report that a child has died, the commissioner shall, within 12 hours of receipt of the report, notify the appropriate law enforcement agency.

Substance-Exposed Infants

This issue is not addressed in the statutes reviewed.

Screening Reports
Citation: Gen. Stat. § 17a-101g

Upon receiving a report of child abuse or neglect in which the alleged perpetrator is a person who is responsible for the child's health, welfare, or care, given access to the child, or entrusted with the care of the child, the commissioner shall cause the report to be classified and evaluated immediately. If the report contains sufficient information to warrant an investigation, best efforts shall be made to commence an investigation of a report concerning an imminent risk of physical harm to a child or other emergency within 2 hours of receipt of the report, and to commence an investigation of all other reports within 72 hours.

If the report is a report of child abuse or neglect in which the alleged perpetrator is not a person specified above, the commissioner shall refer the report to the appropriate local law enforcement authority. If the commissioner determines that abuse or neglect has occurred, the commissioner shall also determine whether there is an identifiable person responsible for the abuse or neglect, and that person poses a risk to the health, safety, or wellbeing of children and should be recommended by the commissioner for placement on the child abuse and neglect registry. If the commissioner makes such a determination, the commissioner shall issue notice of a recommended finding to the person suspected to be responsible for such abuse or neglect.

If the child abuse or neglect resulted in or involves the death of a child, the risk of serious physical injury or emotional harm of a child, serious physical harm of a child, the arrest of a person due to abuse or neglect of a child, or sexual abuse of a child, entry of the finding may be made on the child abuse or neglect registry.

If the commissioner has probable cause to believe that the child or any other child in the household is in imminent risk of physical harm from the child's surroundings and that immediate removal from such surroundings is necessary to ensure the child's safety, the commissioner shall authorize any employee of the department or any law enforcement officer to remove the child and any other child similarly situated from such surroundings without the consent of the child's parent or guardian.

Delaware
Reporting Procedures
Individual Responsibility
Citation: Ann. Code Tit. 16, § 904

Any report required by the reporting laws shall be made to the Division of Child Protective Services in the Department of Services for Children, Youth, and Their Families. An immediate oral report shall be made by telephone or otherwise.

Content of Reports
Citation: Ann. Code Tit. 16, §§ 904; 906

Contents of any written report shall be in accordance with rules and regulations of the division.

When a written report is made, the division will contact the reporter within 48 hours to ensure that full information has been received and to obtain additional information, medical records, or both.

The investigation shall gather pertinent information, including, but not limited to:
- The nature, extent, and cause of the abuse or neglect
- The identity of the alleged perpetrator
- The names and condition of other children and adults in the home
- The home environment
- The relationship of the subject child to the parents or other persons responsible for the child's care
- Any indication of incidents of physical violence against any other household or family member

Special Reporting Procedures
Suspicious Deaths

This issue is not addressed in the statutes reviewed.

Substance-Exposed Infants

This issue is not addressed in the statutes reviewed.

Screening Reports
Citation: Ann. Code Tit. 16, §§ 905; 906; Code of Regs. CDR 9-300-303

The division will maintain a 24-hour toll-free telephone line for accepting reports. Although reports may be made anonymously, the division shall, in all cases, after obtaining relevant information regarding alleged abuse or neglect, request the name and address of any person making a report. When a written report is made by a mandatory reporter, the division shall contact the reporter within 48 hours of the receipt of the report in order to ensure that full information has been received and to obtain any additional information or medical records, or both, that may be pertinent.

Upon receipt of a report, the division shall check the internal information system to determine whether previous reports have been made regarding actual or suspected abuse or neglect of the subject child, any siblings, family members, or the alleged perpetrator.

The division may investigate any report, but shall conduct an investigation involving all reports that involve the commission or attempt to commit a crime against a child by a person responsible for the care, custody, and control of the child. The division will contact the law enforcement agency and provide the agency with a detailed description of the report. The agency will assist the division with the investigation and promptly conduct its own criminal investigation.

In a family assessment and services approach, the division shall assess the service needs of the family from information gathered from the family and other sources and shall identify and provide services for families where it is determined that the child is at risk of abuse or neglect. The division shall:

- Commence an immediate investigation if at any time during the family assessment it determines that an investigation is required or is otherwise appropriate
- Conduct a family assessment on reports initially referred for an investigation, if it is determined that a complete investigation is not required

In regulation: The case finding may indicate that it is substantiated or unsubstantiated. A person who has been substantiated for abuse or neglect must be entered on the Child Protection Registry at one of four designated Child Protection Levels related to the risk of future harm to children:

- Child Protection Level I: Low risk
- Child Protection Level II: Moderate risk
- Child Protection Level III: High risk
- Child Protection Level IV: Highest risk

If the division determines from its investigation not to substantiate the person for abuse or neglect, the person may not be entered on the Child Protection Registry for that reported incident.

District of Columbia
Reporting Procedures
Individual Responsibility
Citation: Ann. Code §§ 4-1321.02; 4-1321.03

A mandated reporter who knows or has reasonable cause to suspect abuse or neglect of a child shall immediately report to the police department or the Child and Family Services Agency.

Each person required to make a report of a known or suspected neglected child shall:

- Immediately make an oral report of the case to the Child and Family Services Agency or the police department
- Make a written report of the case if requested by the agency or police or if the abuse involves drug-related activity

Content of Reports
Citation: Ann. Code § 4-1321.03

The report shall include, but need not be limited to, the following information if it is known to the person making the report:

- The name, age, sex, and address of the child, the child's siblings, other children in the home, and the parents or other persons responsible for the child's care
- The nature and extent of the abuse or neglect and any previous abuse or neglect
- Any other information that might be helpful
- If the source of the report is a mandated reporter, the identity and occupation of the source, how to contact the source, and any action taken by the source concerning the child

Special Reporting Procedures
Suspicious Deaths
This issue is not addressed in the statutes reviewed.

Substance-Exposed Infants
Citation: Ann. Code § 4-1321.02(d)
A licensed health professional, law enforcement officer, or humane officer shall report immediately in writing to the Child and Family Services Agency when there is reasonable cause to believe that a child is abused as a result of inadequate care, control, or subsistence in the home environment due to exposure to drug-related activity.

Screening Reports
Citation: Ann. Code §§ 4-1301.04; 4-1303.03b
The agency shall conduct a thorough investigation of a report of suspected child abuse or neglect to protect the health and safety of the child. The investigation shall commence immediately upon receiving a report indicating that the child's safety or health is in immediate danger; or as soon as possible, and at least within 24 hours, for any report not involving immediate danger to the child.

The initial phase of the investigation shall be completed within 24 hours and include notification and coordination with the police department when there is indication of a crime, including sexual or serious physical abuse, and also include:

- Seeing the child and all other children in the household outside of the presence of the caregivers
- Conducting an interview with the child's caregivers
- Speaking with the source of the report
- Assessing the safety and risk of harm to the child from abuse or neglect in the place where the child lives
- Deciding on the safety of the child and of other children in the household or in the care or custody of the person or persons alleged to be abusing or neglecting the child

The agency shall establish a single reporting line to receive reports of suspected child abuse and neglect. The reporting line shall be maintained by the agency with the assistance and support of the Metropolitan Police Department and shall be staffed 24 hours a day, 7 days a week. Upon receiving reports on the single reporting line, the agency shall:

- Review and screen the reports to collect relevant information from the source of the report
- Transmit the reports to the entity with responsibility under the laws of the District of Columbia, or the appropriate governmental entity in another jurisdiction, for investigation or provision of services

Florida
Reporting Procedures
Individual Responsibility
Citation: Ann. Stat. § 39.201; Admin. Code 65C-29.002

Any person who knows, or has reasonable cause to suspect, that a child is abused, abandoned, or neglected by a parent, legal custodian, caregiver, or other person responsible for the child's welfare, or that a child is in need of supervision and care and has no parent, legal custodian, or responsible adult relative immediately known and available to provide supervision and care shall report such knowledge or suspicion to the Department of Children and Family Services in the manner prescribed below.

Each report shall be made immediately to the department's central abuse hotline. Reports may be made on the single statewide toll-free telephone number or via fax or web-based report.

The names of reporters shall be entered into the record of the report but shall be held confidential and exempt as provided in § 39.202.

In regulation: Professionally mandated reporters are required to provide their names to the abuse hotline when making a report of alleged child maltreatment. A report shall be accepted if it meets statutory criteria for acceptance even if the reporters wish to remain anonymous. Nonprofessionally mandated reporters are not required to provide their names for the acceptance of a report.

Content of Reports
Citation: Ann. Stat. §§ 39.201; 39.301

The department shall voice-record all incoming or outgoing calls that are received or placed by the central abuse hotline that relate to suspected or known child abuse, neglect, or abandonment. The department shall maintain an electronic copy of each fax and web-based report. The recording or electronic copy of each fax and web-based report shall become a part of the record of the report.

The child protective investigation shall gather the following information:
- The composition of the family or household, including the name, address, date of birth, Social Security number, sex, and race of each child named in the report; any siblings or other children in the same household or in the care of the same adults; the parents, legal custodians, or caregivers; and any other adults in the same household
- Indications that any child in the family or household has been abused, abandoned, or neglected; the nature and extent of present or prior injuries, abuse, or neglect, and any evidence thereof
- The person or persons apparently responsible for the abuse, abandonment, or neglect, including the name, address, date of birth, Social Security number, sex, and race of each such person

Special Reporting Procedures
Suspicious Deaths
Citation: Ann. Stat. § 39.201

Any person required to report or investigate cases of suspected child abuse, abandonment, or neglect who has reasonable cause to suspect that a child died as a result of child abuse, abandonment, or neglect shall report his or her suspicion to the appropriate medical examiner. The medical examiner shall accept the report for investigation and shall report his or her findings, in writing, to the local law enforcement agency, the appropriate

State attorney, and the department. Autopsy reports maintained by the medical examiner are not subject to the confidentiality requirements provided for in § 39.202.

Substance-Exposed Infants

This issue is not addressed in the statutes reviewed.

Screening Reports

Citation: Ann. Stat. §§ 39.201; 39.301; Admin. Code 65C-29.002; 65C-29.003

The Department of Children and Family Services shall be capable of receiving and investigating, 24 hours a day, 7 days a week, reports of known or suspected child abuse. If it appears that the immediate safety or well-being of a child is endangered, that the family may flee, or the child will be unavailable for purposes of conducting a child protective investigation, or that the facts otherwise so warrant, the department shall commence an investigation immediately, regardless of the time of day or night. In all other cases, a child protective investigation shall be commenced within 24 hours.

If the report is of an instance of known or suspected child abuse by someone other than a parent, legal custodian, caregiver, or other person responsible for the child's welfare, the report or call shall be immediately electronically transferred to the appropriate county sheriff's office by the central abuse hotline.

Upon receiving a report, the central abuse hotline shall determine if the report requires an immediate onsite protective investigation. For reports requiring an immediate onsite protective investigation, the central abuse hotline shall immediately notify the department.

The department shall immediately forward allegations of criminal conduct to the appropriate law enforcement agency. Upon receiving a written report of an allegation of criminal conduct from the department, the law enforcement agency shall review the information in the report to determine whether a criminal investigation is warranted. If the law enforcement agency accepts the case for criminal investigation, it shall coordinate its investigative activities with the department, when feasible.

The person responsible for the investigation shall determine whether the report is complete. If the investigator finds that the report is incomplete, he or she shall return it without delay to the person or agency originating the report to request additional information in order to complete the report. If the report is complete, but the interests of the child and the public will be best served by providing the child care or other treatment voluntarily accepted by the child and the parents or legal custodians, the protective investigator may refer the parent or legal custodian and child for such care or other treatment. If it is determined that the child is in need of the protection and supervision of the court, the department shall file a petition for dependency.

In regulation: Upon commencement of the investigation, the child protective investigator shall inform all subjects of the report as well as the parent, guardian, legal custodian or other person responsible for the child's welfare, including an adult household member of the following:

- That a report has been received alleging child abuse, neglect or abandonment
- The names of the investigators and identifying credentials
- The purpose of the investigation
- The right to review the investigative records, with the exception of reporter information
- The right to have an attorney present during any interviews

- General information about outcomes and services related to the department's or sheriff's office response and investigation that would assist the family to better understand what they may expect from the investigation
- The commitment of the department or sheriff's office to the safety of the child and the involvement of the family to the fullest extent possible in decisions regarding service planning and provision
- The right of the parent or legal custodian to be involved to the fullest extent possible in determining the nature of the allegation and the nature of any identified problem

Georgia
Reporting Procedures
Individual Responsibility
Citation: Ann. Code §§ 19-7-5; 16-12-100

A mandated reporter who has reasonable cause to believe that a child has been abused shall report or cause reports of that abuse to be made as provided in this section. An oral report shall be made immediately, but in no case later than 24 hours from the time there is reasonable cause to believe a child has been abused, by telephone or otherwise and followed by a report in writing, if requested, to a child welfare agency providing protective services, as designated by the Department of Human Resources, or, in the absence of such agency, to an appropriate police authority or district attorney.

A person who, in the course of processing or producing visual or printed matter either privately or commercially, has reasonable cause to believe that the visual or printed matter submitted for processing or producing depicts a minor engaged in sexually explicit conduct shall immediately report such incident, or cause a report to be made, to the Georgia Bureau of Investigation or the law enforcement agency for the county in which such matter is submitted.

Content of Reports
Citation: Ann. Code § 19-7-5

The report shall contain, if possible:
- The names and addresses of the child and the child's parents or caregivers
- The child's age, if known
- The nature and extent of the child's injuries, including any evidence of previous injuries
- Any other information that might be helpful in establishing the cause of the injuries and the identity of the perpetrator

Special Reporting Procedures
Suspicious Deaths

This issue is not addressed in the statutes reviewed.

Substance-Exposed Infants

This issue is not addressed in the statutes reviewed.

Screening Reports
Citation: Ann. Code § 19-7-5; DHR Proc. Man. §§ 2103.4; 2103.14; 2103.16; 2103.18

If a report of child abuse is made to the child welfare agency or independently discovered by the agency, and the agency has reasonable cause to believe the report is true or the report contains any allegation or evidence of child abuse, then the agency shall immediately notify the appropriate police authority or the district attorney.

In regulation: County departments have responsibility to screen every report received and to assure that timely and appropriate response is initiated. All reports are screened for suitability for CPS investigation, including a thorough history check, and to determine, for a report that meets the criteria for CPS, the response time, according to the following:

- The report is severe and the investigation will begin immediately or within 24 hours. All investigations of abuse or neglect to foster children are included in this category.
- The report is of a less severe nature, and the investigation will begin within 5 days.
- The report does not meet CPS requirements, and no investigation will occur.
- The report does not meet current CPS requirements; however, there have been two or more previous reports on this family, and the report will be assigned for investigation.

Situations that always require an immediate to 24-hour response include:

- The child requires immediate medical attention.
- A child under age 13 alleges maltreatment and expresses fear of returning home.
- A child has a disability or lack of capacity, and the perpetrator will have access to the child within the next 5 days.
- The parent demonstrates physical, emotional, or intellectual instability.
- The nonperpetrating parent is not responding appropriately or protecting the child.
- The child is in severe danger of immediate harm.
- A report from medical personnel indicates that a mother has given birth to an infant, and either the mother or the infant has tested positive for illegal drugs and/or alcohol.
- The child has severe or multiple bruises or welts.
- A child, who is age 8 or younger, who is limited by a disability or lack of capacity, or who is otherwise unable to care for himself or herself, has been left alone.
- The report alleges current sexual abuse involving a child who remains accessible to the alleged perpetrator.
- There is a pattern of ongoing abuse and/or neglect.
- A report contains a self-referral from a parent who states that he or she is unable to cope, feels that he or she will hurt or kill the child, or desires a child's immediate removal and placement away from home.
- A report alleges cruel, callous, or bizarre punishment by the parent.
- A report alleges that the parent of a child is behaving in a bizarre or delusional manner.
- The child presents with an observable emotional or mental health condition that is attributable to his or her emotional maltreatment by the parent.

Any report of conditions or suspicions that indicate allegations of possible child maltreatment will be assigned for investigation. Many reports that can be considered for screening out involve:

- Incidents of child maltreatment that are 6 months old or older
- Reports that are of a criminal nature by a person other than a parent, and negligence on the part of the parent for allowing a child to be exposed to the situation is ruled out
- A report of statutory rape when there is evidence that the parent has protected the child
- Three previous reports of the same allegation made by the same reporter and investigations of these reports revealed no evidence of maltreatment

- An unborn child
- Juvenile delinquency, including truancy, that does not contain a separate allegation of maltreatment
- Other situations where the only indicated concerns contain absolutely no report of any abuse or neglect, e.g., some poverty, educational, or custody issues

Guam
Reporting Procedures
Individual Responsibility
Citation: Ann. Code Tit. 19, § 13203(a)

Mandated reporters shall report cases of suspected abuse to child protective services (CPS) or the police immediately by telephone and follow up in writing within 48 hours. Oral reports shall be made to CPS or to the police department.

Content of Reports
Citation: Ann. Code Tit. 19, § 13203(c)

Reports of child abuse or neglect should contain the following information:
- The name of the person making the report
- The name, age, and sex of the child
- The present location of the child
- The nature and extent of injury
- Any other information, including information that led that person to suspect child abuse, that may be requested by the child protective agency receiving the report

Mandated reporters shall be required to reveal their names.

Other information relevant to the incident of child abuse may also be given to an investigator from a child protective agency who is investigating the known or suspected case of child abuse, including:
- The name of the person or persons responsible for causing the suspected abuse or neglect
- Family composition
- The actions taken by the reporting source, including the taking of photographs and x-rays, removal or keeping of the child, or notification of the medical examiner
- ny other information that the child protective agency may, by regulation, require

Special Reporting Procedures
Suspicious Deaths
Citation: Ann. Code Tit. 19, § 13205

Any mandated reporter who has reasonable cause to suspect that a child has died as a result of abuse shall report that fact to the medical examiner.

The medical examiner shall report any findings to the police department, attorney general's office, and CPS.

Substance-Exposed Infants

This issue is not addressed in the statutes reviewed.

Screening Reports

Citation: Ann. Code Tit. 19, §§ 13209; 13209.1

CPS shall:

- Receive all reports of suspected child abuse or neglect, both oral and written, 7 days a week, 24 hours a day
- Upon receipt of a report, commence within a reasonable time, but no later than 72 hours, an appropriate investigation
- Determine within 60 days whether the report is "indicated," "substantiated," or "unsubstantiated"• If necessary, take a child into protective custody to protect him or her from further abuse
- Based on the investigation and evaluation, provide for the protection of the child in his or her home whenever possible or provide those services necessary for adequate care of the child when placed in protective custody or temporary foster custody

CPS shall develop written procedures for screening each referral for abuse or neglect of a child to assess whether abuse of another family or household member is also occurring. The assessment must include, but is not limited to:

- A check of the criminal record of the parents and the alleged abusive or neglectful person and the alleged perpetrator of family violence, if not a parent of the child
- An inquiry concerning the existence of orders for protection issued to either parent

Hawaii

Reporting Procedures
Individual Responsibility
Citation: Rev. Stat. § 350-1.1

A mandated reporter who has reason to believe that child abuse or neglect has occurred shall immediately report the matter orally to the Department of Human Services or the police department. The initial oral report shall be followed as soon as possible by a report in writing to the department.

Content of Reports
Citation: Rev. Stat. § 350-1.1

All written reports shall contain, if known:

- The name and address of the child and the child's parents or other persons responsible for the child's care
- The child's age
- The nature and extent of the child's injuries
- Any other information that the reporter believes might be helpful or relevant to the investigation

Special Reporting Procedures
Suspicious Deaths

This issue is not addressed in the statutes reviewed.

Substance-Exposed Infants
Citation: Rev. Stat. § 587-89(a)

The Department of Human Services shall implement and operate a statewide program relating to child abuse and neglect that incorporates policies and procedures, including, but not limited to, appropriate referrals to child protective service systems and other appropriate services to address the needs of infants born and identified as being affected by illegal substance abuse or withdrawal symptoms resulting from prenatal drug exposure, including a requirement that health-care providers involved in the delivery or care of an affected infant notify child protective services (CPS) of the condition in the infant.

Screening Reports

Citation: Rev. Stat. §§ 350-2; 587-21; Code of Rules §§ 17-920.1-11; 17-920.1-12; 17-920.1-16

Upon receiving a report concerning child abuse or neglect, the department shall proceed pursuant to chapter 587 and the department's rules. Upon receiving a report that a child is subject to imminent harm, has been harmed, or is subject to threatened harm, the department shall cause such investigation to be made as it deems to be appropriate.

In regulation: The department shall accept reports of alleged abuse, neglect, harm, or threatened harm of children and shall immediately assess the validity of the report to provide appropriate services to the child and family in accordance with the department's guidelines.

The department shall verify or validate the report or complaint in the following manner:

- Evaluate the report or complaint to ensure that it is based on fact
- Take action as soon as possible in order to provide immediate protection to the child
- Discuss the report or complaint directly with the parents, guardians, or custodians, preferably through a home visit by:
  - o Interpreting the department's services and legal authority to protect children
  - o Discussing specific reasons for the department's entry in the particular situation
  - o Evaluating whether the complaint is justified
- See the child as early as possible to evaluate the extent to which the child is threatened with harm Every report or complaint, whether confirmed or unsubstantiated, shall be registered with the State central registry on child abuse and neglect within 60 calendar days from the date of the referral. The department shall, within 60 days, make a clear decision regarding whether abuse, neglect, or exploitation did or will occur. This decision shall be shared with and explained to the family either in writing or orally. If the department confirms abuse, neglect, or exploitation, it shall make a clear decision whether the child is at risk of future abuse, neglect, or exploitation in the child's own home.

The department shall make a clear decision whether abuse, neglect, or exploitation did or will occur. This decision shall be:

- Made within 60 days of the date of complaint
- Clearly recorded in the department's records
- Shared with and explained to the family either in writing or orally
- Shared with the complainant without violating the child's or family's right to confidentiality

A written description of the department's findings shall be given to the family at their request. If the family members cannot be contacted, this fact shall be noted in the department's records.

If the department confirms abuse, neglect, or exploitation, the department shall make a clear decision whether the child is at risk of future abuse, neglect, or exploitation in the child's own home.

Idaho

Reporting Procedures
Individual Responsibility
Citation: Idaho Code § 16-1605

A mandated reporter who has reason to believe that a child has been abused, neglected, or abandoned shall report within 24 hours to a law enforcement agency or the Department of Health and Welfare.

Content of Reports
Citation: Idaho Code § 16-1605

The report shall contain a description of the conditions and circumstances that led to making the report.

Special Reporting Procedures
Suspicious Deaths

This issue is not addressed in the statutes reviewed.

Substance-Exposed Infants

This issue is not addressed in the statutes reviewed.

Screening Reports
Citation: Admin. Code §§ 16.06.01.552; 554; 556; 557; 559; 560

In regulation: Each region of the Department of Health and Welfare shall maintain a system for receiving and responding to reports or complaints on a 24-hour-per-day, 7-day-per-week basis throughout the entire region. The region shall advertise the system to the public throughout the region and ensure the accurate recording of as many facts as possible at the time of the report.

The department shall assign all reports of possible abuse, neglect, or abandonment for risk assessment unless there is information that discredits the report beyond a reasonable doubt. The level of response required will be based on the following criteria:

- Priority I: The department must respond immediately if a child is in immediate danger involving a life-threatening or emergency situation. Law enforcement shall be notified and requested to respond or accompany the family services worker.
- Priority II: A child is not in immediate danger, but there are clear allegations of physical or sexual abuse or medical neglect. Law enforcement shall be notified within 24 hours, and the child seen by the family services worker within 48 hours.
- Priority III: A child may be in a vulnerable situation because of service needs that, if left unmet, may result in harm, or a child is without parental care. A family services worker shall respond within 3 days, and the child must be seen within 5 days.

Possible abuse, abandonment, or neglect of a child who is known or suspected to be Indian shall be reported to appropriate Tribal authorities immediately. If the reported incident occurs off a reservation, the department shall perform the investigation. The department shall also investigate incidents reported on a reservation if requested to do so by appropriate authorities of the Tribe. A record of any response shall be maintained in the case record and written documentation shall be provided to the appropriate Tribal authorities.

Reports involving a military family shall be reported to the appropriate military family advocacy representative. Abuse, neglect, or abandonment of a child on a military reservation falls under Federal jurisdiction.

A risk assessment shall be conducted utilizing statewide risk assessment and multidisciplinary team protocols. When there are findings of moderate or higher risk, a comprehensive risk assessment must be completed within 30 days of the initial contact.

Within 5 days of completion of the risk assessment, the department shall determine whether the report is substantiated or unsubstantiated. A report is unsubstantiated when there is insufficient evidence or facts indicate that the report is erroneous.

Illinois
Reporting Procedures
Individual Responsibility
Citation: Cons. Stat. Ch. 325, § 5/4; 5/7

All reports of suspected child abuse or neglect shall be made immediately by telephone to the central register, on the single, statewide, toll-free telephone number; in person; or by telephone through the nearest Department of Children and Family Services office.

All reports by mandated reporters shall be confirmed in writing to the appropriate child protective service unit, which may be on forms supplied by the department, within 48 hours of any initial report.

Written confirmation reports from persons not required to report may be made to the appropriate child protective service unit.

Content of Reports
Citation: Cons. Stat. Ch. 325, §§ 5/7; 5/9

The initial oral report shall include, if known:
- The name and address of the child and his or her parents or other persons having custody
- The child's age
- The nature of the child's condition including any evidence of previous injuries or disabilities
- Any other information that the person filing the report believes might be helpful in establishing the cause of the abuse or neglect and the identity of the person believed to have caused the abuse or neglect

Initial written reports from the reporting source shall contain the following information to the extent known at the time the report is made
- The names and addresses of the child and his or her parents or other persons responsible for his or her welfare
- The name and address of the school that the child attends or last attended, if the report is written during the summer when school is not in session
- The name of the school district in which the school is located, if applicable
- The child's age, sex, and race
- The nature and extent of the child's abuse or neglect, including any evidence of prior injuries, abuse, or neglect of the child or his or her siblings
- The names of the persons apparently responsible for the abuse or neglect
- Family composition, including names, ages, sexes, and races of other children in the home
- The name of the person making the report, his or her occupation, and where he or she can be reached

- The actions taken by the reporting source, including the taking of photographs and x-rays, placing the child in temporary protective custody, or notifying the medical examiner or coroner
- Any other information the person making the report believes might be helpful

Special Reporting Procedures

Suspicious Deaths

Citation: Cons. Stat. Ch. 325, § 5/4.1

A mandated reporter or any other person who has reasonable cause to believe that a child has died as a result of abuse or neglect shall report to the appropriate medical examiner.

The medical examiner or coroner shall investigate the report and communicate any apparent gross findings orally, immediately upon completion of the gross autopsy, but in all cases within 72 hours, and within 21 days in writing, to the local law enforcement agency, the appropriate State's attorney, the department, and, if the institution making the report is a hospital, the hospital.

Substance-Exposed Infants

Citation: Cons. Stat. Ch. 325, § 5/7.3b

All mandated reporters may refer to the department any pregnant person who is addicted as defined in the Alcoholism and Other Drug Abuse and Dependency Act.

Screening Reports

Citation: Cons. Stat. Ch. 325, §§ 5/7.3; 5/7.4; 7.12 Admin. Code Tit. 89, §§ 300.100; 300.110

The department shall be the sole agency responsible for receiving and investigating reports of child abuse or neglect, except where investigations by other agencies may be required with respect to reports alleging the death, serious injury, or sexual abuse to a child. The department shall be capable of receiving reports of suspected child abuse or neglect 24 hours a day, 7 days a week.

If it appears that the immediate safety or well-being of a child is endangered, that the family may flee, or the child disappear, child protection services (CPS) shall commence an investigation immediately, regardless of the time of day or night. In all other cases, an investigation shall begin within 24 hours.

After seeing to the safety of the child or children, the department shall notify the subjects of the report in writing of the existence of the report and their rights in regard to amendment or expunction.

The CPS unit shall determine, within 60 days, whether the report is ''indicated'' or ''unfounded'' and report it forthwith to the central register. When it is not possible to initiate or complete an investigation within 60 days, the report may be deemed ''undetermined'' provided every effort has been made to undertake a complete investigation. The department may extend the period in which such determinations must be made in individual cases for additional periods of up to 30 days each for good cause shown.

In regulation: When a report of child abuse or neglect is received, the department shall make an initial investigation to validate whether there is reasonable cause to believe that child abuse or neglect exists. When investigative staff make a determination that there is reasonable cause to believe that child abuse or neglect exists, a formal investigation shall be made.

Upon completion of a formal investigation of abuse or neglect, investigative staff shall make a final determination as to whether a child was abused or neglected. Allegations may be determined to be indicated, undetermined, or unfounded.

- When credible evidence of abuse or neglect has been obtained pertinent to an allegation, the allegation is indicated.
- When credible evidence of abuse or neglect has not been obtained, the allegation is unfounded.
- When investigative staff have been unable, for good cause, to gather sufficient facts to support a decision within 60 days of the date the report was received, the allegation shall be considered undetermined.

Indiana
Reporting Procedures
Individual Responsibility
Citation: Ann. Code §§ 31-33-5-1 to 31-33-5-4
A mandated reporter who has reason to believe that a child is a victim of abuse or neglect shall immediately make an oral report to the Department of Child Services or a local law enforcement agency.

Content of Reports
Citation: Ann. Code § 31-33-7-4
The department shall make a written report of a child who may be a victim of child abuse or neglect no later than 48 hours after receipt of the oral report.

Written reports must be made on forms supplied by the administrator. The written reports must include, if known, the following information:
- The names and addresses of the child and the child's parents, guardian, custodian, or other person responsible for the child's care
- The child's age and sex
- The nature and apparent extent of the child's injuries, abuse, or neglect, including any evidence of prior injuries of the child or abuse or neglect of the child or the child's siblings
- The name of the person allegedly responsible for causing the injury, abuse, or neglect
- The source of the report
- The name of the person making the report and where the person can be reached
- The actions taken by the reporting source, including the following:
o   Taking of photographs and x-rays
o   Removing or keeping of the child
o   Notifying the coroner
- The written documentation required by § 31-34-2-3 if a child was taken into custody without a court order
- Any other information that the director requires by rule or the person making the report believes might be helpful

Special Reporting Procedures
Suspicious Deaths
Citation: Ann. Code §§ 31-33-7-5; 31-33-7-6
A copy of the written report of the local child protection service shall immediately be made available to the coroner for the coroner's consideration in a case involving death. Upon receiving a written report, the coroner shall accept the report for investigation and report the findings to:

- The appropriate law enforcement agency
- The prosecuting attorney
- The department
- The hospital, if the institution making the report is a hospital

Substance-Exposed Infants

This issue is not addressed in the statutes reviewed.

Screening Reports

Citation: Ann. Code §§ 31-33-7-1; 31-33-8-1; 31-33-8-7(a); 31-33-8-12(a)

The department shall arrange for receipt, on a 24-hour, 7-day per week basis, of all reports of suspected child abuse or neglect.

The department shall initiate an immediate and appropriately thorough child protection investigation of every report of known or suspected child abuse or neglect the department receives.

- If the report alleges a child may be a victim of child abuse, the investigation shall be initiated immediately, but not later than 24 hours after receipt of the report.
- If reports of child neglect are received, the investigation shall be initiated within a reasonably prompt time, but not later than 5 days, with the primary consideration being the well-being of the child who is the subject of the report.
- If the immediate safety or well-being of a child appears to be endangered or the facts otherwise warrant, the investigation shall be initiated regardless of the time of day.
- If the department has reason to believe that the child is in imminent danger of serious bodily harm, the department shall initiate an immediate, onsite investigation within 1 hour.

The department's investigation, to the extent that is reasonably possible, must include the following:

- The nature, extent, and cause of the known or suspected child abuse or neglect
- The identity of the person allegedly responsible for the child abuse or neglect
- The names and conditions of other children in the home
- An evaluation of the parent, guardian, custodian, or person responsible for the care of the child
- An evaluation of the home environment and the relationship of the child to the parent, guardian, custodian, or other persons responsible for the child's care
- All other data considered pertinent

Upon completion of an investigation, the department shall classify reports as substantiated, indicated, or unsubstantiated.

Iowa

Reporting Procedures
Individual Responsibility
Citation: Ann. Stat. § 232.70

Each report made by a mandated reporter shall be made both orally and in writing. Each report made by a permissive reporter may be oral, written, or both.

The oral report shall be made by telephone or otherwise to the Department of Human Services. If the person making the report has reason to believe that immediate protection for the child is advisable, that person shall also make an oral report to an appropriate law enforcement agency.

The written report shall be made to the Department of Human Services within 48 hours after the oral report.

Content of Reports
Citation: Ann. Stat. § 232.70

The oral and written reports shall contain as much of the following information as the reporter is able to furnish:

- The names and home addresses of the child and the child's parent(s) or other persons responsible for the child's care
- The child's present whereabouts if not the same as the parents' home address
- The child's age
- The nature and extent of the child's injuries, including any evidence of prior injury
- The name, age, and condition of other children in the same home
- Any other information which the person making the report believes might be helpful in establishing the cause of the injury to the child, the identity of the person or persons responsible for the injury, or in providing assistance to the child
- The name and address of the person making the report

Special Reporting Procedures
Suspicious Deaths

This issue is not addressed in the statutes reviewed.

Substance-Exposed Infants
Citation: Ann. Stat. § 232.77(2)

If a health practitioner discovers in a child physical or behavioral symptoms of the effects of exposure to cocaine, heroin, amphetamine, methamphetamine, or other illegal drugs, or combinations or derivatives thereof, that were not prescribed by a health practitioner, or if the health practitioner has determined through examination of the natural mother of the child that the child was exposed in utero, the health practitioner may perform or cause to be performed a medically relevant test, as defined in § 232.73, on the child. The practitioner shall report any positive results of such a test on the child to the department. The department shall begin an assessment pursuant to § 232.71B upon receipt of such a report. A positive test result obtained prior to the birth of a child shall not be used for the criminal prosecution of a parent for acts and omissions resulting in intrauterine exposure of the child to an illegal drug.

Screening Reports
Citation: Ann. Stat. §§ 232.70; 232.71B; Admin. Code § 441-175.22

Upon receipt of a report the department shall do all of the following:

- Immediately, upon receipt of an oral report, make a determination as to whether the report constitutes an allegation of child abuse as defined in § 232.68
- Notify the appropriate county attorney of the receipt of the report

If the department determines a report alleges child abuse, it shall begin an appropriate assessment within 24 hours of receiving the report. The primary purpose of the assessment shall be the protection of the child named in the report. The secondary purpose of the assessment shall be to engage the child's family in services to enhance family strengths and to address needs. The assessment shall include the following:

- Identification of the nature, extent, and cause of the injuries, if any, to the child named in the report
- Identification of the person or persons responsible for the alleged child abuse
- A description of the name, age, and condition of other children in the same home as the child named in the report
- An evaluation of the home environment
- An interview of the person alleged to have committed the child abuse, if the person's identity and location are known

The department, upon completion of the assessment, shall make a written report of the assessment. The written assessment shall:

- Incorporate the information required above
- Be completed within 20 business days of the receipt of the report
- Include a description of the child's condition, identification of the injury or risk to which the child was exposed, the circumstances that led to the injury or risk to the child, and the identity of any person alleged to be responsible for the injury or risk to the child
- Identify the strengths and needs of the child, and of the child's parent, home, and family
- Identify services available from the department and informal and formal services and other support available in the community to address the strengths and needs identified in the assessment

In regulation: Reports of child abuse shall be received by the department, central abuse registry, or child abuse hotline. Any report that alleges child abuse shall be accepted for assessment. Reports that do not meet the legal definition of child abuse shall become rejected intakes.

If a report does not meet the legal definition of child abuse, but a criminal act harming a child is alleged, the department shall immediately refer the matter to the appropriate law enforcement agency. If a report alleges child sexual abuse that involves a person who was not a caregiver, the department shall refer the report to law enforcement orally as soon as practicable, and follow up in writing within 72 hours of receiving the report.

Kansas
Reporting Procedures
Individual Responsibility
Citation: Ann. Stat. § 38-2223

When any mandated reporter has reason to suspect that a child has been harmed as a result of physical, mental, or emotional abuse or neglect or sexual abuse, the person shall report the matter promptly as provided below. The report may be made orally and shall be followed by a written report if requested.

Reports shall be made to the secretary of Social and Rehabilitation Services, except as follows:

- When the Department of Social and Rehabilitation Services is not open for business, reports shall be made to the appropriate law enforcement agency. On the next day that the department is open for business, the law enforcement agency shall report to the department any report received and any investigation initiated pursuant to § 38-2226. The reports may be made orally or, on request of the secretary, in writing.

- Reports of child abuse or neglect occurring in an institution operated by the Department of Social and Rehabilitation Services or the Department of Juvenile Justice shall be made to the attorney general.
- Reports of child abuse or neglect committed by persons employed by the Department of Social and Rehabilitation Services, or the children of employees, shall be made to the appropriate law enforcement agency.

Content of Reports
Citation: Ann. Stat. § 38-2223

Every report shall contain, if known:

- The names and addresses of the child and the child's parents or other persons responsible for the child's care
- The location of the child if other than the child's residence
- The child's gender, race, and age
- The reasons the reporter suspects the child may be a child in need of care
- The nature and extent of the harm to the child, including any evidence of previous harm
- Any other information that the reporter believes might be helpful in establishing the cause of the harm and the identity of the persons responsible for the harm

When reporting a suspicion that a child may be in need of care, the reporter shall disclose protected health information freely and cooperate fully with the secretary and law enforcement throughout the investigation and any subsequent legal process.

Special Reporting Procedures
Suspicious Deaths
Citation: Ann. Stat. §§ 38-2223; 22a-242

A mandated reporter who has information relating to the death of a child shall immediately notify the coroner, as provided by § 22a-242.

When a child dies, a law enforcement officer, health-care provider, or any other person having knowledge of the death shall immediately notify the coroner of the known facts concerning the time, place, manner, and circumstances of the death.

Substance-Exposed Infants

This issue is not addressed in the statutes reviewed.

Screening Reports
Citation: Ann. Stat. §§ 38-2226; 38-2230; Pol. Man. §§ 1310; 1320; 1521

The department and law enforcement officers shall have the duty to receive and investigate reports of child abuse or neglect to determine whether the report is valid and whether action is required to protect the child from further abuse or neglect.

If the department and officers determine that no action is necessary to protect the child but that a criminal prosecution should be considered, the case shall be referred to the appropriate law enforcement agency.

Whenever any person furnishes information to the secretary that a child appears to be a child in need of care, the department shall make a preliminary inquiry to determine whether the interests of the child require further action. Whenever practicable, the inquiry shall include a preliminary investigation of the circumstances that were the subject of the information, including the home and environmental situation and the previous history of the child. If reasonable grounds exist to support the allegations of abuse or neglect, immediate steps shall be taken to protect the health and welfare of the abused or neglected child as well as that of any other child under the same care who may be harmed by abuse or neglect. After the inquiry, if the secretary determines it is not otherwise possible to provide the services necessary to protect the interests of the child, the secretary shall recommend to the county or district attorney that a petition be filed.

In regulation: The report shall be screened to determine if it meets statutory and regulatory definitions. If the report does not fall within the definitions, the report may be screened out. Reports may also be screened out when:

- The child has not been harmed or is not likely to be harmed.
- It concerns ''lifestyle'' issues that do not directly harm a child or place a child at risk of harm.
- Credible information indicates concern is minimal or remote; the incident was reported as accidental or as a single, minor incident.
- It concerns abuse or neglect that occurred in the past.
- It fails to provide the information necessary to locate the child.
- It is known to be fictitious and/or malicious.
- The incident has been or is being assessed by the department and/or law enforcement.

A preliminary inquiry may be made to gain additional information to determine whether the concern is currently being addressed by the family and community, or whether the interests of the child require further action. Requests for additional information must be made within 3 working days. This option must not be used when it appears likely that a child may be harmed within the preliminary inquiry period.

If efforts to yield sufficient information require a face-to-face interview with a child or caregiver, the case must be assigned for assessments of safety and risk of future maltreatment. If, following an initial interview with an alleged victim, there is clearly no evidence to support the allegations of abuse or neglect, the report may be screened out based on the information provided.

When a report alleging child abuse or neglect is assigned for assessment, the supervisor shall determine the appropriate response time consistent with the facts reported, and according to the following criteria:

- Same Day: When there is reason to believe that a child has been seriously injured or is in immediate serious danger
- 72 Hours: All other reports

Kentucky
Reporting Procedures
Individual Responsibility
Citation: Rev. Stat. § 620.030

Any person who knows or has reasonable cause to believe that a child is abused or neglected shall immediately make an oral or written report, by telephone or otherwise, to a local law enforcement agency, the Department of Kentucky State Police, the Cabinet for

Health and Family Services or its designated representative, the Commonwealth attorney, or the county attorney.

A mandated reporter shall file a written report within 48 hours of the original report, if requested.

Content of Reports
Citation: Rev. Stat. § 620.030

The written report shall contain

- The names and addresses of the child and the child's parents or other persons exercising control or
- supervision over the child
- The child's age
- The nature and extent of the child's alleged dependency, neglect, or abuse, including any previous charges of dependency, neglect, or abuse to the child or any siblings
- The name and address of the person allegedly responsible for the abuse or neglect
- Any other information that the reporter believes may be helpful

Special Reporting Procedures
Suspicious Deaths

This issue is not addressed in the statutes reviewed.

Substance-Exposed Infants
Citation: Rev. Stat. § 214.160(2)-(6)

Any physician attending a pregnant woman may perform a screening for alcohol or substance dependency or abuse, including a comprehensive history of such behavior. Any physician may administer a toxicology test to a mother under the physician's care within 8 hours after she has delivered a baby to determine whether there is evidence that she has ingested alcohol or a controlled substance or if she has obstetrical complications that are a medical indication of possible use of any such substance for a nonmedical purpose.

Any physician attending a mother may administer to each newborn infant born to that mother a toxicology test to determine whether there is evidence of prenatal exposure to alcohol or a controlled substance, if the attending person has reason to believe, based on a medical assessment of either patient, that the mother used any such substance for a nonmedical purpose during the pregnancy.

The circumstances surrounding any positive toxicology finding shall be evaluated by the attending person to determine if abuse or neglect of the infant, as defined under § 600.020(1), has occurred and whether investigation by the Cabinet for Health and Family Services is necessary.

No prenatal screening for alcohol or other substance abuse or positive toxicology finding shall be used as prosecutorial evidence. No person shall conduct or cause to be conducted any toxicological test pursuant to this section on any pregnant woman without first informing her of the purpose of the test.

Screening Reports
Citation: Rev. Stat. § 620.040; Admin. Reg. Tit. 922, § 1:330

Based upon the allegation in the report, the cabinet shall immediately make an initial determination as to the risk of harm and immediate safety of the child. Based upon the level of risk determined, the cabinet shall investigate the allegation or accept the report for an assessment of family needs and, if appropriate, may provide or make referral to any community-based services necessary to reduce risk to the child and to provide family support.

A report of sexual abuse shall be considered high risk and shall not be referred to any other community agency.

The cabinet shall, within 72 hours, exclusive of weekends and holidays, make a written report to the Commonwealth's or county attorney and the local enforcement agency or the State Police concerning the action that has been taken on the investigation.

If the report alleges abuse or neglect by someone other than a parent, guardian, or person exercising custodial control or supervision, the cabinet shall immediately notify the Commonwealth or county attorney and the local law enforcement agency or the State police.

In regulation: Cabinet staff shall attempt to elicit from the reporter as much information as possible about the child's circumstances. If a report does not meet the criteria for investigation or family-in-need-of-services assessment, the cabinet shall not accept the report for investigation or assessment but shall refer the caller to a community resource that may meet family needs and keep a record of the report.

Based upon an accepted report of child abuse, neglect, or dependency, the cabinet shall make an initial determination as to the immediate safety and risk of harm to a child. The following timeframes apply:

- If the report indicates imminent danger, the investigation shall be initiated within 1 hour.
- If the report indicates nonimminent danger of physical abuse, efforts shall be made to have face-to-face contact with the child and family within 24 hours.
- If the report indicates nonimminent danger, not involving physical abuse, efforts shall be made to have face-to-face contact with the child and family within 48 hours.
- An investigation or an assessment shall be initiated within 48 hours within a report of dependency if a child is not in imminent danger.

Louisiana
Reporting Procedures
Individual Responsibility
Citation: Ch. C. art. 610

Reports of abuse where the abuser is believed to be a caregiver shall be made immediately to the local child protection unit.

Reports of abuse where the abuser is believed to be someone other than a caregiver shall be made immediately to a law enforcement agency. Dual reporting to both the local child protection unit of the Department of Social Services and the local or State law enforcement agency is permitted.

Mandated reporters must file a written report within 5 days of the initial oral report.

Any commercial film processor who has knowledge of any film, photograph, videotape, negative, or slide depicting a child under age 17 in an activity that constitutes child pornography shall report immediately to the local law enforcement agency. The reporter shall provide a copy of the film, photograph, videotape, negative, or slide to the agency receiving the report.

Content of Reports
Citation: Ch. C. art. 610
The report shall contain the following information, if known:

- The name, address, age, sex, and race of the child
- The nature, extent, and cause of the child's injuries or endangered condition, including any previous known or suspected abuse of the child or the child's siblings
- The names and addresses of the child's parents or other caregivers
- The names and ages of all other members of the child's household
- The name and address of the reporter
- An account of how the child came to reporter's attention
- Any explanation of the cause of the child's injury or condition offered by the child, the caregiver, or any other person
- The number of times the reporter has filed a report on the child or the child's siblings
- The person or persons who are thought to have caused or contributed to the child's condition, if known, and any person named by the child
- Any other information the reporter believes might be important or relevant

Special Reporting Procedures

Suspicious Deaths

Citation: Ch. C. art. 610(A), (E)

Reports of abuse or neglect that were a contributing factor in a child's death, where the abuser is believed to be a caregiver, shall be made to the local child protection unit.

A local child protection unit shall report all cases of child death that involve a suspicion of abuse or neglect to the local or State law enforcement agency, the office of the district attorney, and the coroner.

Substance-Exposed Infants

Citation: Ch. C. art. 610(G)

If a physician has cause to believe that a mother of an infant unlawfully used during pregnancy a controlled dangerous substance, the physician shall order a toxicology test upon the infant, without the consent of the infant's parents or guardian, to determine whether there is evidence of prenatal neglect. If the test results are positive, the physician shall report the results as soon as possible. If the test results are negative, all identifying information shall be obliterated if the record is retained, unless the parent approves the inclusion of identifying information. Positive test results shall not be admissible in a criminal prosecution.

The version below, as amended by Acts 2007, No. 396, § 1, shall not become effective unless and until sufficient funds are appropriated by the legislature for such purposes.

If a physician has cause to believe that a newborn was exposed in utero to an unlawfully used controlled dangerous substance, the physician shall order a toxicology test upon the newborn, without the consent of the newborn's parents or guardian, to determine whether there is evidence of prenatal neglect. If the test results are positive, the physician shall issue a report, as soon as possible, in accordance with this Article. If the test results are negative, all identifying information shall be obliterated if the record is retained, unless the parent approves the inclusion of identifying information. Positive test results shall not be admissible in a criminal prosecution.

If there are symptoms of withdrawal in the newborn or other observable and harmful effects in his or her physical appearance or functioning that a physician has cause to believe are due to the chronic or severe use of alcohol by the mother during pregnancy, the physician shall issue a report in accordance with this Article.

Screening Reports

Citation: Ch. C. art. 610; 612; 615

All reports received by a law enforcement agency that involve a caregiver shall be referred to a local child protection unit.

All reports received by the child protection unit that involve someone other than a caregiver shall be referred to a local law enforcement agency. Reports involving a felony-grade crime against a child shall be promptly communicated to the appropriate law enforcement authorities.

Upon receiving a report of abuse or neglect of a child, the local child protection unit of the department shall promptly assign a level of risk to the child based on the information provided by the reporter.

Reports of high and intermediate levels of risk shall be investigated promptly. This investigation shall include a preliminary investigation as to the nature, extent, and cause of the abuse or neglect and the identity of the person actually responsible for the child's condition.

In lieu of an investigation, reports of low levels of risk may be assessed promptly through interviews with the family to identify needs and available match to community resources. If, during this assessment, it is determined that a child is at immediate substantial risk of harm, the local child protection unit shall promptly conduct or participate in an intensive investigation.

After investigation, the local child protection unit shall make one of the following determinations:

- The child appears to be a child in need of care and immediate removal is necessary for his or her protection from further abuse or neglect.
- The report appears to be justified in that there is evidence of child abuse or neglect, and:
  o A protective order would eliminate the need for removal of the child in order to protect him or her from further abuse, in which case it may apply for a temporary restraining order or protective order.
  o All pertinent information shall be reported to the district attorney as soon as possible, but in no case more than 30 days after the determination is made.
- The report is inconclusive in that the evidence tends to support a finding of abuse or neglect, but there is not enough information to confirm a justified report.
- The report does not appear justified as the evidence does not support a finding of child abuse or neglect.
- The investigation indicates the report appears to be false and that the reporter knowingly made a false report in which case all pertinent information shall be forwarded to the district attorney for a determination of whether the evidence supports a finding of a false public report.

In addition to investigation or assessment of reports, or both, the local child protection family services unit may offer available information, referrals, or services to the family when there appears to be some need for medical, mental health, social, basic support, supervision, or other services.

Maine
Reporting Procedures
Individual Responsibility
Citation: Ann. Stat. Tit. 22, §§ 4011-A; 4012

A mandated reporter shall immediately report or cause a report to be made to the Department of Human Services when he or she knows or has reasonable cause to suspect that a child has been or is likely to be abused or neglected.

When, while acting in a professional capacity, a mandated reporter knows or has reasonable cause to suspect that a child has been abused or neglected by a person not responsible for the child, he or she immediately shall report or cause a report to be made to the appropriate district attorney's office.

Any person may make a report if that person knows or has reasonable cause to suspect that a child has been or is likely to be abused or neglected.

An oral report shall be followed by a written report within 48 hours, if requested by the department.

Content of Reports
Citation: Ann. Stat. Tit. 22, § 4012

The reports shall include the following information, if known:
- The name and address of the child and the persons responsible for the child's care or custody
- The child's age and sex
- The nature and extent of the abuse or neglect, including a description of any injuries and the explanation given for them
- A description of sexual abuse or exploitation, if applicable
- Family composition
- Any evidence of prior abuse of the child or any siblings
- The source of report
- Any action taken by the reporter, including a description of photographs or x-rays taken
- Any other information that the reporter believes may be helpful

Special Reporting Procedures
Suspicious Deaths
Citation: Ann. Stat. Tit. 22, §§ 4011-A; 4022(12)

A mandated reporter shall immediately report or cause a report to be made to the department when the he or she knows or has reasonable cause to suspect that a suspicious child death has occurred.

When, while acting in a professional capacity, a mandated reporter has reasonable cause to suspect that a suspicious child death has been caused by a person not responsible for the child, he or she immediately shall report or cause a report to be made to the appropriate district attorney's office.

Any person may make a report if that person knows or has reasonable cause to suspect that there has been a suspicious child death.

''Suspicious child death'' means the death of a child under circumstances in which there is reasonable cause to suspect that abuse or neglect was a cause of or factor contributing to the child's death.

Substance-Exposed Infants
Citation: Ann. Stat. Tit. 22, § 4011-B; 4004-B

If a health-care provider involved in the delivery or care of an infant knows or has reasonable cause to suspect that the infant has been affected by illegal substance abuse or is suffering from withdrawal symptoms resulting from prenatal drug exposure, whether or not the prenatal exposure was to legal or illegal drugs, the provider shall notify the department. The report must be made in the same manner as reports of abuse or neglect.

The department shall act to protect newborn infants identified as being affected by illegal substance abuse or suffering from withdrawal symptoms resulting from prenatal drug exposure, whether or not the prenatal exposure was to legal or illegal drugs, regardless of whether or not the infant is abused or neglected. The department shall:

- Receive reports of infants who may be affected by illegal substance abuse or suffering from prenatal drug exposure
- Promptly investigate all reports to determine whether each infant reported is affected by an illegal substance
- Determine whether or not each infant reported is affected by illegal substance abuse or suffers from withdrawal symptoms resulting from prenatal drug exposure
- Determine whether or not the infant is abused or neglected and, if so, determine the degree of harm or threatened harm in each case
- For each infant whom the department determines to be affected by illegal substance abuse or to be suffering from withdrawal symptoms resulting from prenatal drug exposure, develop, with the assistance of any health care provider involved in the mother's or the child's medical or mental health care, a plan for the safe care of the infant and, in appropriate cases, refer the child or mother or both to a social service agency or voluntary substance abuse prevention service

Screening Reports
Citation: Ann. Stat. Tit. 22, § 4004; CFS Pol. Man. §§ IV.C; IV.D-1

The department shall act to protect abused and neglected children, and children in circumstances that present a substantial risk of abuse and neglect, to prevent further abuse and neglect, to enhance the welfare of these children and their families, and to preserve family life wherever possible. The department shall:

- Receive reports of abuse and neglect and suspicious child deaths
- Promptly investigate all abuse and neglect cases and suspicious child deaths coming to its attention
- If, after investigation, the department does not file a petition under § 4032 but does open a case to provide services to the family to alleviate child abuse and neglect in the home, assign a caseworker, who shall:
  - o Provide information about rehabilitation and other services that may be available to assist the family
  - o Develop with the family a written child and family plan
- File a petition under § 4032 if, after investigation, the department determines that a child is in immediate risk of serious harm or in jeopardy
- In the case of a suspicious child death, determine:
  - o Whether abuse or neglect was a cause or factor contributing to the child's death
  - o The degree of threatened harm to any other child for whom the person responsible for the deceased child may be responsible in the future

In regulation: All calls that relate to suspected child abuse and/or neglect will be immediately routed to the Child Protective Intake Unit. The Intake Unit will determine if the report is appropriate. The intake worker will gather facts from the reporter regarding:

- The identity and location of the parents, children, and relative resources
- The nature of suspected abuse or neglect and the impact on the child
- The reporter's actions taken thus far, if any
- Other persons who may have direct knowledge, and how to contact them

If the information is not sufficient to determine whether the report is appropriate or inappropriate, the worker may, with supervisor approval, contact at least one professional person, if available, whom the worker believes will have direct knowledge of the child's current condition. The intake worker will also review previous child welfare history regarding the family and the alleged abuser(s).

The worker will analyze the information to determine if the report indicates that there is immediate risk of serious harm. If it appears that the child is in immediate risk of serious harm, the worker will contact the intake supervisor immediately and the intake supervisor will review the report immediately and notify the appropriate district office supervisor.

Reports may be classified as follows:

- ''Substantiated'' means that, by a preponderance of the evidence, a parent or caregiver has caused and/or is likely to cause high severity child abuse and neglect. This person is considered a danger to children.
- ''Indicated'' means that, by a preponderance of the evidence, a parent or caregiver has caused and/or is likely to cause low/moderate severity child abuse. Signs of risk may also be present.
- ''Unsubstantiated'' means that, by a preponderance of the evidence, a parent or caregiver did not abuse or neglect a child. However, signs of risk may be present.

Maryland
Reporting Procedures
Individual Responsibility
Citation: Fam. Law § 5-704

A mandated reporter shall make an oral report, by telephone or direct communication, as soon as possible:

- To the local Department of Social Services or appropriate law enforcement agency if the person has reason to believe that the child has been subjected to abuse
- To the local department if the person has reason to believe that the child has been subjected to neglect The mandated reporter shall make a written report to the local department no later than 48 hours after the contact, examination, attention, or treatment that caused the individual to believe that the child had been subjected to abuse or neglect and shall submit a copy to the local State's attorney if the individual has reason to believe that the child has been subjected to abuse.

Content of Reports
Citation: Fam. Law § 5-704

Insofar as is reasonably possible, an individual who makes a report under this section shall include in the report the following information:

- The name, age, and home address of the child
- The name and home address of the child's parent(s) or other person responsible for the child's care
- The whereabouts of the child
- The nature and extent of the abuse or neglect of the child, including any evidence or information available to the reporter concerning possible previous instances of abuse or neglect
- Any other information that might be helpful to determine the cause of the suspected abuse or neglect and the identity of any individual responsible for the abuse or neglect

Special Reporting Procedures
Suspicious Deaths
This issue is not addressed in the statutes reviewed.
Substance-Exposed Infants
This issue is not addressed in the statutes reviewed.
Screening Reports
Citation: Fam. Law §§ 5-701; 5-706; 5-706.1
Within 24 hours after receiving a report of suspected physical or sexual abuse of a child, and within 5 days after receiving a report of suspected neglect or suspected mental injury of a child, the local department or the appropriate law enforcement agency shall:

- See the child
- Attempt to have an on-site interview with the child's caregiver
- Decide on the safety of the child, wherever the child is, and of other children in the household
- Decide on the safety of other children in the care or custody of the alleged abuser

To the extent possible, an investigation shall be completed within 10 days after receipt of the first notice of the suspected abuse or neglect by the local department or law enforcement agencies. An investigation that is not completed within 30 days shall be completed within 60 days of receipt of the first notice of the suspected abuse or neglect.

Reports may be classified as follows:

- ''Indicated'' means a finding that there is credible evidence, which has not been satisfactorily refuted, that abuse, neglect, or sexual abuse did occur.
- ''Unsubstantiated'' means a finding that there is an insufficient amount of evidence to support a finding of indicated or ruled out.
- ''Ruled out'' means a finding that abuse, neglect, or sexual abuse did not occur.

Massachusetts
Reporting Procedures
Individual Responsibility
Citation: Ann. Laws Ch. 119, § 51A(a)
A mandated reporter shall immediately communicate orally with the Department of Children and Families when, in his or her professional capacity, he or she has reasonable cause to believe that a child is suffering physical or emotional injury resulting from:

- Abuse that causes harm or substantial risk of harm to the child's health or welfare, including sexual abuse
- Neglect, including malnutrition
- Within 48 hours, a written report shall be filed with the department detailing the suspected abuse or neglect.

Content of Reports
Citation: Ann. Laws Ch. 119, § 51A(d)

A report filed under this section shall contain:

- The names and addresses of the child and the child's parents or other person responsible for the child's care, if known
- The child's age and sex
- The nature and extent of the child's injuries, abuse, maltreatment, or neglect, including any evidence of prior injuries, abuse, maltreatment, or neglect
- The circumstances under which the person required to report first became aware of the child's injuries, abuse, maltreatment, or neglect
- Whatever action, if any, was taken to treat, shelter, or otherwise assist the child
- The name of the person or persons making the report
- Any other information that the person reporting believes might be helpful in establishing the cause of the injuries
- The identity of the person or persons responsible for the neglect or injuries
- Other information required by the department

Special Reporting Procedures
Suspicious Deaths
Citation: Ann. Laws Ch. 119, § 51A(e)

A mandated reporter who has reasonable cause to believe that a child has died as a result of any of the conditions listed above shall report the death to the district attorney for the county in which the death occurred and the Office of the Chief Medical Examiner.

Substance-Exposed Infants
Citation: Ann. Laws Ch. 119, § 51A(a)

A mandated reporter shall immediately communicate orally with the Department of Children and Families when, in his or her professional capacity, he or she has reasonable cause to believe that a child is suffering physical or emotional injury resulting from physical dependence upon an addictive drug at birth.

Screening Reports
Citation: Ann. Laws Ch. 119, § 51B; Code of Regs. Tit. 110, §§ 4.21; 4.27; 4.31; 4.32

Upon receipt of a report, the department shall investigate the suspected child abuse or neglect, provide a written evaluation of the household of the child, including the parents and home environment, and make a written determination relative to the safety of and risk posed to the child and whether the suspected child abuse or neglect is substantiated.

Upon completion of the investigation and evaluation, the department shall make a written determination relative to:

- The safety of the child, the risk of physical or emotional injury to that child, and the safety of and risk to any other children in the household
- Whether the suspected child abuse or neglect is substantiated

If the department has reasonable cause to believe a child's health or safety is in immediate danger from abuse or neglect, the department shall take a child into immediate temporary custody if it has reasonable cause to believe that the removal is necessary to protect the child from abuse or neglect. The investigation and evaluation shall commence within 2 hours of initial contact and an interim report with an initial determination regarding the child's safety and custody shall be completed as soon as possible but not more than 24 hours after initial contact. The final report required under this section shall be complete within 5 business days of initial contact. If a child is taken into immediate temporary custody, the department shall make a written report stating the reasons for such removal and shall file a care and protection petition under section 24 on the next court day.

If the department does not have reasonable cause to believe that a child's health or safety is in immediate danger from abuse or neglect, the investigation and evaluation shall commence within 2 business days of initial contact and a determination shall be made within 15 business days, unless a waiver has been approved by the area director or requested by law enforcement.

In regulation: Upon receipt of a report, the department shall immediately screen such report to distinguish the need for an emergency or nonemergency response.

At the time of the first contact with parents or caregivers, the investigator shall deliver to the individual a statement of rights that shall include written notice that report has been made, the nature and possible effects of the investigation, and that information given could and might be used in subsequent court hearings. Such notice shall be in a form prescribed by the department.

The investigation of all emergency reports shall commence within 2 hours of initial contact and shall be completed within 24 hours after the emergency designation of the report by the department. The investigation of all nonemergency reports shall commence within 2 working days of initial contact and shall be completed within 10 calendar days following the receipt of the report.

After completion of its investigation, the department shall make a determination as to whether the allegations in the report received are ''supported'' or ''unsupported.'' To support a report means that the department has reasonable cause to believe that an incident (reported or discovered during the investigation) of abuse or neglect by a caregiver did occur.

Michigan
Reporting Procedures
Individual Responsibility
Citation: Comp. Laws § 722.623(1)

A mandated reporter who has reasonable cause to suspect child abuse or neglect shall make immediately, by telephone or otherwise, an oral report, or cause an oral report to be made, of the suspected child abuse or neglect to the Family Independence Agency (department). Within 72 hours after making the oral report, the reporting person shall file a written report.

Content of Reports
Citation: Comp. Laws § 722.623(2)

The written report shall contain:
- The name of the child and a description of the abuse or neglect
- If possible, the names and addresses of the child's parents, guardian, or persons with whom the child resides, and the child's age

- Other information available to the reporting person that might establish the cause of the abuse or neglect, and the manner in which the abuse or neglect occurred

Special Reporting Procedures

Suspicious Deaths

Citation: Comp. Laws § 722.628b

If a central registry case involves a child's death, the department shall refer the case to the prosecuting attorney for the county in which the child is located.

Substance-Exposed Infants

Citation: Comp. Laws § 722.623a

A mandated reporter who knows, or from the child's symptoms has reasonable cause to suspect, that a newborn infant has any amount of alcohol, a controlled substance, or a metabolite of a controlled substance in his or her body, shall report to the department in the same manner as other reports.

Screening Reports

Citation: Comp. Laws § 722.623; 722.628; 722.628d

Within 24 hours after receiving a report, the department shall refer the report to the prosecuting attorney and the local law enforcement agency if the report indicates that the suspected abuse or neglect was a criminal act, was committed by an individual who is not a person responsible for the child's health or welfare, or involves allowing a child to be exposed to methamphetamine production, or shall commence an investigation of the child suspected of being abused or neglected or exposed to or who has had contact with methamphetamine production.

At the time that an investigator contacts an individual about whom a report has been made, the investigator shall advise that individual of the investigator's name, whom the investigator represents, and the specific complaints or allegations made against the individual.

In the course of its investigation, the department shall determine if the child is abused or neglected. In conducting its investigation, the department shall seek the assistance of and cooperate with law enforcement officials within 24 hours after becoming aware that one or more of the following conditions exist:

- Abuse or neglect is the suspected cause of a child's death.
- The child is the victim of suspected sexual abuse or sexual exploitation.
- Abuse or neglect resulting in severe physical injury to the child requires medical treatment or hospitalization.
- Law enforcement intervention is necessary for the protection of the child, a department employee, or another person involved in the investigation.
- The alleged perpetrator of the child's injury is not a person responsible for the child's health or welfare.
- The child has been exposed to or had contact with methamphetamine production.

Allegations of child abuse may be classified as follows:

- Category V: Services not needed. There is no evidence of child abuse or neglect
- Category IV: Community services recommended. There is not a preponderance of evidence of child abuse or neglect, but there is an indication of future risk of harm to the child.

- Category III: Community services needed. There is a preponderance of evidence of child abuse or neglect, and an indication of low or moderate risk of future harm to the child.
- Category II: Child protective services required. There is evidence of child abuse or neglect, and an indication of high or intensive risk of future harm to the child. The department shall open a protective services case, provide services, and list the perpetrator on the central registry.
- Category I: Court petition required. There is evidence of child abuse or neglect, the child is not safe, and a petition for removal is needed.

Minnesota
Reporting Procedures
Individual Responsibility
Citation: Ann. Stat. § 626.556, Subd. 3, 7

A person who knows or has reason to believe a child is being neglected or physically or sexually abused, or a child has been neglected or physically or sexually abused within the preceding 3 years, shall immediately report the information to the local welfare agency, agency responsible for assessing or investigating the report, police department, or the county sheriff.

An oral report shall be made immediately by telephone or otherwise. An oral report made by a mandated reporter shall be followed within 72 hours, exclusive of weekends and holidays, by a report in writing to the appropriate police department, the county sheriff, the agency responsible for assessing or investigating the report, or the local welfare agency, unless the appropriate agency has informed the reporter that the oral information does not constitute a report.

Content of Reports
Citation: Ann. Stat. § 626.556, Subd. 7

Any report shall be of sufficient content to identify:
- The child
- Any person believed to be responsible for the abuse or neglect, if known
- The nature and extent of the abuse or neglect
- The name and address of the reporter

Special Reporting Procedures
Suspicious Deaths
Citation: Ann. Stat. § 626.556, Subd. 9

When a mandated reporter knows or has reason to believe that a child has died as a result of neglect, physical abuse, or sexual abuse, the reporter shall immediately report that information to the appropriate medical examiner or coroner instead of the local welfare agency, police department, or county sheriff.

Medical examiners or coroners shall notify the local welfare agency, police department, or county sheriff in instances in which they believe that the child has died as a result of neglect, physical abuse, or sexual abuse. The medical examiner or coroner shall complete an investigation as soon as feasible and report the findings to the police department or county sheriff and the local welfare agency.

Substance-Exposed Infants

Citation: Ann. Stat. §§ 626.5561; 626.5562; 626.5563

A mandated reporter shall immediately report to the local welfare agency when there is reason to believe that a pregnant woman has used a controlled substance for a nonmedical purpose, including, but not limited to, tetrahydrocannabinol, or has consumed alcoholic beverages during the pregnancy in any way that is habitual or excessive. An oral report shall be made immediately by telephone or otherwise. An oral report made by a mandated reporter shall be followed within 72 hours by a written report. Any report shall be of sufficient content to identify the pregnant woman, the nature and extent of the use, if known, and the name and address of the reporter.

A physician shall administer a toxicology test to a mother within 8 hours after delivery to determine whether there is evidence that she has ingested a controlled substance, if the woman has obstetrical complications that are an indication of possible use of a controlled substance for a nonmedical purpose. A physician shall administer to each newborn infant born under the physician's care a toxicology test to determine whether there is evidence of prenatal exposure to a controlled substance, if the physician has reason to believe based on a medical assessment of the mother or the infant that the mother used a controlled substance for a nonmedical purpose during the pregnancy. If the results of either test are positive, the physician shall report the results as neglect under § 626.556.

If a mandated reporter knows or has reason to believe that a woman is pregnant and has knowingly abused alcohol after she knows of the pregnancy, the person may:

- Arrange for a chemical use assessment conducted according to rules adopted by the commissioner of human services, and confirm that the recommendations indicated by the assessment are followed
- Immediately report to the local welfare agency or maternal child substance abuse project

Screening Reports

Citation: Ann. Stat. § 626.556, Subd. 7, 10, 10e

The local welfare agency shall determine if the report is accepted for an assessment or investigation as soon as possible but in no event longer than 24 hours after the report is received.

Upon receipt of a report, the local welfare agency shall determine whether to conduct a family assessment or an investigation. The agency shall conduct:

- An investigation on reports involving substantial child endangerment
- A family assessment for reports that do not allege substantial child abuse

If the report alleges maltreatment by a parent or other family member, the agency shall immediately conduct the assessment or investigation. If the report alleges a violation of a criminal statute involving sexual abuse, physical abuse, neglect, or endangerment, a law enforcement agency and welfare agency shall coordinate the planning and execution of their respective investigation and assessment efforts to avoid a duplication of fact-finding efforts and multiple interviews.

If the information collected early in an assessment shows no basis for a full assessment or investigation, the local welfare agency or the agency responsible for assessing or investigating the report may make a determination of no maltreatment, and close the case. Upon receipt of a report, the local welfare agency shall conduct a face-to-

face contact with the child reported to be maltreated and with the child's primary caregiver sufficient to complete a safety assessment and ensure the immediate safety of the child. The face-to-face contact with the child and primary caregiver shall occur immediately if substantial child endangerment is alleged and within 5 calendar days for all other reports.

The local welfare agency shall conclude the family assessment or the investigation within 45 days of the receipt of a report. After conducting a family assessment, the local welfare agency shall:

- Determine whether services are needed to address the safety of the child and other family members and the risk of subsequent maltreatment
- Make two determinations: first, whether maltreatment has occurred; and second, whether child protective services are needed

Mississippi

Reporting Procedures
Individual Responsibility
Citation: Ann. Code § 43-21-353

A mandated reporter who has reasonable cause to suspect that a child is abused or neglected shall immediately make an oral report to the Department of Human Services, to be followed as soon as possible by a written report.

Content of Reports
Citation: Ann. Code § 43-21-353

Any report to the department shall contain:

- The names and addresses of the child, the child's parents, or other persons responsible for the child's care
- The child's age
- The nature and extent of injuries, including any evidence of prior injuries
- Any other information that might be helpful in establishing the cause of the injury and the identity of the perpetrator

Special Reporting Procedures
Suspicious Deaths

This issue is not addressed in the statutes reviewed.

Substance-Exposed Infants

This issue is not addressed in the statutes reviewed.

Screening Reports

Citation: Ann. Code §§ 43-21-353; 43-21-357; Code of Rules, 11-111-001, Sec. B

When the department receives a report, it shall immediately make a referral to the Youth Court intake unit. The intake unit shall promptly comply with § 43-21-357.

At the initial time of contact with the person about whom a report has been made or the person responsible for the health or welfare of a child about whom a report has been made, the department of shall inform the person of the specific complaints or allegations made against him or her. The identity of the person who made the report shall not be disclosed.

Upon receiving a report that a child has been abused in such a manner as to cause serious bodily harm or abuse that would be a felony under State or Federal law, the department shall immediately notify the law enforcement agency in whose jurisdiction the abuse occurred and shall notify the appropriate prosecutor within 48 hours. The law enforcement agency and the department shall investigate the reported abuse immediately and shall file a preliminary report with the appropriate prosecutor's office within 24 hours and shall make additional reports as new or additional information or evidence becomes available.

If the Youth Court intake unit receives a neglect or abuse report, the intake unit shall immediately forward the complaint to the Department of Human Services to promptly make an investigation or report concerning the child and any other children in the same environment and promptly present the findings to the Youth Court intake unit. If it appears from the preliminary inquiry that the child or other children in the same environment are within the jurisdiction of the court, the intake unit shall recommend to the Youth Court:

- That the Youth Court take no action
- That the Department of Human Services monitor the child, family, and other children in the same environment
- That a petition be filed

In regulation: The CPS intake unit of the department receives and evaluates reports of suspected child abuse, neglect, and exploitation. Any report received for investigation by the department should be thoroughly screened to determine if the following criteria are met:

- The individual being reported as abused or neglected must be younger than age 18.
- The individual must fall under the statutory jurisdiction of the Youth Court.
- The allegations must be subject to investigation in accordance with statutory definitions of abused/neglected child and department policies and procedures.
- An element of risk or endangerment must be present or indicated.

All investigations of abuse that should be considered a felony crime under State or Federal law shall be initiated immediately. Investigation of all other reports must be initiated within 24 hours of receipt of report. The level of risk to the child is determined from the evidence gathered during the investigation, an analysis of its reliability and importance, and an evaluation of how the various risk factors interrelate. The interaction between the child, family, and environment requires careful analysis in order to assess accurately risk of harm to the child. Case dispositions are:

- Evidence of Abuse/Neglect: An investigation concludes that there is evidence that a child has been abused and/or neglected. In all cases where there is evidence of abuse/neglect, a service case shall be opened to provide services and to lower risk.
- No Evidence: An investigation determines that the allegations cannot be supported, there is no concrete evidence (physical, medical, psychological, or other), or there is insufficient information available to conclude the abuse or neglect of a child did occur.

All cases with a high level of risk should remain open. Cases are opened to provide prevention services, protection services, or placement services.

Missouri
Reporting Procedures
Individual Responsibility
Citation: Ann. Stat. § 210.115

When a mandated reporter has reasonable cause to suspect that a child has been or may be subjected to abuse or neglect, that person shall immediately cause an oral report to be made to the Children's Division of the Department of Social Services.
Content of Reports

Citation: Ann. Stat. § 210.130

Reports shall contain the following information:

- The names and addresses of the child, the child's parents, or other persons responsible for the child's care
- The child's age, sex, and race
- The nature and extent of the child's injuries, abuse, or neglect, including any evidence of previous injuries, abuse, or neglect to the child or the child's siblings
- The name, age, and address of the person responsible for the child's injuries, if known
- Family composition
- The source of the report
- The name, address, occupation, and contact information of the reporter
- Actions taken by the reporter
- Any other information that might be helpful

Special Reporting Procedures

Suspicious Deaths

Citation: Ann. Stat. § 210.115

Any mandated reporter who has probable cause to suspect that a child has died as a result of abuse or neglect shall report that fact to the medical examiner or coroner.

Substance-Exposed Infants

Citation: Ann. Stat. § 191.737

Any physician or health-care provider may refer to the Department of Health and Senior Services families in which children may have been exposed to a controlled substance or alcohol, as evidenced by:

- Medical documentation of signs and symptoms consistent with controlled substances or alcohol exposure at birth
- Results of a confirmed toxicology test performed on the mother or the child at the child's birth
- A written assessment made by a physician, health-care provider, or the Division of Family Services that documents the child as being at risk of abuse or neglect Nothing in this section shall preclude a physician or other mandated reporter from reporting abuse or neglect of a child as required by the provisions of § 210.115.

Screening Reports

Citation: Ann. Stat. § 210.145; Code of Regs. Tit. 13, § 35-20.010

The division shall utilize structured decision-making protocols for classification purposes of all child abuse and neglect reports. The protocols developed by the division shall give priority to ensuring the well-being and safety of the child. All child abuse and neglect reports shall be initiated within 24 hours and shall be classified based upon the reported risk and injury to the child.

The local office shall contact the appropriate law enforcement agency immediately upon receipt of a report that division personnel determine merits an investigation and provide such agency with a detailed description of the report received. In such cases the local division office shall request the assistance of the local law enforcement agency in all aspects of the investigation.

In regulation: All reports received by the hotline shall be screened within 24 hours of receipt and shall be classified based upon the reported safety risk and injury to the child. In all cases, the division must have face-to-face contact with all children in the alleged victim's household within 72 hours.

If the call is screened in, it will be accepted as a CA/N report and sent to the county office. If the call is screened out, the call will be documented and entered into the database, but no further action will be taken, unless the division decides to refer it for appropriate community service. After response assignment, the report is sent to the local division office for review. The local division office has the option to change the response assignment, given additional information or prior history with the family. Each investigation will be classified as a 3-hour, 24-hour, or 72-hour call, based upon information received by the hotline.

Montana
Reporting Procedures
Individual Responsibility
Citation: Ann. Code § 41-3-201

When a mandated reporter knows or has reasonable cause to suspect, as a result of information they receive in their professional or official capacity, that a child is abused or neglected, he or she shall promptly make a report to the Department of Public Health and Human Services.

Content of Reports
Citation: Ann. Code § 41-3-201

The report must contain:
- The names and addresses of the child and the child's parents or other persons responsible for the child's care
- To the extent known, the nature and extent of the child's injuries, including any evidence of prior injuries
- Any other information that the reporter believes might be helpful in establishing the cause of the injuries or showing the willful neglect and the identity of the person or persons responsible for the injury or neglect
- The facts that led the reporter to believe that the child suffered injury or willful neglect

Special Reporting Procedures
Suspicious Deaths
Citation: Ann. Code § 41-3-206

A mandated reporter who has reasonable cause to suspect that a child has died as a result of abuse or neglect shall report that suspicion to the appropriate medical examiner or law enforcement officer.

Substance-Exposed Infants
Citation: Ann. Code § 41-3-201(3)

A physician or other health-care professional involved in the delivery or care of an infant shall report to the department any infant known to the professional to be affected by a dangerous drug, as defined in § 50-32-101.

Screening Reports
Citation: Ann. Code § 41-3-202; Admin. Rules R. 37.47.302; 37.47.303

Upon receipt of a report that a child is or has been abused or neglected, the department shall promptly assess the information contained in the report and make a determination regarding the level of response required and the timeframe within which action must be initiated. If the department determines that an investigation is required, a social worker, the county attorney, or a peace officer shall promptly conduct a thorough investigation into the circumstances surrounding the allegations of abuse or neglect of the child.

An initial investigation of alleged abuse or neglect may be conducted when an anonymous report is received. However, the investigation must within 48 hours result in the development of independent, corroborative, and attributable information in order for the investigation to continue. Without the development of independent, corroborative, and attributable information, a child may not be removed from the home.

In regulation: All reports of child abuse or neglect must be made through the child abuse hotline. When the child abuse hotline receives an incoming communication, the intake specialist will use standardized questions to screen the communication and determine:

- The type of child abuse or neglect alleged
- The level of response required
- How the report will be classified

When the incoming communication received by the hotline contains an allegation of child abuse or neglect requiring investigation, the intake specialist shall transmit the report to a local office for a response pursuant to § 41-3-202.

When an incoming communication received by the hotline results in a report alleging child abuse or neglect that indicates a child may be in immediate danger of serious harm, thus requiring an immediate response, the intake specialist will promptly contact the appropriate social worker in the field designated to receive those reports and verbally inform the field social worker of:

- The nature of the concerns
- Where the child or children of concern can be located
- Any other information necessary to facilitate protection of the child or children

Nebraska
Reporting Procedures
Individual Responsibility
Citation: Rev. Stat. § 28-711

When a mandated reporter has reasonable cause to believe that a child has been subjected to abuse or neglect, he or she shall report to the proper law enforcement agency or the Department of Health and Human Services on the toll-free number.

The report may be made orally by telephone with the caller giving his or her name and address, and shall be followed by a written report.

Content of Reports
Citation: Rev. Stat. § 28-711

The report shall contain:

- The address and age of the child
- The address of the person having custody of the child
- The nature and extent of the abuse or neglect or the conditions or circumstances that would reasonably result in abuse or neglect
- Any evidence of previous abuse or neglect

- Any other information that in the opinion of the reporter may be helpful in establishing the cause of the child abuse or neglect and the identity of the perpetrator or perpetrators

Special Reporting Procedures

Suspicious Deaths

This issue is not addressed in the statutes reviewed.

Substance-Exposed Infants

This issue is not addressed in the statutes reviewed.

Screening Reports

Citation: Rev. Stat. §§ 28-711; 28-713; 28-720; HHS Man. §§ 3-006.02; 4-008.01

The department shall establish a statewide toll-free number to be used by any person any hour of the day or night, any day of the week, to make reports of child abuse or neglect.

It is the duty of the law enforcement agency to investigate the report, to take immediate steps to protect the child, and to institute legal proceedings if appropriate. The law enforcement agency may request assistance from the department during the investigation and shall, by the next working day, notify either the hotline or the department of receipt of the report, including whether or not an investigation is being undertaken by the law enforcement agency. A copy of all reports, whether or not an investigation is being undertaken, shall be provided to the department.

The department shall, by the next working day after receiving a report, make a written report or a summary on forms provided by the department to the proper law enforcement agency and enter the report in the tracking system of child protection cases.

All cases entered into the central register shall be classified as one of the following:

- Court substantiated: if a court of competent jurisdiction has entered a judgment of guilty against the subject of the report of child abuse or neglect upon a criminal complaint, indictment, or information, or there has been an adjudication of jurisdiction of a juvenile court over the child that relates to the report of child abuse or neglect
- Court pending: if a criminal complaint, indictment, or information or a juvenile petition that relates to the subject of the report of abuse or neglect has been filed and is pending in a court of competent jurisdiction
- Inconclusive: if the evidence indicates, by a preponderance of the evidence, that child abuse or neglect probably did not occur

In regulation: Allegations that meet the definition of child abuse and neglect will be assigned for assessment. When law enforcement has investigated a report and has reported its findings to the department, the department will enter the findings in the central registry. The department will not begin another assessment unless the law enforcement investigation indicates the child is at continued risk or the information on the family is incomplete.

Cases classified as follows will not be entered into the registry:

- Unable to locate: when the subjects of the report cannot be found
- Unfounded: all cases that cannot be otherwise classified

Nevada
Reporting Procedures
Individual Responsibility
Citation: Rev. Stat. §§ 432B.220(1)-(2); 432B.230

A mandated reporter who, in his or her professional or occupational capacity, knows or has reasonable cause to believe that a child has been abused or neglected shall:

- Report the abuse or neglect of the child to an agency that provides child welfare services or to a law enforcement agency
- Make such a report as soon as reasonably practicable but no later than 24 hours after the person knows or has reasonable cause to believe that the child has been abused or neglected

If a mandated reporter knows or has reasonable cause to believe that the abuse or neglect of the child involves an act or omission of a person directly responsible or serving as a volunteer for or an employee of a public or private home, institution or facility where the child is receiving child care outside of his or her home for a portion of the day, the person shall make the report to a law enforcement agency.

If a mandated reporter knows or has reasonable cause to believe that the abuse or neglect of the child involves an act or omission of an agency that provides child welfare services or a law enforcement agency, the person shall make the report to an agency other than the one alleged to have committed the act or omission.

A person may make a report by telephone or, in light of all the surrounding facts and circumstances that are known or that reasonably should be known to the person at the time, by any other means of oral, written, or electronic communication that a reasonable person would believe, under those facts and circumstances, is a reliable and swift means of communicating information to the person who receives the report. If the report is made orally, the person who receives the report must reduce it to writing as soon as reasonably practicable.

Content of Reports
Citation: Rev. Stat. § 432B.230

The report must contain the following information, if obtainable:

- The name, address, age, and sex of the child
- The name and address of the child's parents or other person responsible for the child's care
- The nature and extent of the abuse or neglect of the child, the effect of prenatal illegal substance abuse on the newborn infant, or the nature of the withdrawal symptoms resulting from prenatal drug exposure
- Any evidence of previously known or suspected abuse or neglect of the child or the child's siblings, effects of prenatal illegal substance abuse, or evidence of withdrawal symptoms resulting from prenatal drug exposure of the newborn infant
- The name, address, and relationship, if known, of the person who is alleged to have abused or neglected the child
- Any other information known to the person making the report that the agency that provides child welfare services considers necessary

Special Reporting Procedures
Suspicious Deaths
Citation: Rev. Stat. § 432B.220(6)

If a mandated reporter knows or has reasonable cause to believe that a child has died as a result of abuse or neglect, the person shall, as soon as reasonably practicable, report this belief to an agency that provides child welfare services or a law enforcement agency. If the report is made to a law enforcement agency, the law enforcement agency shall notify an agency that provides child welfare services and the appropriate medical examiner or coroner of the report. If such a report is made to an agency that provides child welfare services, the agency shall notify the appropriate medical examiner or coroner of the report.

The medical examiner or coroner shall investigate the report and submit his or her written findings to the appropriate child welfare agency, the appropriate district attorney, and a law enforcement agency. The written findings must include, if obtainable, the information required by § 432B.230(2).

Substance-Exposed Infants
Citation: Rev. Stat. § 432B.220(3)
Any mandated reporter who delivers or provides medical services to a newborn infant and knows or has reasonable cause to believe that the newborn infant has been affected by prenatal substance abuse or has withdrawal symptoms resulting from prenatal drug exposure shall, as soon as reasonably practicable but no later than 24 hours after the person knows, notify an agency that provides child welfare services of the condition of the infant and refer each person who is responsible for the welfare of the infant for appropriate counseling, training, or other services.

Screening Reports
Citation: Rev. Stat. § 432B.260; Admin. Code § 432B.170
Upon the receipt of a report concerning the possible abuse or neglect of a child, a child welfare agency or a law enforcement agency shall promptly notify the appropriate licensing authority, if any. A law enforcement agency shall promptly notify a child welfare agency of any report it receives. Upon receipt of a report concerning the possible abuse or neglect of a child, a child welfare agency or a law enforcement agency shall immediately initiate an investigation if the report indicates that:
- The child is age 5 or younger.
- There is a high risk of serious harm to the child.
- The child has suffered a fatality.
- The child is living in a household in which another child has died, or the child is seriously injured or has visible signs of physical abuse.

In other cases, a child welfare agency shall conduct an evaluation no later than 3 days after the report or notification was received to determine whether an investigation is warranted. For the purposes of this subsection, an investigation is not warranted if:
- The child is not in imminent danger of harm.
- The child is not vulnerable as the result of any untreated injury, illness, or other physical, mental, or emotional condition that threatens his or her immediate health or safety.
- The alleged abuse or neglect could be eliminated if the child and his or her family receive or participate in social or health services offered in the community, or both.
- The agency determines that the alleged abuse or neglect was the result of the reasonable exercise of discipline by a parent or guardian.

If the agency determines that an investigation is warranted, the agency shall initiate the investigation no later than 3 days after the evaluation is completed.

In regulation: After the investigation of a report of the abuse or neglect of a child, an agency that provides child welfare services shall determine its case findings based on whether there is reasonable cause to believe a child is abused or neglected or threatened with abuse or neglect, and whether there is credible evidence of alleged abuse or neglect of the child. The agency shall make one of the following findings:

- The allegation of abuse or neglect is substantiated.
- The allegation of abuse or neglect is unsubstantiated.

New Hampshire
Reporting Procedures
Individual Responsibility
Citation: Rev. Stat. § 169-C:30

A mandated reporter shall immediately make an oral report to the Department of Health and Human Services by telephone or otherwise, followed within 48 hours by a written report, if so requested by the department.

Content of Reports
Citation: Rev. Stat. § 169-C:30

The report shall contain, if known:

- The name and address of the child and the person responsible for the child's welfare
- The nature and extent of the child's injuries, including any evidence of prior injury
- The identity of the person suspected of being responsible for the abuse or neglect
- Any other information that might be helpful in establishing the neglect or abuse or that may be required by the department

Special Reporting Procedures
Suspicious Deaths

This issue is not addressed in the statutes reviewed.

Substance-Exposed Infants

This issue is not addressed in the statutes reviewed.

Screening Reports
Citation: Rev. Stat. §§ 169-C:34; 169-C:38-a

If it appears that the immediate safety or well-being of a child is endangered, the family may flee or the child disappear, or the facts otherwise so warrant, the department shall commence an investigation immediately after receipt of a report. In all other cases, a child protective investigation shall be commenced within 72 hours of receipt of the report.

For each report it receives, the department shall promptly perform a child protective investigation to determine:

- The composition of the family or household, including:
  - The name, address, age, sex, and race of each child named in the report
  - Any siblings or other children in the same household or in the care of the same adults . The parents or other persons responsible for the welfare of the children
  - Any other adults in the same household
- Whether there is probable cause to believe that any child in the family or household is abused or neglected, including a determination of:

- o Harm or threatened harm to each child
- o The nature and extent of present or prior injuries, abuse, or neglect, and any evidence thereof. The person or persons apparently responsible for the abuse or neglect
- The immediate and long-term risk to each child if the child remains in the existing home environment
- The protective treatment and ameliorative services that appear necessary to help prevent further child abuse or neglect and to improve the home environment and the parents' ability to adequately care for the children

At the first contact in person, any person investigating a report of abuse or neglect on behalf of the department shall verbally inform the parents of a child suspected of being a victim of abuse or neglect of the specific nature of the charges and that they are under no obligation to allow a social worker or State employee on their premises or surrender their children to interviews unless that social worker or State employee is in possession of a court order to that effect. Upon receiving such information, the parent shall sign a written acknowledgement indicating that the information required under this paragraph was provided by the person conducting the investigation. The parent and department shall each retain a copy of the acknowledgment.

The Department of Health and Human Services and the Department of Justice shall jointly develop a standardized protocol for the interviewing of victims and the investigation and assessment of cases of child abuse and neglect. The protocol shall seek to minimize the impact on the victim. The protocol shall also be designed to protect the rights of all parties affected, and specifically address the need to establish safe and appropriate places for interviewing children.

New Jersey
Reporting Procedures
Individual Responsibility
Citation: Ann. Sat. § 9:6-8.10
Any person who has reasonable cause to believe that a child has been subjected to abuse or neglect shall report the same to the Division of Youth and Family Services by telephone or otherwise.
Content of Reports
Citation: Ann. Stat. § 9:6-8.10
The report, where possible, shall contain:
- The names and addresses of the child and the child's parent, guardian, or other person having custody
- If known, the child's age
- The nature and possible extent of injuries, including any evidence of prior injury
- Any other information that might be helpful with respect to the child abuse and the identity of the perpetrator
Special Reporting Procedures
Suspicious Deaths
This issue is not addressed in the statutes reviewed.

Substance-Exposed Infants

This issue is not addressed in the statutes reviewed.

Screening Reports

Citation: Ann. Stat. § 9:6-8.11; Admin. Code Tit. 10, §§ 129-2.1; 129-2.3; 129-5.2; 129-5.3

Upon receipt of a report, the division shall immediately take such action as shall be necessary to insure the safety of the child and to that end may request and shall receive appropriate assistance from local and State law enforcement officials. The division shall initiate an investigation within 24 hours of receipt of the report, unless a delay is authorized based upon the request of a law enforcement official. The division shall also, within 72 hours, forward a report of such matter to the child abuse registry.

In regulation: The central registry shall deem a call to be a report if it contains at least one allegation that, if true, would constitute abuse or neglect, as defined by law. Child protective services (CPS) shall investigate each new report, regardless of whether or not the alleged child victim and his or her family are known to the department. CPS shall investigate each report alleging abuse or neglect on a military installation, to the extent permitted by the base commander.

CPS shall start the investigation of a report within either 2 hours or 24 hours of the central registry determining the timeframe. Each report that meets one or more of the following criteria shall be investigated within 2 hours of receipt:

- Law enforcement personnel request an immediate response.
- An immediate response will prevent the loss of evidence.
- A child has died due to abuse or neglect and a sibling remains under the care of a parent or guardian.
- A child is a boarder baby left in a hospital or born drug-exposed.
- A child under age 6 is alone at the time of the report.
- A child requires medical attention at the time of the report.
- A child is being seriously physically abused at the time of the report.

The child protective investigator shall, upon initial contact, inform each person specifically alleged to be a perpetrator of abuse or neglect that he or she has been named the alleged perpetrator of abuse or neglect, unless the police, prosecutor, or deputy attorney general advises the child protective investigator to delay providing the information, or when providing such information will jeopardize the investigation.

The child protective investigator shall evaluate the available information and, for each allegation, determine whether abuse or neglect has occurred, and shall make a finding of either substantiated or unfounded. The child protective investigator shall make every reasonable effort to identify the perpetrator for each allegation of abuse or neglect.

New Mexico

Reporting Procedures

Individual Responsibility

Citation: Ann. Stat. § 32A-4-3(A)

A mandated reporter who knows or has reasonable suspicion that a child is abused or neglected shall report the matter immediately to:

- A local law enforcement agency
- The Children, Youth and Families Department
- The Tribal law enforcement or social services agency for an Indian child residing in Indian country

Content of Reports

Citation: Ann. Stat. § 32A-4-3(B)

The written report shall contain:

The names and addresses of the child and the child's parents, guardian, or custodian

The child's age

The nature and extent of the child's injuries, including any evidence of previous injuries

Any other information that the reporter believes might be helpful in establishing the cause of the injuries and the identity of the person responsible for the injuries

Special Reporting Procedures

Suspicious Deaths

This issue is not addressed in the statutes reviewed.

Substance-Exposed Infants

This issue is not addressed in the statutes reviewed.

Screening Reports

Citation: Ann. Stat. §§ 32A-4-3; 32A-4-4; Admin. Code Tit. 8, §§ 10.2.14; 10.3.10; 10.3.11; 10.3.12; 10.3.17

A law enforcement agency receiving the report shall immediately transmit the facts of the report by telephone to the department and a written report within 48 hours. The department shall immediately transmit the facts of the report by telephone to a local law enforcement agency and a written report within 48 hours.

The recipient of a report shall take immediate steps to ensure prompt investigation of the report, and take steps to protect the health or welfare of the alleged child victim, as well as any other child under the same care who may be in danger of abuse or neglect. A local law enforcement officer trained in the investigation of child abuse and neglect is responsible for investigating reports of alleged child abuse or neglect at schools, daycare facilities or child care facilities. Reports alleging neglect or abuse shall be referred to the department.

In regulation: The department will refer all screened out reports to other agencies as resources exist or as required by law. When the alleged perpetrator is not a caregiver or household member, the allegation will be forwarded within 48 hours for investigation to law enforcement. When the report received involves an Indian child on a reservation or pueblo, the department will immediately transmit the information to Tribal law enforcement or Tribal social services.

Emergency and priority 1 reports are assigned for investigation immediately upon receipt of the report. Reports received under safe haven and on children in foster care or preadoptive homes are emergency reports. Priority 2 reports are assigned for investigation no later than 24 hours from receipt of the report. Investigations are conducted within the following timeframes:

- Emergency reports are initiated within 3 hours of receipt.
- Priority 1 reports are initiated within 24 hours of receipt.
- Priority 2 reports are initiated within 5 calendar days of receipt.

The department shall, at the initial time of contact with the subjects of the investigation, advise them of the allegations made and their basic rights. The investigation shall be completed within a reasonable period of time from the date the report was made. The investigation decision includes a determination of substantiated or unsubstantiated on each of the allegations in the report.

New York
Reporting Procedures
Individual Responsibility
Citation: Soc. Serv. Law §§ 413(1); 415

Mandated reporters shall immediately make an oral or electronic report to the statewide central register when they have reasonable cause to suspect that a child has been abused or neglected by a person responsible for that child's care. Oral reports shall be followed by written reports within 48 hours.

Content of Reports
Citation: Soc. Serv. Law § 415

Written reports shall be made in a manner prescribed and on forms supplied by the commissioner of the Office of Children and Family Services and shall include the following information:

- The names and addresses of the child and the child's parents or other person responsible for the child's care
- The child's age, sex, and race
- The nature and extent of any injury, abuse, or maltreatment, including any evidence of prior injuries, abuse, or maltreatment to the child or the child's siblings
- The name of the person or persons alleged to be responsible for causing the injury, abuse, or maltreatment, if known
- Family composition
- The source of the report
- The name and contact information of the person making the report
- Actions taken by the reporting source
- Any other information that the reporter believes may be helpful or required by regulation

Special Reporting Procedures
Suspicious Deaths
Citation: Soc. Serv. Law § 418

Any mandated reporter, including workers of the local child protective service agency or an official of the State agency responsible for investigation of a report of abuse or maltreatment of a child in residential care, who has reasonable cause to suspect that a child has died as a result of abuse or maltreatment shall report that fact to the appropriate medical examiner or coroner.

The medical examiner or coroner shall accept the report for investigation and shall issue a preliminary written report of his or her findings within 60 days of the date of death, absent extraordinary circumstances, and his or her final written report promptly to the police, the appropriate district attorney, the local child protective service, the Office of Children and Family Services, and, if the institution making the report is a hospital, the hospital. The Office of Children and Family Services shall promptly provide a copy of the preliminary and final reports to the statewide central register of child abuse and maltreatment.

Substance-Exposed Infants
This issue is not addressed in the statutes reviewed.
Screening Reports
Citation: Soc. Serv. Law § 424
Each child protective service shall:

- Receive on a 24-hour, 7-day-a-week basis all reports of suspected child abuse or maltreatment
- Transmit a copy of each written report to the State central register
- No later than 7 days after receipt of the initial report send a preliminary written report of the initial investigation, including evaluation and actions taken or contemplated, to the central register
- Upon receipt of a report, commence, within 24 hours, an appropriate investigation that shall include: . An evaluation of the environment of the child named in the report and any other children in the same home
  - A determination of the risk to such children if they continue to remain in the existing home environment
  - A determination of the nature, extent, and cause of any condition enumerated in the report . The names, ages, and conditions of other children in the home
  - After seeing to the safety of the child or children, notify the subjects of the report and other persons named in the report in writing of the existence of the report and their respective rights
- Determine, within 60 days, whether the report is ''indicated'' or ''unfounded''
- Take a child into protective custody to protect him or her from further abuse or maltreatment when appropriate and in accordance with the provisions of the family court act

North Carolina

Reporting Procedures
Individual Responsibility
Citation: Gen. Stat. § 7B-301
A mandated reporter who has cause to suspect that a child is abused, neglected, or dependent shall report the case to the Department of Social Services in the county where the child resides. The report may be made orally, by telephone, or in writing.
Content of Reports
Citation: Gen. Stat. § 7B-301
The report shall contain information as is known to the reporter, including:

-
- The name and address of the child and the child's parent(s), guardian, or caregiver
- The age of the child
- The names and ages of other children in the home
- The present whereabouts of the child, if not at the home address
- The nature and extent of any injury or condition resulting from abuse or neglect
- Any other information that the reporter believes might be helpful in establishing the need for protective services or court intervention

Special Reporting Procedures
Suspicious Deaths
Citation: Gen. Stat. §§ 7B-301; 7B-302

A mandated reporter who has cause to believe that a child has died as a result of maltreatment shall report the case to the department.

The department shall immediately ascertain if other children are in the home and in need of protective services or immediate removal from the home.

Substance-Exposed Infants

This issue is not addressed in the statutes reviewed.

Screening Reports
Citation: Gen. Stat. §§ 7B-301; 7B-302;
Admin. Code Tit. 10A, § 70A.0106

Upon receipt of any report of sexual abuse of the child in a child care facility, the director shall notify the State Bureau of Investigation within 24 hours or on the next workday.

When a report is received, the department shall promptly assess the extent of the abuse or neglect, and the risk of harm to the child, in order to determine whether protective services should be provided or a complaint filed. When the report alleges abuse, the assessment must begin within 24 hours. When the report alleges neglect or dependency, the assessment must begin within 72 hours. When the report alleges abandonment, the department must immediately begin an assessment, take appropriate steps to assume temporary custody of the child, and take appropriate steps to secure an order for nonsecure custody of the child.

In regulation: When a report is received, the county director shall check the county agency's records and the State central registry to ascertain if any previous reports have been made concerning the alleged victim child or children.

The county director shall implement a structured decision-making process that includes assessments of the immediate safety and future risk of harm to the child or children, and the family's strengths and needs. In addition, there shall be documentation of an assessment of all of the information obtained during the investigation, any safety response plan, and the case decision.

North Dakota

Reporting Procedures
Individual Responsibility
Citation: Cent. Code § 50-25.1-04

All mandated reporters shall immediately report cases of known or suspected abuse or neglect to the Department of Human Services. Oral reports must be followed by written reports within 48 hours if requested by the department.

Content of Reports
Citation: Cent. Code § 50-25.1-04

A requested written report must include information specifically sought by the department if the reporter possesses or has reasonable access to the information.

Special Reporting Procedures
Suspicious Deaths

This issue is not addressed in the statutes reviewed.

Substance-Exposed Infants

This issue is not addressed in the statutes reviewed.

Screening Reports

Citation: Cent. Code § 50-25.1-05;

Admin. Code § 75-03-19-03

The department immediately shall initiate an assessment of any report of child abuse or neglect received. If the report alleges a violation of a criminal statute involving sexual or physical abuse, the department and an appropriate law enforcement agency shall coordinate the planning and execution of their investigation efforts to avoid a duplication of fact-finding efforts and multiple interviews. The department or the law enforcement agency may refer the case to a children's advocacy center for a forensic interview, forensic medical examination, and other services.

In regulation: All nonemergency child abuse or neglect assessments must be initiated no later than 72 hours after receipt of a report by the assessing agency unless the department prescribes a different time in a particular case. In cases involving a serious threat or danger to the life or health of a child, the assessment and any appropriate protective measures must commence immediately upon receipt of the report. An assessment is initiated by a search of records for information relating to the report, contact with a subject of the report, or with a collateral contact.

Northern Mariana Islands

Reporting Procedures

Individual Responsibility

Citation: Commonwealth Code Tit. 6, § 5313(a)

Any mandated reporter who knows or has reasonable cause to suspect a child is or was abused or neglected shall report promptly to the Department of Public Safety. This notification shall be made within 24 hours.

Content of Reports

Citation: Commonwealth Code Tit. 6, § 5313(a)

The report shall contain a statement of the time, date, circumstances, and information that gave rise to the reporter's belief that abuse or neglect occurred or will occur.

Special Reporting Procedures

Suspicious Deaths

Citation: Commonwealth Code Tit. 6, § 5313(c)

A mandated reporter who has reasonable cause to suspect that a child has died as a result of abuse shall report that fact to the medical examiner.

Substance-Exposed Infants

This issue is not addressed in the statutes reviewed.

Screening Reports

Citation: Commonwealth Code Tit. 6, § 5313(c); 5322

The Department of Public Safety shall promptly, within 24 hours, notify the Office of the Attorney General and Division of Youth Services of all reported cases.

If a child is taken into custody, the division shall immediately commence a child protective investigation to determine if it is necessary to make the child a ward of the court. The division shall make a recommendation to the Attorney General's Office within 24 hours of the initiation of protective custody regarding whether it is necessary to make the child a ward of the court.

Ohio

Reporting Procedures
Individual Responsibility
Citation: Rev. Stat. § 2151.421

A mandated reporter who knows or has reasonable cause to suspect that a child has suffered or faces a threat of suffering abuse or neglect shall immediately make a report to the county public children services agency (PCSA) or a peace officer in the county in which the child resides or the abuse or neglect occurred.

The report shall be made either by telephone or in person and shall be followed by a written report, if requested by the receiving agency or officer.

Content of Reports
Citation: Rev. Stat. § 2151.421

The written report shall contain:

- The names and addresses of the child and the child's parents or persons having custody
- The child's age
- The nature and extent of any injuries, abuse, or neglect, including any evidence of prior injuries, abuse, or neglect
- Any other information that might be helpful in establishing the cause of the injury, abuse, or neglect that is known or reasonably suspected or believed to have occurred or of the threat of injury, abuse, or neglect that is known or reasonably suspected or believed to exist

Special Reporting Procedures
Suspicious Deaths
Citation: Rev. Stat. § 2151.421(H)(4)

If a report has been made, and if for any reason the child dies before reaching age 18, the PCSA or peace officer to which the report was made or referred shall, upon request of the Child Fatality Review Board, submit a summary of the report to the Child Fatality Review Board.

Substance-Exposed Infants

This issue is not addressed in the statutes reviewed.

Screening Reports
Citation: Rev. Stat. § 2151.421(F)(1);
Admin. Code § 5101:2-34-32

The PCSA shall investigate, within 24 hours, each report of child abuse or child neglect or threat of abuse or neglect that is known or reasonably suspected or believed to have occurred. The investigation shall be made in cooperation with the law enforcement agency. The PCSA shall, at the time of initial contact with the person subject to the investigation, inform the person of the specific complaints or allegations made against the person.

In regulation: Upon receipt of a report, the PCSA shall determine the immediacy of need for agency response based on information from the referent or reporter and child protective services records for the family, and collateral sources.

The PCSA shall consider the report an emergency when there is an imminent threat to the child's safety or there is insufficient information to determine whether or not the child is safe at the time of the report. For emergency reports, the PCSA shall attempt a face-to-face contact with the alleged child victim within 1 hour of the receipt of the report. For all other reports, contact must be made within 24 hours with a principal or collateral source to ensure that the child is safe, and attempt face-to-face contact with the alleged child victim within 3 calendar days.

Oklahoma
Reporting Procedures
Individual Responsibility
Citation: Ann. Stat. Tit. 10, §§ 7103; 7104

A mandated reporter who has reason to believe that a child is a victim of abuse or neglect shall report the matter promptly to the Department of Human Services. Such reports may be made by telephone, in writing, in person, or by any other method prescribed by the department.

A health professional attending to a victim of what appears to be criminally injurious conduct, including physical or sexual abuse, shall report the matter promptly to the nearest law enforcement agency.

Content of Reports
Citation: Ann. Stat. Tit. 10, § 7103

The written report shall contain:
- The names and addresses of the child and the child's parents or persons responsible for the child
- The child's age
- The nature and extent of the abuse or neglect, including any evidence of previous injuries
- Whether the child has tested positive for alcohol or a controlled dangerous substance
- Any other information that the reporter believes might be helpful in establishing the cause of the injuries and the identity of the person or persons responsible for the abuse if such information is known to the person making the report

Special Reporting Procedures
Suspicious Deaths

This issue is not addressed in the statutes reviewed.

Substance-Exposed Infants
Citation: Ann. Stat. Tit. 10, § 7103

Every health care professional attending the birth of a child who tests positive for alcohol or a controlled dangerous substance shall report the matter promptly to the Department of Human Services.

Screening Reports
Citation: Ann. Stat. Tit. 10, §§ 7106; 7108;
Admin. Code Tit. 340, 75-3-7; 75-3-7.1

A county office of the department shall promptly respond to a report by initiating an investigation or an assessment of the family in accordance with guidelines established by the department. The department may assign priorities to reports of alleged child abuse or neglect based on the severity and immediacy of the alleged harm to the child. The primary purpose of the investigation or assessment shall be the protection of the child.

At the initial time of contact with a parent or other person who is the subject of an investigation, the child protective services (CPS) worker shall advise such person of the specific complaint or allegation made against the person.

In regulation: All reports are screened to determine whether allegations meet the definition of child abuse or neglect and are within the scope of a CPS investigation or assessment. If the allegations are not appropriate for CPS, the reporter may be given an explanation why an investigation or assessment will not be conducted and, if appropriate, where a referral may be made to assist the family.

Intervention is limited to current situations as the CPS focus is on identifying and protecting children who are presently at risk or will be at risk if safety measures are not put in place.

When a report is received that is not appropriate for CPS and services are needed, the child welfare worker may make a referral within the department, to outside resources, or both, for emergency food, shelter, medical services, or counseling. In situations that indicate the child and family are in need of services, referrals to community agencies or contract providers may be offered to the family.

Priority guidelines have been established to assist staff in determining how quickly an initial response must be made to a report.

- Priority I: A Priority I report indicates that the child is in imminent danger of serious physical injury and must be responded to immediately, but no later than 24 hours after receipt of the report.
- Priority II: Priority II reports indicate that there is no imminent danger of severe injury, but without intervention and safety measures it is likely that the child will not be safe. Priority II investigations or assessments are initiated from within 2 to 15 calendar days from the date that the report was accepted for investigation or assessment.

Oregon
Reporting Procedures
Individual Responsibility
Citation: Rev. Stat. § 419B.015

A person making a report shall make an oral report, by telephone or otherwise, to:
- The local office of the Department of Human Services or a designee of the department
- A law enforcement agency in the county where the person is located

Content of Reports
Citation: Rev. Stat. § 419B.015

The report shall contain, if known:
- The names and addresses of the child and the child's parents or other persons responsible for the child
- The child's age
- The nature and extent of the abuse, including any evidence of previous abuse
- The explanation given for the abuse

- Any other information that the reporter believes might be helpful in establishing the cause of the abuse and the identity of the perpetrator

Special Reporting Procedures

Suspicious Deaths

This issue is not addressed in the statutes reviewed.

Substance-Exposed Infants

This issue is not addressed in the statutes reviewed.

Screening Reports

Citation: Rev. Stat. § 419B.017;

Admin. Rules §§ 413-015-0205;

413-015-0210; 413-015-1000

The department shall adopt rules establishing the time within which the notification required above must be made. At a minimum, these rules shall:

- Establish which reports of child abuse require notification within 24 hours after receipt
- Provide that all other reports require notification within 10 days after receipt
- Establish criteria that enable the department or law enforcement agency to quickly and easily identify reports that require notification within 24 hours

In regulation: On the same day a report is received by the department, screeners must use the guided assessment screening template to collect critical information in order to effectively evaluate the presence of safety threats.

A child protective services (CPS) assessment is required if the screener determines that the information received constitutes a report of child abuse with a familial protection issue. If an assessment is required, the screener must determine the response timeframe:

- Within 24 hours if there is an immediate threat to safety
- Within 5 days if the threat to safety is not immediate

Following the completion of the CPS assessment, the worker must determine whether there is reasonable cause to believe that child abuse occurred. The possible determinations are:

- ''Founded'': There is reasonable cause to believe that abuse occurred.
- ''Unfounded'': No evidence of child abuse was identified or disclosed.
- ''Unable to determine'': There was insufficient data to conclude whether there was reasonable cause to believe that abuse occurred.

Pennsylvania

Reporting Procedures

Individual Responsibility

Citation: Cons. Stat. Tit. 23 §§ 6311; 6313

A mandated reporter who has reasonable cause to suspect that a child is an abused or neglected child shall make a report to the Department of Public Welfare.

An oral report shall be made immediately, to be followed by a written report within 48 hours.

Written reports shall be made to the appropriate county agency in a manner and on forms the department prescribes by regulation.

Content of Reports
Citation: Cons. Stat. Tit. 23 § 6313
The written reports shall include the following information if available:

- The names and addresses of the child and the child's parents or other persons responsible for the care of the child, if known
- Where the suspected abuse occurred
- The age and sex of subjects of the report
- The nature and extent of the suspected abuse, including any evidence of prior abuse to the child or siblings of the child
- The name and relationship of the person responsible for causing the suspected abuse, if known, and any evidence of prior abuse by that person
- Family composition
- The source of the report
- The name and contact information of the person making the report
- Any actions taken by the source
- Any other information that the department may require by regulation

Special Reporting Procedures
Suspicious Deaths
Citation: Cons. Stat. Tit. 23 § 6317
A mandated reporter who has reasonable cause to suspect that a child has died as a result of abuse or neglect shall report that suspicion to the appropriate coroner. The coroner shall accept the report for investigation and shall report his finding to the police, the district attorney, the appropriate county agency and, if the report is made by a hospital, the hospital.

Substance-Exposed Infants
This issue is not addressed in the statutes reviewed.

Screening Reports
Citation: Cons. Stat. Tit. 23 §§ 6334; 6368
If the complaint received does not suggest suspected child abuse, but does suggest a need for social services or other services or investigation, the department shall transmit the information to the county agency or other public agency for appropriate action. The information shall not be considered a child abuse report unless the agency to which the information was referred has reasonable cause to suspect after investigation that abuse occurred. If the agency has reasonable cause to suspect that abuse occurred, the agency shall notify the department, and the initial complaint shall be considered to have been a child abuse report.

Upon receipt of each report of suspected child abuse, the county agency shall immediately commence an appropriate investigation and see the child immediately if emergency protective custody is required or if it cannot be determined from the report whether emergency protective custody is needed. Otherwise, the county agency shall commence an appropriate investigation and see the child within 24 hours of receipt of the report. The investigation shall include a determination of the risk of harm to the child or children if they are to remain in the existing home environment, as well as a determination of the nature, extent, and cause of any condition enumerated in the report and any action necessary to provide for the safety of the child or children.

The investigation by the county agency to determine whether the report is "founded," "indicated," or "unfounded," and whether to accept the family for service, shall be completed within 60 days in all cases.

Puerto Rico
Reporting Procedures
Individual Responsibility
Citation: Ann. Laws Tit. 8, § 446

Any person who has knowledge of or suspects that a child may be a victim abuse or neglect, or is at risk of becoming a victim, must report to the hotline of the Department of the Family, the police, or the local office of the department.

Every processor of film or photographs who has knowledge of or observes any motion picture, photograph, videotape, negatives, or slides that depict a minor involved in a sexual activity must make a report.

Mandated reporters must complete a form furnished by the department within 48 hours after the oral report. The written report shall be sent to the central register.

Content of Reports
Citation: Ann. Laws Tit. 8, § 446

Reports shall contain, but not be limited to, all information that confirms the abuse.

Every motion picture, photograph, videotape, negative, or slide that shows a minor involved in a sexual activity shall be delivered to the nearest police station.

Special Reporting Procedures
Suspicious Deaths
Citation: Ann. Laws Tit. 8, § 446

Mandated reporters who have knowledge of or suspect that a minor has died as a result of abuse or neglect shall report that fact to the police or the hotline of the department.

Substance-Exposed Infants

This issue is not addressed in the statutes reviewed.

Screening Reports
Citation: Ann. Laws Tit. 8, § 444a

The department shall be responsible for investigating and attending to situations of abuse, institutional abuse, neglect, and/or institutional neglect. Likewise, it shall be responsible for instituting programs for the prevention, identification, investigation, and provision of the necessary services, pursuant to the public policy established in this chapter and the needs of minors and their families in any situation of abuse, institutional abuse, neglect, and/or institutional neglect.

The department shall investigate, order, or refer for investigation referrals of abuse, institutional abuse, neglect, and/or institutional neglect, making use, for this purpose, of all procedures, services, and means required to guarantee the most expeditious and effective attention to such investigations.

Rhode Island

Reporting Procedures

Individual Responsibility

Citation: Gen. Laws §§ 40-11-3; 40-11-6

Any person who has reasonable cause to know or suspect that a child has been abused, neglected, or sexually abused by another child shall report the information within 24 hours to the Department of Children, Youth and Families.

A physician or registered nurse practitioner who has cause to suspect that a child is abused or determines that a child under age 12 is suffering from any sexually transmitted disease shall report his or her suspicions to the department. An immediate oral report shall be made by telephone or otherwise, to both the department and law enforcement agency, and shall be followed by a report, in writing, to the department and law enforcement agency explaining the extent and nature of the abuse or neglect the child is alleged to have suffered.

Content of Reports

Citation: Gen. Laws § 40-11-6

A written report shall follow the oral report. The written report will explain the extent and nature of the abuse or neglect the child is alleged to have suffered.

Special Reporting Procedures

Suspicious Deaths

Citation: Gen. Laws § 40-11-3.1

Any mandated reporter who has reasonable cause to know or suspect that a child has died as a result of child abuse or neglect shall immediately report that information to the department, which shall cause the report to be investigated immediately. Upon receipt of the report, the department shall immediately refer the information to the local law enforcement agency or the State police as well as to the office of the medical examiner.

The office of the medical examiner shall investigate the report and communicate its preliminary findings, orally within 72 hours, and in writing within 7 working days, to the appropriate law enforcement agency, to the department, and if the person who made the report is an employee or a member of the staff of a hospital, to the hospital.

Substance-Exposed Infants

This issue is not addressed in the statutes reviewed.

Screening Reports

Citation: Gen. Laws § 40-11-7;

Admin. Rules 500.0010; 500.0015; 500.0070; 500.0085

The Department of Children, Youth and Families shall investigate each report to determine the circumstances surrounding the alleged abuse or neglect and its cause. The investigation shall include personal contact with the child named in the report and any other children in the same household.

In regulation: The department has established criteria for accepting or rejecting a child abuse/neglect report for investigation. The circumstances reported, if true, must constitute child abuse or neglect as defined by statute. There must be reasonable cause to believe that abuse/neglect circumstances exist.

Intake workers initially set the response priority for each referral of child abuse or neglect. Response priorities delineate the time limit for the intake workers to process the child protective services (CPS) report and for the initiation of an investigation. Response priorities are categorized into three types:

- Emergency Response: The CPS report must be processed within 10 minutes after the call is completed. A child protection investigator (CPI) must respond to the report within 10 minutes of assignment.
- Immediate Response: The CPS report must be processed within 1 hour after the call is completed. A CPI must respond to the report within the shift in which the call was received.
- Routine Response: The CPS report must be processed within 1 hour after the call is completed. A CPI must respond to the report within 24 hours of assignment. Routine Response criteria are used for all other reports in which there is minimal risk of harm to the child.

Assessment of risk is the process by which a CPI determines the current safety of a child and the prospects of future harm through child abuse or neglect. This assessment process is the focal point of each investigation and is the basis of most investigative decisions. It is an ongoing process that should occur each time a new piece of evidence/ information is obtained. Failure to make a thorough and up-to-date assessment could later jeopardize the safety of the child.

A notification will be made to a person who is alleged to have perpetrated abuse and/or neglect upon a child, to inform that person whether the department's CPS investigation will be ''indicated'' or ''unfounded,'' and to identify the allegations that have been ''indicated'' or ''unfounded.''

South Carolina
Reporting Procedures
Individual Responsibility
Citation: Ann. Code § 63-7-310

A mandated reporter shall report to the Department of Social Services or a law enforcement agency when the reporter has reason to believe that a child may have been abused or neglected.

The report is made to a law enforcement agency when abuse is committed by someone other than a person responsible for the child's welfare.

Reports may be made orally by telephone or otherwise to the county Department of Social Services or to a law enforcement agency in the county where the child resides or is found.

Content of Reports
Citation: Ann. Code § 63-7-310

Reports must include the identity of the reporter, which is kept confidential.

Special Reporting Procedures
Suspicious Deaths
Citation: Ann. Code § 63-7-310

A mandated reporter who has reason to believe that a child has died as a result of abuse or neglect shall report the information to the appropriate medical examiner or coroner.

The medical examiner or coroner shall accept the report for investigation and shall report his or her findings to the appropriate law enforcement agency, circuit solicitor's office, the county Department of Social Services, and if the institution making a report is a hospital, to the hospital.

Substance-Exposed Infants

This issue is not addressed in the statutes reviewed.

Screening Reports

Citation: Ann. Code §§ 63-7-340; 63-7-350; 63-7-910; 63-7-920; 63-7-930

When a report is referred to the department for an investigation, the department must determine whether previous reports have been made regarding the same child or the same subject of the report.

If the department does not conduct an investigation, the department must make a record of the report and classify the record as a Category IV unfounded report. The department and law enforcement are authorized to use information from the report for purposes of assessing risk and safety if additional contacts are made concerning the child, the family, or the subject of the report.

The department may maintain a toll-free number available to persons throughout the State for the reporting of known or suspected cases of child abuse or neglect.

Within 24 hours of the receipt of a report of suspected child abuse or neglect, the department must begin an appropriate and thorough investigation to determine whether a report of suspected child abuse or neglect is ''indicated'' or ''unfounded.'' The finding must be made no later than 45 days from the receipt of the report.

The department must furnish to parents or guardians on a standardized form the following information as soon as reasonably possible after commencing the investigation:

- The allegations being investigated
- Whether the person's name has been recorded by the department as a suspected perpetrator of abuse or neglect
- How information provided by the parent or guardian may be used
- The possible outcomes of the investigation

Reports of child abuse and neglect must be classified in the department's data system and records in one of three categories: suspected, unfounded, or indicated. All initial reports must be considered suspected. Reports must be maintained in the category of suspected for no more than 60 days after the report was received. By the end of the 60-day time period, suspected reports must be classified as either unfounded or indicated based on the investigation.

Indicated findings must be based upon a finding of the facts available to the department that there is a preponderance of evidence that the child is an abused or neglected child. All reports that are not indicated at the conclusion of the investigation and all records of information for which an investigation was not conducted must be classified as unfounded. Unfounded reports must be further classified as Category I, Category II, Category III, or Category IV:

- Category I unfounded reports are those in which abuse and neglect were ruled out following the investigation. A report falls in this category if evidence of abuse or neglect as defined in this chapter was not found regardless of whether the family had other problems or was in need of services.
- Category II unfounded reports are those in which the investigation did not produce a preponderance of evidence that the child is an abused or neglected child.
- Category III unfounded reports are those in which an investigation could not be completed because the department was unable to locate the child or family or for some other compelling reason.

- Category IV unfounded reports are records of information received pursuant to § 63-7-350 but were not investigated by the department.

South Dakota
Reporting Procedures
Individual Responsibility
Citation: Ann. Laws § 26-8A-8

Reports required from mandated reporters shall be made immediately orally by telephone or otherwise to the State's attorney, the Department of Social Services, or a law enforcement officer.

Content of Reports
Citation: Ann. Laws § 26-8A-10

The report to the department shall include:

- The child's name, address, date, and place of birth
- The name and address of the child's parents, guardian, custodian, or responsible persons
- The date of the report
- Suspected or proven instances of abuse

Special Reporting Procedures
Suspicious Deaths
Citation: Ann. Laws § 26-8A-4

Any person who has reasonable cause to suspect that a child has died as a result of abuse or neglect shall report that information to the medical examiner or coroner. Upon receipt of the report, the medical examiner or coroner shall cause an investigation to be made and submit written findings to the State's attorney and the Department of Social Services.

Substance-Exposed Infants

This issue is not addressed in the statutes reviewed.

Screening Reports
Citation: Ann. Laws §§ 26-8A-8; 26-8A-9; Admin. Code § 67:14:30:06

The State's attorney or law enforcement officers, upon receiving a report, shall immediately notify the Department of Social Services.

Upon receipt of a report, the department or law enforcement officers shall investigate. Investigating personnel may personally interview a child out of the presence of the child's parents, guardian, or custodian without advance notice or consent. If the investigation and report indicate that child abuse or neglect has occurred, the State's attorney shall take appropriate action immediately.

In regulation: The department shall provide for 24-hour receipt of reports of child abuse or neglect through agreements with law enforcement agencies, hospitals, courts, or other community-based human service agencies.

The department shall provide immediate or prompt investigation of situations in which a child is alleged to be in need of protective service by reason of a report to the department by a State's attorney, or by any person who shall or may make a report under the reporting laws.

If a report received by the department implicates involvement of a foster parent or person employed by the department, the department shall request an investigation by the State's attorney. The department shall offer protective service to the family and may make referral to the court of competent jurisdiction upon confirmation of need for child protection service.

Tennessee
Reporting Procedures
Individual Responsibility
Citation: Ann. Code §§ 37-1-403; 37-1-605

Any person who has knowledge of or is called upon to render aid to any child who is suffering from or has sustained any wound, injury, disability, or physical or mental condition shall report such harm immediately if the harm is of such a nature as to reasonably indicate that it has been caused by brutality, abuse, or neglect, or that, on the basis of available information, reasonably appears to have been caused by brutality, abuse, or neglect.

Any person with knowledge of the type of harm described above shall report it, by telephone or otherwise, to:
- The judge having juvenile jurisdiction over the child
- The Department of Children's Services, either by contacting a local representative of the department or by utilizing the department's centralized intake procedure
- The sheriff of the county where the child resides
- The chief law enforcement official of the municipality where the child resides

Every physician who makes a diagnosis of any sexually transmitted disease in a child who is age 13 or younger shall report the case immediately, in writing, to the Department of Health. If sexual abuse is suspected, the Department of Health will report the case to the Department of Children's Services.

Any person who knows or has reasonable cause to suspect that a child has been sexually abused shall report such knowledge or suspicion to the department. Each report of known or suspected child sexual abuse shall be made immediately to the local office of the department responsible for the investigation of reports, the judge having juvenile jurisdiction, or to the office of the sheriff or the chief law enforcement official of the municipality where the child resides.

Content of Reports
Citation: Ann. Code § 37-1-403

To the extent known by the reporter, the report shall include:
- The name, address, and age of the child
- The name and address of the person responsible for the care of the child
- The facts requiring the report
- Any other pertinent information

Special Reporting Procedures
Suspicious Deaths
Citation: Ann. Code §§ 37-1-403; 37-1-605

A mandated reporter who has reasonable cause to suspect that a child has died as a result of child abuse or neglect or sexual abuse shall report such suspicion to the medical examiner. The medical examiner shall accept the report for investigation and shall report the medical examiner's findings, in writing, to the local law enforcement agency, the appropriate district attorney general, and the department.

Substance-Exposed Infants

This issue is not addressed in the statutes reviewed.

Screening Reports

Citation: Ann. Code §§ 37-1-406; 37-1-606

The department shall be capable of receiving and investigating reports of child abuse 24 hours a day, 7 days a week. The county office shall make a thorough investigation promptly after receiving a report of harm. All representatives of the child protective services agency shall, at the initial time of contact with the subject of a child abuse and neglect investigation, advise the individual of the complaints or allegations made against him or her. If it appears that the immediate safety or well-being of a child is endangered, that the family may flee or the child will be unavailable, or the facts otherwise warrant, the department shall commence an investigation immediately, regardless of the time of day or night.

In cases involving child sexual abuse, the investigation shall be conducted by a child protective investigation team. In the event an immediate investigation has been initiated, the department shall notify the child protection team as soon as possible, and the team shall proceed with the investigation. Other cases of child abuse may be investigated by the team at the discretion of each individual team.

No later than 60 days after receiving the initial report, the department or team shall determine whether the reported abuse was indicated or unfounded, and report its findings to the department's abuse registry.

Texas

Reporting Procedures

Individual Responsibility

Citation: Fam. Code §§ 261.101; 261.103

Any person who has cause to believe that a child has been adversely affected by abuse or neglect shall immediately make a report.

A professional who has cause to believe that a child has been abused or neglected or may be abused or neglected shall make a report no later than 48 hours after the professional first suspects that the child has been or may be abused or neglected.

The report shall be made to a law enforcement agency, the department, the agency that operates or licenses the facility where the abuse or neglect occurred, or to the agency designated by the court to be responsible for the protection of children.

The report must be made to the department if the alleged or suspected abuse or neglect involves a person responsible for the care, custody, or welfare of the child.

Content of Reports

Citation: Fam. Code § 261.104

The person making a report shall identify, if known:

•   The name and address of the child

•   The name and address of the person responsible for the care, custody, or welfare of the child

•   Any other pertinent information concerning the alleged abuse or neglect

Special Reporting Procedures

Suspicious Deaths

Citation: Fam. Code § 261.105

The department or designated agency shall immediately notify the law enforcement agency of any report it receives that concerns the death of a child from abuse or neglect.

Substance-Exposed Infants

This issue is not addressed in the statutes reviewed.

Screening Reports

Citation: Fam. Code §§ 261.105; 301; 3015; Admin. Code Tit. 40, §§ 700.505; 511

If the department determines that the abuse or neglect does not involve a person responsible for the child's care, it shall refer the report to a law enforcement agency for further investigation. The department shall make a prompt and thorough investigation of a report of child abuse or neglect allegedly committed by a person responsible for a child's care.

The department shall assign priorities and prescribe investigative procedures for investigations based on the severity and immediacy of the alleged harm to the child. The department is required to:

- Immediately respond to a report that involves circumstances in which the death of the child or substantial bodily harm to the child would result unless the department immediately intervenes
- Respond within 24 hours to a report that is assigned the highest priority
- Respond within 72 hours to a report that is assigned the second highest priority

An investigation of a report that alleges that a child has been or may be the victim of a criminal offense, that poses an immediate risk of physical or sexual abuse that could result in the death of or serious harm to the child, shall be conducted jointly by the department and a peace officer.

The department shall establish a flexible response system to allow the department to make the most effective use of resources by investigating serious cases of abuse and neglect and by screening out less serious cases of abuse and neglect if the department determines that the child's safety can be assured without further investigation. The department may administratively close the less serious cases without providing services or by making a referral to another entity for assistance.

A case is considered to be a less serious case of abuse or neglect if the circumstances of the case do not indicate an immediate risk of abuse or neglect that could result in the death of or serious harm to the child.

In regulation: Child Protective Services (CPS) assigns priorities for reports of abuse and neglect based on the assessment of the immediacy of the risk and the severity of the possible harm to the child.

- Priority I reports concern children who appear to face an immediate risk of abuse or neglect that could result in death or serious harm.
- Priority II reports are all other reports of abuse or neglect that are not assigned a Priority I. CPS must:
- Respond immediately to a report of abuse or neglect that is assigned as a Priority I and involves circumstances in which the death of the child or substantial bodily harm to the child will imminently result unless the department immediately intervenes
- Respond within 24 hours a report of abuse or neglect that is assigned a Priority I, other than a report described above

- Respond within 72 hours to a report of abuse or neglect that is assigned a Priority II by initiating an investigation or by forwarding the report to specialized screening staff

The finding made in the investigation about each individual allegation of abuse/neglect that was identified at intake or during the investigation is assigned one of the following allegation dispositions:

- Reason-to-believe: Based on a preponderance of evidence, staff conclude that abuse or neglect has occurred.
- Ruled-out: Staff determine, based on available information, that it is reasonable to conclude that the abuse or neglect has not occurred.
- Moved: Before staff could draw a conclusion, the persons involved in the allegation moved and could not be located.
- Unable-to-determine: Staff conclude that none of the dispositions specified above is appropriate.
- Administrative closure: Information received after a case was assigned for investigation reveals that continued intervention is unwarranted.

Utah
Reporting Procedures
Individual Responsibility
Citation: Ann. Code §§ 62A-4a-403; 62A-4a-408
When a mandated reporter has reason to believe that a child has been subjected to abuse or neglect, or who observes a child being subjected to conditions or circumstances that would reasonably result in abuse or neglect, he or she shall immediately notify a peace officer, a law enforcement agency, or the Division of Child and Family Services.

Content of Reports
Citation: Ann. Code § 62A-4a-403
The report shall include the reporter's observations of the conditions or circumstances of the child that led to the suspicion that the child was being abused or neglected.

Special Reporting Procedures
Suspicious Deaths
Citation: Ann. Code § 62A-4a-405
Any person who has reason to believe that a child has died as a result of abuse or neglect shall report that fact to:

- The local law enforcement agency, who shall report to the county attorney or district attorney
- The appropriate medical examiner

he medical examiner shall investigate and report his or her findings to the police, the appropriate county attorney or district attorney, the Attorney General's Office, the division, and if the institution making the report is a hospital, to that hospital.

Substance-Exposed Infants
Citation: Ann. Code § 62A-4a-404
Any person who attends the birth or cares for a child and determines that the child, at the time of birth, has fetal alcohol syndrome or fetal drug dependency shall report that determination to the division as soon as possible.

Screening Reports
Citation: Ann. Code §§ 62A-4a-101; 62A-4a-409; Admin. Code R512-200-3

The division shall make a thorough preremoval investigation upon receiving either an oral or written report of alleged abuse, neglect, fetal alcohol syndrome, or fetal drug dependency, when there is reasonable cause to suspect that a situation of abuse, neglect, fetal alcohol syndrome, or fetal drug dependency exists. The primary purpose of the investigation shall be protection of the child.

The division shall make a written report of its investigation that shall include a determination regarding whether the alleged abuse or neglect is supported, unsupported, or without merit.

- ''Supported'': a finding by the division based on the evidence available at the completion of an investigation that there is a reasonable basis to conclude that abuse, neglect, or dependency occurred
- ''Unsupported'': a finding at the completion of an investigation that there is insufficient evidence to conclude that abuse, neglect, or dependency occurred
- ''Without merit'': a finding at the completion of an investigation by the division, or a judicial finding, that the alleged abuse, neglect, or dependency did not occur, or that the alleged perpetrator was not responsible for the abuse, neglect, or dependency

In regulation: The division will maintain a system for receiving referrals or reports about child abuse, neglect, or dependency. The system shall supply workers with a complete previous division history for each child, including siblings, foster care episodes, all reports of abuse, neglect, or dependency, treatment plans, and casework deadlines.

The division shall establish priority timeframes as follows:

- A Priority 1 response shall be assigned when the child referred is in need of immediate protection.
- A Priority 2 response shall be assigned when physical evidence is at risk of being lost or the child is at risk of further abuse, neglect, or dependency, but the child does not have immediate protection and safety needs, as determined by the Intake checklist. Intake will begin to collect information as soon as possible after the completion of the initial contact from the reporter and notify the child protection services (CPS) worker. The CPS worker then has 24 hours to initiate efforts to make face-to-face contact with the alleged victim.
- A Priority 3 response shall be assigned when potential for further harm to the child and the loss of physical evidence is low. The CPS worker will make face-to-face contact with the alleged victim within a reasonable period of time.
- A Priority 4 response shall be assigned when one or more of the following apply and there are no safety or protection issues identified:
- A juvenile court or district court orders an investigation where there are no specific allegations of abuse, neglect, or dependency.
    o There is an alleged out-of-home perpetrator (an alleged perpetrator who does not reside with or have access to the child) and there is no danger that critical evidence will be lost.
    o An agency outside the State of Utah requests a courtesy investigation, and the circumstances in the case do not meet the definition of a priority 1, 2, or 3.

Vermont
Reporting Procedures
Individual Responsibility
Citation: Ann. Stat. Tit. 33, §§ 4913; 4914

A mandated reporter who has reasonable cause to believe that a child has been abused or neglected shall report within 24 hours.

A report shall be made orally or in writing to the Department of Social and Rehabilitation Services.

Content of Reports
Citation: Ann. Stat. Tit. 33, § 4914

The report shall contain:

- The name and address of the reporter
- The names and addresses of the child and the child's parents or other persons responsible for the child, if known
- The age of the child
- The nature and extent of the child's injuries, including any evidence of previous abuse and neglect of the child or the child's siblings
- Any other information that the reporter believes might be helpful in establishing the cause of the injuries or the reasons for the neglect

Special Reporting Procedures
Suspicious Deaths

This issue is not addressed in the statutes reviewed.

Substance-Exposed Infants

This issue is not addressed in the statutes reviewed.

Screening Reports
Citation: Ann. Stat. Tit. 33, §§ 4912; 4915

Upon receipt of a report of abuse or neglect, the department shall promptly determine whether the report constitutes an allegation of child abuse or neglect. If the report is accepted as a valid allegation of abuse or neglect, the department shall determine whether to conduct an assessment or an investigation. The department shall begin either an assessment or an investigation within 72 hours after the receipt of a report, provided that it has sufficient information to proceed.

The decision to conduct an assessment shall include consideration of the following factors:

- The nature of the conduct and the extent of the child's injury, if any
- The accused person's prior history of child abuse or neglect, or lack thereof
- The accused person's willingness or lack thereof to accept responsibility for the conduct and cooperate in remediation

The department shall conduct an investigation when an accepted report involves allegations indicating substantial child endangerment. For purposes of this section, ''substantial child endangerment'' includes conduct by an adult involving or resulting in sexual abuse, and conduct by a person responsible for a child's welfare involving or resulting in abandonment, child fatality, malicious punishment, or abuse or neglect that causes serious physical injury. The department may conduct an investigation of any report.

''Substantiated report'' means that the commissioner has determined after investigation that a report is based upon accurate and reliable information that would lead a reasonable person to believe that the child has been abused or neglected.

Virgin Islands
Reporting Procedures
Individual Responsibility
Citation: Ann. Code Tit. 5, §§ 2533; 2534

When a mandated reporter has reasonable cause to suspect that a child has been subjected to abuse, sexual abuse, or neglect, he or she shall immediately make a report by telephone or otherwise to the the U.S. Virgin Islands Police Department (VIPD) or the Department of Social Welfare (department).

At the request of the department, an oral report shall be followed by a written report within 48 hours.

Content of Reports
Citation: Ann. Code Tit. 5, § 2534(b)

To the extent possible, the reports shall include the following information:
- The names and addresses of the child and the child's parents or other persons responsible for the child's care
- The child's age and sex
- The nature and extent of the injuries, sexual abuse, or neglect to the child or to other children in the same home
- The name and address of the person responsible for the injuries, sexual abuse, or neglect
- Family composition
- The source of the report, including the name, occupation, and contact information of the person making the report
- Any action taken by the reporter, including the taking of x-rays or color photographs
- Any other information that the reporter believes might be helpful

Special Reporting Procedures
Suspicious Deaths

This issue is not addressed in the statutes reviewed.

Substance-Exposed Infants

This issue is not addressed in the statutes reviewed.

Screening Reports
Citation: Ann. Code Tit. 5, § 2536

The department shall receive all reports of alleged child abuse, sexual abuse, or neglect; provide or arrange for emergency temporary care and protection of victims of alleged abuse; and within 24 hours of notification of an alleged case, commence a thorough investigation of the report.

The department shall, within 90 days of receipt of the initial report, prepare a progress report, including a determination that the report is founded or unfounded, a plan for rehabilitative or ameliorative treatment, services offered and accepted or refused, and the present status of the case. Within 7 days of termination of a case, a report indicating the final disposition shall be prepared.

The VIPD shall, on its own initiative where appropriate or at the request of the department, investigate reports of alleged child abuse, sexual abuse, or neglect, and shall convey the results of such investigation to the department and, where a petition or complaint has been filed, to the Superior Court. If the report of child abuse or neglect involves the acts or omissions of the department, the VIPD shall investigate such report and shall convey the results of such report to the Department of Law, which shall take appropriate action.

Virginia
Reporting Procedures
Individual Responsibility
Citation: Ann. Code § 63.2-1509

A mandated reporter who has reason to suspect that a child is an abused or neglected child shall report the matter immediately to the local department of the county or city wherein the child resides or wherein the abuse or neglect is believed to have occurred or to the toll-free child abuse and neglect hotline of the Department of Social Services.

If an employee of the local department is suspected of abusing or neglecting a child, the report shall be made to the court of the county or city where the abuse or neglect was discovered. Upon receipt of such a report by the court, the judge shall assign the report to a local department that is not the employer of the suspected employee for investigation or family assessment.

The initial report may be an oral report but such report shall be reduced to writing by the child abuse coordinator of the local department on a form prescribed by the State Board of Social Services.

Content of Reports
Citation: Ann. Code § 63.2-1509

A mandated reporter shall disclose all information that is the basis for his or her suspicion of abuse or neglect of the child and, upon request, shall make available to the child protective services coordinator and the local department that is the agency of jurisdiction any information, records, or reports that document the basis for the report.

Special Reporting Procedures
Suspicious Deaths
Citation: Ann. Code § 63.2-1503(D)-(E)

The local department shall upon receipt of a complaint, report immediately to the attorney for the Commonwealth and the local law enforcement agency and make available to them the records of the local department when abuse or neglect is suspected in any case involving the death of a child.

When abuse or neglect is suspected in any case involving the death of a child, the local department shall report the case immediately to the regional medical examiner and the local law enforcement agency.

Substance-Exposed Infants
Citation: Ann. Code § 63.2-1503(D)

The local department shall upon receipt of a complaint, report immediately to the attorney for the Commonwealth and the local law enforcement agency and make available to them the records of the local department when abuse or neglect is suspected in any case involving any felony or Class 1 misdemeanor drug offense involving a child.

Screening Reports
Citation: Ann. Code §§ 63.2-1504; 1505; 1506; 1516.01;
Admin. Code Tit. 22, § 40-705-10

The department shall implement a child protective services differential response system that will allow local departments to respond to valid reports of child abuse or neglect by conducting either an investigation or a family assessment.

An investigation will determine:

- The immediate safety needs of the child
- Risk of future harm to the child
- Whether abuse or neglect has occurred
- If abuse or neglect has occurred, who abused or neglected the child
- A finding of either founded or unfounded based on the facts collected during the investigation If the local department responds to the report or complaint by conducting an investigation, the local department shall make immediate investigation and determine within 45 days if a report of abuse or neglect is founded or unfounded. It will transmit a report to such effect to the Department of Social Services and to the person who is the subject of the investigation.

A family assessment will determine:

- The immediate safety needs of the child
- The protective and rehabilitative services needs of the child and family
- Risk of future harm to the child
- Alternative plans for the child's safety if protective and rehabilitative services are indicated and the family is unable or unwilling to participate

If the local department responds to the report or complaint by conducting an investigation, the local department shall make immediate investigation and determine within 45 days if a report of abuse or neglect is founded or unfounded. It will transmit a report to such effect to the Department of Social Services and to the person who is the subject of the investigation.

An immediate investigation will be commenced if, at any time during the completion of the family assessment, the local department determines that an investigation is required. The following valid reports of child abuse or neglect shall be investigated:

- Sexual abuse
- Child fatality
- Abuse or neglect resulting in serious injury
- A child taken into the custody by the local department
- Cases involving a caregiver at a child care center, school, hospital, or any institution

The local department shall, at the initial time of contact with the person subject to an investigation, advise such person of the complaints or allegations made against the person, in a manner that is consistent with laws protecting the rights of the person making the report or complaint.

In regulation: ''Founded'' means that a review of the facts shows by a preponderance of evidence that child abuse and/or neglect has occurred. ''Unfounded'' means that a review of the facts does not show by a preponderance of evidence that child abuse or neglect occurred.

Valid complaints or reports shall be screened for high priority based on the following:

- The immediate danger to the child
- The severity of the type of abuse or neglect alleged

- The age of the child
- The circumstances surrounding the alleged abuse or neglect
- The physical and mental condition of the child
- Reports made by mandated reporters

Washington
Reporting Procedures
Individual Responsibility
Citation: Rev. Code § 26.44.030; 26.44.040

When any mandated reporter has reasonable cause to believe that a child has suffered abuse or neglect, he or she shall make a report to the law enforcement agency or to the Department of Social and Health Services.

An oral report shall be made at the first opportunity but no longer than 48 hours after there is reasonable cause. The oral report must be followed by a report in writing.

When any person, in his or her official supervisory capacity with a nonprofit or for-profit organization, has reasonable cause to believe that a child has suffered abuse or neglect caused by a person over whom he or she regularly exercises supervisory authority, he or she shall report such incident, or cause a report to be made, to the proper law enforcement agency, if the person alleged to have caused the abuse or neglect is employed by, contracted by, or volunteers with the organization and coaches, trains, educates, or counsels a child or children or regularly has unsupervised access to a child or children as part of the employment, contract, or voluntary service. No one shall be required to report when he or she obtains the information solely as a result of a privileged communication.

An immediate oral report must be made by telephone or otherwise to the proper law enforcement agency or the Department of Social and Health Services and, upon request, must be followed by a report in writing.

Content of Reports
Citation: Rev. Code §§ 26.44.030; 26.44.040

The reports must contain the following information, if known:
- The name, address, and age of the child
- The name and address of the child's parents, stepparents, guardians, or other persons having custody of the child
- The nature and extent of alleged injuries, neglect, or sexual abuse
- Any evidence of previous injuries, including their nature and extent
- Any other information that might be helpful in establishing the cause of the child's death, injury, or injuries, and the identity of the alleged perpetrator or perpetrators

Special Reporting Procedures
Suspicious Deaths
Citation: Rev. Code § 26.44.030(4), (5)

If the report involves a child who has died:
- The department shall notify the proper law enforcement agency.
- The law enforcement agency shall report the incident in writing to the proper county prosecutor or city attorney and notify the department.

Substance-Exposed Infants
Citation: Rev. Code §§ 26.44.170; 26.44.200

When an investigation is made that includes an in-person contact with the person alleged to have committed abuse, there shall be a determination of whether it is probable that the use of alcohol or controlled substances is a contributing factor.

If, in the course of investigating an allegation relating to the manufacture of methamphetamine or possession of ephedrine or any of its salts or isomers or salts of isomers, pseudoephedrine or any of its salts or isomers or salts of isomers, pressurized ammonia gas, or pressurized ammonia gas solution with intent to manufacture methamphetamine, a law enforcement agency discovers that a child is present at the site, the agency shall contact the department immediately.

Screening Reports
Citation: Rev. Code §§ 26.44.030; 26.44.050

The department, upon receiving a report of alleged abuse or neglect involving a child who has died, physical injury inflicted upon a child by other than accidental means, or alleged sexual abuse, shall report the incident to the law enforcement agency. In emergency cases, where the child's welfare is endangered, the department shall notify the law enforcement agency within 24 hours. In all other cases, the department shall notify the law enforcement agency within 72 hours.

Upon receiving a report of alleged abuse or neglect, the department shall make reasonable efforts to learn the name, address, and telephone number of each person making a report. The department shall provide assurances of appropriate confidentiality of the identification of persons reporting under this section. If the department is unable to learn the information required under this subsection, the department shall only investigate cases in which:

- The department believes there is a serious threat of substantial harm to the child.
- The report indicates conduct involving a criminal offense that has, or is about to occur, in which the child is the victim.
- The department has a prior founded report of abuse or neglect with regard to a member of the household that is within 3 years of receipt of the referral.

For reports of alleged abuse or neglect that are accepted for investigation by the department, the investigation shall be conducted within timeframes established by the department in rule. In no case shall the investigation extend longer than 90 days from the date the report is received, unless a law enforcement agency or prosecuting attorney has determined that a longer investigation period is necessary. At the completion of the investigation, the department shall make a finding that the report of child abuse or neglect is founded or unfounded.

The department shall use a risk assessment process when investigating alleged child abuse and neglect referrals. The department shall present the risk factors at all hearings in which the placement of a dependent child is an issue. Substance abuse must be a risk factor. The department shall offer enhanced community-based services to persons who are determined not to require further State intervention.

West Virginia
Reporting Procedures
Individual Responsibility
Citation: Ann. Code §§ 49-6A-2; 49-6A-5

When a mandated reporter has reasonable cause to suspect that a child is abused or neglected, he or she shall report to the Department of Health and Human Resources immediately, and not more than 48 hours after suspecting abuse or neglect.

If the reporter believes the child has suffered serious physical or sexual abuse, a report shall be made to the State Police or any law enforcement agency.

Reports of child abuse and neglect shall be made immediately by telephone to the child protective service agency and shall be followed by a written report within 48 hours if so requested by the receiving agency.

Content of Reports
Citation: Ann. Code § 49-6A-2
The report shall contain the reporter's observations of the conditions or circumstances that led to the suspicion that a child was an abused or neglected child.

Special Reporting Procedures
Suspicious Deaths
Citation: Ann. Code § 49-6A-3
Any mandated reporter who has reasonable cause to suspect that a child has died as a result of child abuse or neglect shall report that fact to the appropriate medical examiner or coroner.

Upon the receipt of such a report, the medical examiner or coroner shall cause an investigation to be made and report the findings to the police, the appropriate prosecuting attorney, the local child protective service agency and, if the institution making a report is a hospital, to the hospital.

Substance-Exposed Infants
This issue is not addressed in the statutes reviewed.
Screening Reports
Citation: Ann. Code § 49-6A-9
Each local child protective service office shall:
- Receive all reports of children known or suspected to be abused or neglected on a 24-hour, 7-day-a-week basis
- Provide or arrange for emergency children's services to be available at all times
- Upon notification of suspected child abuse or neglect, commence a thorough investigation of the report and the child's environment
- Respond immediately to all allegations of imminent danger to the physical well-being of the child or of serious physical abuse
- Within 72 hours, conduct a face-to-face interview with the child or children, and develop a protection plan that may involve law enforcement officers or the court The local child protective service office shall be responsible for providing, directing, or coordinating the appropriate and timely delivery of services to any child suspected or known to be abused or neglected, including services to the child's family and those responsible for the child's care.

Wisconsin
Reporting Procedures
Individual Responsibility
Citation: Ann. Stat. § 48.981(3)

A mandated reporter who has reasonable cause to suspect that a child has been abused or neglected shall immediately inform, by telephone or personally, the county department or, in a county having a population of 500,000 or more, the Department of Children and Families, a licensed child welfare agency under contract with the department, the sheriff, or city, village, or town police department.

Content of Reports
Citation: Ann. Stat. § 48.981(3)

The report must include the facts and circumstances contributing to a suspicion of child abuse or neglect or of unborn child abuse or to a belief that abuse or neglect will occur.

Special Reporting Procedures
Suspicious Deaths
Citation: Ann. Stat. § 48.981(5)

A mandated reporter who has reasonable cause to suspect that a child has died as a result of abuse or neglect shall report that fact to the appropriate medical examiner or coroner. The medical examiner or coroner shall accept the report for investigation and shall report the findings to the appropriate district attorney, the department, and if the institution making the report initially is a hospital, to the hospital.

Substance-Exposed Infants

This issue is not addressed in the statutes reviewed.

Screening Reports
Citation: Ann. Stat. § 48.981(3)

The sheriff or police department may refer to the department a report in which a person who is not a caregiver is suspected of abuse or of threatened abuse of a child. The department shall, within 12 hours, refer to the sheriff or police department all cases of suspected or threatened abuse reported to it.

If the report is of suspected or threatened abuse, the sheriff or police department and the department shall coordinate the planning and execution of the investigation of the report.

If the sheriff or police department determines that criminal action is necessary, the sheriff or police department shall refer the case to the district attorney for criminal prosecution. Within 24 hours after receiving a report, the agency shall evaluate the report to determine whether there is reason to suspect that a caregiver has abused or neglected the child, has threatened the child with abuse or neglect, or failed to prevent the suspected or threatened abuse or neglect. If the agency makes such a determination, or cannot determine who abused or neglected the child, within 24 hours after receiving the report, the agency shall initiate a diligent investigation to determine if the child is in need of protection or services.

If the investigation is of suspected or threatened child abuse or neglect by a caregiver who continues to have access to the child, or of a report that does not disclose who is suspected of the child abuse or neglect, the investigation shall also include observation of or an interview with the child, or both, and, if possible, an interview with the child's parents, guardian, or legal custodian. The department shall determine, within 60 days after receipt of a report, whether abuse or neglect has occurred or is likely to occur. The determination shall be based on a preponderance of evidence.

Immediately after receiving a report, the county department shall evaluate the report to determine whether there is reason to suspect that a caregiver has abused or neglected the child, has threatened the child with abuse or neglect, or has facilitated or failed to take action to prevent the suspected or threatened abuse or neglect. If the agency determines that a caregiver is suspected of abuse or neglect or of threatened abuse or neglect of the child, or that a caregiver is suspected of facilitating or failing to take action to prevent the suspected or threatened abuse or neglect of the child, or cannot determine who abused or neglected the child, it will, within 24 hours after receiving the report, initiate a diligent investigation to determine if the child is in need of protection or services. If the agency determines that a person who is not a caregiver is suspected of abuse or of threatened abuse, the agency may initiate a diligent investigation to determine if the child is in need or protection or services.

The county department shall determine, within 60 days after receipt of a report, whether abuse or neglect has occurred or is likely to occur. The determination shall be based on a preponderance of evidence produced by the investigation. In making a determination that emotional damage has occurred, the county department shall give due regard to the culture of the subjects.

Wyoming
Reporting Procedures
Individual Responsibility
Citation: Ann. Stat. § 14-3-205
Any person who knows or has reasonable cause to believe that a child has been abused or neglected shall immediately report it to the child protective agency or local law enforcement agency.
Content of Reports
Citation: Ann. Stat. § 14-3-206
The report shall provide to law enforcement or the local child protective agency the following, to the extent available:
- The name, age, and address of the child
- The name and address of any person responsible for the child's care
- The nature and extent of the child's condition
- The basis of the reporter's knowledge
- The names and conditions of any other children relevant to the report
- Any evidence of previous injuries to the child
- Photographs, videos, and x-rays with the identification of the person who created the evidence and the date the evidence was created
Special Reporting Procedures
Suspicious Deaths
Citation: Ann. Stat. § 14-3-207
Any person who knows or has reasonable cause to suspect that a child has died as a result of abuse or neglect shall report to the appropriate coroner. The coroner shall investigate the report and submit his or her findings in writing to the law enforcement agency, the appropriate district attorney, and the local child protective agency.
Substance-Exposed Infants
This issue is not addressed in the statutes reviewed.
Screening Reports
Citation: Ann. Stat. § 14-3-206; Wyo. Rules § 049-240-002
The State agency shall receive reports of child abuse or neglect 24 hours, 7 days a week.

In regulation: Reports of suspected child abuse or neglect shall be made to any field office of the Department of Family Services or to any law enforcement center at any time. All reports are screened to determine whether the allegations meet the statutory definitions of child abuse/neglect and are within the scope of Child Protective Services. The verification process will begin within 24 hours. The department shall check records, including the central registry, to obtain pertinent information, including past department involvement.

A safety assessment will be initiated within 24 hours and completed within 7 calendar days for all accepted reports to determine if the case is appropriate for investigation or assessment. Accepted reports where criminal charges appear unlikely, children do not appear to be in imminent danger, or removal from the home appears unlikely may be assigned for assessment. The case will be referred for investigation if the safety assessment indicates a child is in imminent danger.

The investigative process begins when a report is accepted. All investigations may be teamed with law enforcement. The appropriate law enforcement agency will be contacted for assistance and consideration of criminal investigation in the following types of cases:

- A child may have died as a result of abuse or neglect.
- Imminent danger, sexual abuse, or major injury to the child is suspected.
- The situation necessitates the removal of the child from the home.

A safety assessment shall be completed for each child and a safety plan initiated when appropriate. A risk assessment also shall be completed for each child.

Upon completion of an investigation of abuse or neglect, the department shall make a final determination in a written report as to whether a child was abused or neglected. This determination shall be based upon whether the information and evidence gathered during the investigation constitutes credible evidence of child abuse or neglect.

Allegations must be determined to be substantiated or unsubstantiated:

- When credible evidence of abuse or neglect has been determined, the allegation is substantiated.
- In the absence of credible evidence, the allegations and the investigation shall be unsubstantiated and the investigation closed. Services may be offered.

End Notes

[1] See Child Welfare Information Gateway's Mandatory Reporters of Child Abuse and Neglect:
www.childwelfare.gov/systemwide/laws policies/statutes/manda.cfm

[2] Alabama, Arizona, California, Colorado, Connecticut, Hawaii, Illinois, Iowa, Louisiana, Maryland, Massachusetts, Michigan, Minnesota, Mississippi, Nebraska, Nevada, New York, Pennsylvania, Rhode Island, and Washington.

[3] Georgia, Kansas, Kentucky, Maine, New Hampshire, North Dakota, Ohio, and West Virginia.

[4] The word approximately is used to stress the fact that States frequently amend their laws. This information is current through January 2009. The 31 States that provide procedures for reporting suspicious child deaths are Arkansas, California, Colorado, Connecticut, Florida, Illinois, Indiana, Kansas, Louisiana, Maine, Massachusetts, Michigan, Minnesota, Missouri, Montana, Nevada, New York, North Carolina, Ohio, Pennsylvania, Rhode Island, South Carolina, South Dakota, Tennessee, Texas, Utah, Virginia, Washington, West Virginia, Wisconsin, and Wyoming.

[5] 42 U.S.C. 5106a(b)(2)(A)(ii).

[6] Arizona, California, Hawaii, Illinois, Iowa, Kentucky, Louisiana, Maine, Massachusetts, Michigan, Minnesota, Missouri, Montana, Nevada, Oklahoma, Utah, Virginia, and Washington.

[7] See Child Welfare Information Gateway's Parental Drug Use as Child Abuse: www.childwelfare. gov/systemwide/laws

[8] For an overview of the process, see Child Welfare Information Gateway's How the Child Welfare System Works: www.childwelfare.gov/pubs/factsheets/cpswork.cfm

[9] See Child Welfare Information Gateway's Definitions of Child Abuse and Neglect: www.childwelfare.gov/systemwide/laws

[10] Alabama, Arizona, Arkansas, California, Connecticut, Florida, Georgia, Idaho, Illinois, Indiana, Kansas, Kentucky, Louisiana, Maryland, Massachusetts, Missouri, Montana, Nevada, New Hampshire, New Jersey, New Mexico, North Carolina, North Dakota, Ohio, Oklahoma, Oregon, Pennsylvania, Rhode Island, Texas, and Utah.

[11] Arizona, Delaware, Kentucky, Louisiana, Minnesota, Nevada, Oklahoma, Texas, Vermont, Virginia, and Wyoming.

[12] Alaska, Florida, Illinois, Iowa, Kansas, Louisiana, Maryland, Michigan, Minnesota, Mississippi, North Carolina, North Dakota, Texas, Washington, and Wyoming.

[13] Alaska, Connecticut, Florida, Iowa, Kentucky, Louisiana, Michigan, New Mexico, and Texas.

[14] See Child Welfare Information Gateway's Cross-Reporting Among Responders to Child Abuse and Neglect: www.childwelfare.gov/systemwide/laws. cfm

In: Reporting Child Abuse and Neglect
Editor: Henry J. Pervall

ISBN: 978-1-62100-157-7
© 2012 Nova Science Publishers, Inc.

Chapter 5

PENALTIES FOR FAILURE TO REPORT AND FALSE REPORTING OF CHILD ABUSE AND NEGLECT: SUMMARY AND STATE LAWS[*][1]

United States Department of Health and Human Services

Many cases of child abuse and neglect are not reported, even when mandated by law. Therefore, nearly every State and U.S. territory imposes penalties, often in the form of a fine or imprisonment, on mandatory reporters who fail to report suspected child abuse or neglect as required by law.[1] In addition, to prevent malicious or intentional reporting of cases that are not founded, many States and the U.S. Virgin Islands impose penalties against any person who files a report known to be false.

PENALTIES FOR FAILURE TO REPORT

Approximately 47 States, the District of Columbia, American Samoa, Guam, the Northern Mariana Islands, and the Virgin Islands impose penalties on mandatory reporters who knowingly or willfully fail to make a report when they suspect that a child is being abused or neglected.[2] Failure to report is classified as a misdemeanor in 39 States and American Samoa, Guam, and the Virgin Islands.[3] In Arizona, Florida, and Minnesota, misdemeanors are upgraded to felonies for failure to report more serious situations, while in Illinois and Guam, second or subsequent violations are classified as felonies.

Twenty States and the District of Columbia, Guam, the Northern Mariana Islands, and the Virgin Islands specify in the reporting laws the penalties for failure to report.[4] Upon conviction, a mandated reporter who fails to report can face jail terms ranging from 10 days

---

[*] This is an edited, reformatted and augmented version of the United States Department of Health and Human Services publication, dated December 2009.

[1] This material may be freely reproduced and distributed. However, when doing so, please credit Child Welfare Information Gateway.

to 5 years or fines ranging from $100 to $5,000. In seven States and American Samoa, in addition to any criminal penalties, the reporter may be civilly liable for any damages caused by the failure to report.[5]

PENALTIES FOR FALSE REPORTING

Approximately 28 States carry penalties in their civil child protection laws for any person who willfully or intentionally makes a report of child abuse or neglect that the reporter knows to be false.[6] In New York, Ohio, and the Virgin Islands, making false reports of child maltreatment is made illegal in criminal sections of State code.

Twenty States and the Virgin Islands classify false reporting as a misdemeanor or similar charge.[7] In Florida, Tennessee, and Texas, false reporting is a felony, while in Arkansas, Illinois, Indiana, Missouri, and Virginia, second or subsequent offenses are upgraded to felonies. In Michigan, false reporting can be either a misdemeanor or a felony, depending on the seriousness of the alleged abuse in the report. No criminal penalties are imposed in California, Maine, Montana, Minnesota, and Nebraska; however, immunity from civil or criminal action that is provided to reporters of abuse or neglect is not extended to those who make a false report.

Eleven States and the Virgin Islands specify the penalties for making a false report.[8] Upon conviction, the reporter can face jail terms ranging from 30 days to 5 years or fines ranging from $200 to $5,000. Florida imposes the most severe penalties:

In addition to a court sentence of 5 years and $5,000, the Department of Children and Family Services may fine the reporter up to $10,000. In six States the reporter may be civilly liable for any damages caused by the report.[9]

This publication is a product of the State Statutes Series prepared by Child Welfare Information Gateway. While every attempt has been made to be complete, additional information on these topics may be in other sections of a State's code as well as in agency regulations, case law, and informal practices and procedures.

Alabama
Failure to Report Ala. Code § 26-14-13
Any person who knowingly fails to make the report required by the reporting laws shall be guilty of a misdemeanor and shall be punished by a sentence of not more than 6 months imprisonment or a fine of not more than $500.
False Reporting
This issue is not addressed in the statutes reviewed.

Alaska
Failure to Report
Alaska Stat. § 47.17.068
A person who fails to comply with the laws requiring reports of child abuse or neglect or child pornography and who knew or should have known that the circumstances gave rise to the need for a report is guilty of a Class A misdemeanor.

False Reporting

This issue is not addressed in the statutes reviewed.

American Samoa
Failure to Report
Ann. Code § 45.2002(d)

Any person who willfully violates the provisions of subsection (a) [requiring certain persons to report]:

- Commits a Class A misdemeanor
- Is liable for damages proximately caused

False Reporting

This issue is not addressed in the statutes reviewed.

Arizona
Failure to Report
Rev. Stat. § 13-3620(O)

A person who violates this section requiring the reporting of child abuse or neglect is guilty of a Class 1 misdemeanor, except if the failure to report involves a reportable offense, in which case the person is guilty of a Class 6 felony.

False Reporting
Rev. Stat. § 13-3620.01

A person acting with malice who knowingly and intentionally makes a false report of child abuse or neglect, or a person acting with malice who coerces another person to make a false report of child abuse or neglect, is guilty of a Class 1 misdemeanor.

A person who knowingly and intentionally makes a false report that another person made a false report is guilty of a Class 1 misdemeanor.

Arkansas

Failure to Report
Ann. Code §§ 12-18-201; 12-18-202; 12-18- 206

A person commits the offense of failure to notify by a mandated reporter in the first degree if he or she:

- Is a mandated reporter under this chapter
- Has:
  - Reasonable cause to suspect that a child has been subjected to child maltreatment
  - Reasonable cause to suspect that a child has died as a result of child maltreatment
  - Observes a child being subjected to conditions or circumstances that would reasonably result in child maltreatment
- Knowingly fails to notify the Child Abuse Hotline of the child maltreatment or suspected child maltreatment Failure to notify by a mandated reporter in the first degree is a Class A misdemeanor.

A person commits the offense of failure to notify by a mandated reporter in the second degree if he or she:

- Is a mandated reporter under this chapter
- Has:
  - Reasonable cause to suspect that a child has been subjected to child maltreatment
  - Reasonable cause to suspect that a child has died as a result of child maltreatment
  - Observes a child being subjected to conditions or circumstances that would reasonably result in child maltreatment
- Recklessly fails to notify the Child Abuse Hotline of the child maltreatment or suspected child maltreatment

Failure to notify by a mandated reporter in the second degree is a Class C misdemeanor.

A person required to make a report of child maltreatment or suspected child maltreatment to the Child Abuse Hotline who purposely fails to do so is civilly liable for damages proximately caused by that failure.

False Reporting
Ann. Code § 12-18-203

A person commits the offense of making a false report under this chapter if he or she purposely makes a report containing a false allegation to the Child Abuse Hotline knowing the allegation to be false.

A first offense of making a false report under this chapter is a Class A misdemeanor. A subsequent offense of making a false report under this chapter is a Class D felony.

California

Failure to Report
Penal Code §§ 11166(c); 11166.01

Any mandated reporter who fails to report an incident of known or reasonably suspected child abuse or neglect is guilty of a misdemeanor punishable by up to 6 months in a county jail, by a fine of $1,000, or both. If a mandated reporter intentionally conceals his or her failure to report an incident known by the mandated reporter to be abuse or severe neglect, the failure to report is a continuing offense until an agency specified in § 11165.9 discovers the offense.

Any supervisor or administrator who violates § 11166(1) [that prohibits impeding others from making a report], shall be punished by not more than 6 months in a county jail, by a fine of not more than $1,000, or both.

Any mandated reporter who willfully fails to report abuse or neglect, or any person who impedes or inhibits a report of abuse or neglect, where that abuse or neglect results in death or great bodily injury, shall be punished by not more than 1 year in a county jail, by a fine of not more than $5,000, or both.

False Reporting
Penal Code § 11172(a)

Any person reporting a known or suspected instance of child abuse or neglect shall not incur civil or criminal liability as a result of any report unless it can be proven that a false report was made and the person knew that the report was false or was made with reckless disregard of the truth or falsity of the report.

Any person who makes a report of child abuse or neglect known to be false or with reckless disregard of the truth or falsity of the report is liable for any damages caused.

Colorado
Failure to Report
Rev. Stat. § 19-3-304(4)
Any mandatory reporter who willfully fails to report as required by § 19-3-304(1):
- Commits a Class 3 misdemeanor and shall be punished as provided by law
- Shall be liable for damages proximately caused

False Reporting
Rev. Stat. § 19-3-304(3.5), (4)
No person, including a mandatory reporter, shall knowingly make a false report of abuse or neglect to a county department or local law enforcement agency.

Any person who violates this provision:
- Commits a Class 3 misdemeanor and shall be punished as provided by law
- Shall be liable for damages proximately caused

Connecticut

Failure to Report Gen. Stat. § 17a-101a
Any person who is required to report who fails to make such report shall be:

- Fined not less than $500 nor more than $2,500
- Required to participate in an educational and training program pursuant to § 17a-101(d)

False Reporting
Gen. Stat. § 17a-101e(c)
Any person who knowingly makes a false report of child abuse or neglect shall be fined not more than $2,000, imprisoned for not more than 1 year, or both.

Delaware
Failure to Report
Ann. Code Tit. 16, § 914
Any person who violates § 903 of this title [that requires certain persons to report suspected child abuse or neglect] shall be liable for a civil penalty not to exceed $5,000 for the first violation and not to exceed $50,000 for any subsequent violation.

In any action brought under this section, if the court finds a violation, the court may award costs and attorneys' fees.

False Reporting
This issue is not addressed in the statutes reviewed.

District of Columbia

Failure to Report
Ann. Code § 4-1321.07

Any person required to make a report under the reporting laws who willfully fails to make such a report shall be fined not more than $300, imprisoned for not more than 90 days, or both.

False Reporting

This issue is not addressed in the statutes reviewed.

Florida

Failure to Report
Ann. Stat. § 39.205(1)-(2)

A person who is required to report known or suspected child abuse or neglect, and who knowingly and willfully fails to do so, or who knowingly and willfully prevents another person from doing so, is guilty of a misdemeanor of the first degree. Upon conviction, the person may be:

- Imprisoned for a term not to exceed 1 year
- Fined $1,000

Unless the court finds that the person is a victim of domestic violence or that other mitigating circumstances exist, a person who is 18 years of age or older and lives in the same house or living unit as a child who is known or suspected to be a victim of child abuse, neglect of a child, or aggravated child abuse, and knowingly and willfully fails to report the child abuse, commits a felony of the third degree. Upon conviction, the person may be:

- Imprisoned for a term not to exceed 5 years
- Fined $5,000

False Reporting
Ann. Stat. §§ 39.205(6); 39.206(1)

A person who knowingly and willfully makes a false report of child abuse, abandonment, or neglect, or who advises another to make a false report, is guilty of a felony of the third degree. Upon conviction, the person may be:

- Imprisoned for a term not to exceed 5 years
- Fined $5,000

In addition to any other penalty authorized by this section or other law, the Department of Children and Family Services may impose a fine, not to exceed $10,000 for each violation, upon a person who knowingly and willfully makes a false report of abuse, abandonment, or neglect of a child, or a person who counsels another to make a false report.

Georgia

Failure to Report Ann. Code § 19-7-5(h)

Any person or official required by law to report a suspected case of child abuse who knowingly and willfully fails to do so shall be guilty of a misdemeanor.

False Reporting

This issue is not addressed in the statutes reviewed.

Guam
Failure to Report
Ann. Code Tit. 19, § 13207
Any person required to report who fails to report an instance of child abuse that he or she knows to exist or reasonably should know to exist is guilty of a misdemeanor that is punishable by imprisonment for a term not to exceed 6 months, a fine of not more than $1,000, or both.

A second or subsequent conviction shall be a felony in the third degree.
False Reporting
This issue is not addressed in the statutes reviewed.

Hawaii
Failure to Report Rev. Stat. § 350-1.2
Any mandatory reporter who knowingly prevents another person from reporting, or who knowingly fails to provide information as required by the reporting laws, shall be guilty of a petty misdemeanor.
False Reporting
This issue is not addressed in the statutes reviewed.

Idaho
Failure to Report
Idaho Code § 16-1605(4)
Failure to report as required by the reporting laws shall be a misdemeanor.
False Reporting
Idaho Code § 16-1607
Any person who makes a report or allegation of child abuse, abandonment, or neglect knowing the report is false, or who reports or alleges the same in bad faith or with malice, shall be liable to the party or parties against whom the report was made for the amount of actual damages sustained or statutory damages of $2,500, whichever is greater, plus attorney's fees and costs of suit.

If the court finds that the defendant acted with malice or oppression, the court may award treble actual damages or treble statutory damages, whichever is greater.

Illinois
Failure to Report
Comp. Stat. Ch. 325, §§ 5/4.02; 5/4
Any physician who willfully fails to report suspected child abuse or neglect shall be referred to the Illinois State Medical Disciplinary Board for action in accordance with the Medical Practice Act of 1987. Any dentist or dental hygienist who willfully fails to report suspected child abuse or neglect shall be referred to the Department of Professional Regulation for action in accordance with the Illinois Dental Practice Act.

Any mandatory reporter who willfully fails to report suspected child abuse or neglect shall be guilty of a Class A misdemeanor for a first violation and a Class 4 felony for a second or subsequent violation.

Any person who knowingly and willfully violates any provision of this Section is guilty of a Class A misdemeanor for a first violation and a Class 4 felony for a second or subsequent violation.

If the person acted as part of a plan or scheme having as its object the prevention of discovery of an abused or neglected child by lawful authorities for the purpose of protecting or insulating any person or entity from arrest or prosecution, the person is guilty of a Class 4 felony for a first offense and a Class 3 felony for a second or subsequent offense (regardless of whether the second or subsequent offense involves any of the same facts or persons as the first or other prior offense).

False Reporting
Comp. Stat. Ch. 325, § 5/4

Any person who knowingly transmits a false report to the department commits the offense of disorderly conduct. Any person who violates this provision a second or subsequent time shall be guilty of a Class 3 felony.

Indiana
Failure to Report
Ann. Code § 31-33-22-1

A person who knowingly fails to make a report required by law commits a Class B misdemeanor.

A person who, in his or her capacity as a staff member of a medical or other institution, school, facility, or agency, is required to make a report to the individual in charge of the institution, school, facility, or agency, or his or her designated agent, as required by § 31-33-5-2, and who knowingly fails to make a report commits a Class B misdemeanor. This penalty is imposed in addition to the penalty imposed above.

False Reporting
Ann. Code § 31-33-22-3(a)-(b)

A person who intentionally communicates to a law enforcement agency or the department a report of child abuse or neglect, knowing the report to be false, commits a Class A misdemeanor. The offense is a Class D felony if the person has a previous unrelated conviction for making a report of child abuse or neglect knowing the report to be false.

A person who intentionally communicates to a law enforcement agency or the department a report of child abuse or neglect knowing the report to be false is liable to the person accused of child abuse or neglect for actual damages. The finder of fact may award punitive damages and attorney's fees in an amount determined by the finder of fact against the person.

Iowa
Failure to Report
Ann. Stat. § 232.75(1)-(2)

Any person, official, agency, or institution required to report a suspected case of child abuse who knowingly and willfully fails to do so is guilty of a simple misdemeanor.

Any person, official, agency, or institution required by § 232.69 to report a suspected case of child abuse who knowingly fails to do so, or who knowingly interferes with the making of such a report in violation of § 232.70, is civilly liable for the damages proximately caused by such failure or interference.

False Reporting
Ann. Stat. § 232.75(3)

A person who reports or causes to be reported to the Department of Human Services false information regarding an alleged act of child abuse, knowing that the information is false or that the act did not occur, commits a simple misdemeanor.

Kansas
Failure to Report
Ann. Stat. § 38-2223(e)

Willful and knowing failure to make a report required by this section is a Class B misdemeanor. It is not a defense that another mandatory reporter made a report.

Intentionally preventing or interfering with the making of a report required by this section is a Class B misdemeanor.

False Reporting
Ann. Stat. § 38-2223(e)

Any person who willfully and knowingly makes a false report pursuant to this section or makes a report that such person knows lacks factual foundation is guilty of a Class B misdemeanor.

Kentucky
Failure to Report
Rev. Stat. § 620.990(1)

Any person intentionally violating the provisions of this chapter shall be guilty of a Class B misdemeanor.

False Reporting
Rev. Stat. § 620.050(1)

Any person who knowingly makes a false report and does so with malice shall be guilty of a Class A misdemeanor.

Louisiana
Failure to Report
Children's Code art. 609; Rev. Stat. 14:403(A)(1)

Violation of the duties imposed upon a mandatory reporter subjects the offender to criminal prosecution.

Any person who is required to report the abuse or neglect or sexual abuse of a child and knowingly and willfully fails to do so shall be guilty of a misdemeanor and upon conviction shall be fined not more than $500, imprisoned for not more than 6 months, or both.

False Reporting
Children's Code art. 609; Rev. Stat. 14:403(A)(3)

The filing of a report, known to be false, may subject the offender to criminal prosecution.

Any person who reports a child as abused or neglected or sexually abused to the department or to any law enforcement agency, knowing that such information is false, shall be guilty of a misdemeanor and upon conviction shall be fined not more than $500, imprisoned for not more than 6 months, or both.

Maine
Failure to Report
Rev. Stat. Tit. 22, § 4009
A person who knowingly violates a provision of this chapter commits a civil violation for which a forfeiture of not more than $500 may be adjudged.
False Reporting
Rev. Stat. Tit. 22, § 4014(1)
Immunity from any criminal or civil liability for the act of reporting or participating in the investigation or proceeding is not extended in instances when a false report is made and the person knows the report is false. Nothing in this section may be construed to bar criminal or civil action regarding perjury.

Maryland
Failure to Report
This issue is not addressed in the statutes reviewed. False Reporting
This issue is not addressed in the statutes reviewed.

Massachusetts
Failure to Report
Gen. Laws Ch. 119, § 51A
Any mandatory reporter who fails to report shall be punished by a fine of not more than $1,000.
False Reporting
Gen. Laws Ch. 119, § 51A
Whoever knowingly and willfully files a frivolous report of abuse or neglect under this section shall be punished by a fine of not more than $1,000.
Effective July 1, 2010
Whoever knowingly and willfully files a frivolous report of child abuse or neglect under this section shall be punished by:
- A fine of not more than $2,000 for the first offense
- Imprisonment for not more than 6 months and a fine of not more than $2,000 for the second offense
- Imprisonment for not more than 2 1/2 years and a fine of not more than $2,000 for the third and subsequent offenses

Michigan

Failure to Report
Comp. Laws § 722.633(1), (2)

A mandatory reporter who fails to report as required is civilly liable for the damages proximately caused by the failure.

A mandatory reporter who knowingly fails to report as required is guilty of a misdemeanor punishable by one or both of the following:

- Imprisonment for not more than 93 days
- A fine of not more than $500

False Reporting
Comp. Laws § 722.633(5)

Any person who intentionally makes a false report of child abuse or neglect knowing that the report is false is guilty of a crime as follows:

- If the child abuse or neglect would not constitute a crime but would constitute a misdemeanor if the report were true, the person is guilty of a misdemeanor punishable by imprisonment for not more than 93 days or a fine of not more than $100, or both.
- If the child abuse or neglect reported would constitute a felony if the report were true, the person is guilty of a felony punishable by the lesser of the following:
  o The penalty for the child abuse or neglect falsely reported
  o Imprisonment for not more than 4 years or a fine of not more than $2,000, or both

Minnesota
Failure to Report
Ann. Stat. § 626.556, Subd. 6

A mandatory reporter who knows or has reason to believe that a child is neglected or physically or sexually abused, or has been neglected or physically or sexually abused within the preceding 3 years, and fails to report the abuse is guilty of a misdemeanor.

A mandatory reporter who knows or has reason to believe that two or more children not related to the perpetrator have been physically or sexually abuse by the same perpetrator within the preceding 10 years, and fails to report is guilty of a gross misdemeanor.

A parent, guardian, or caregiver who knows or reasonably should know that the child's health is in serious danger and who fails to report:

- Is guilty of a gross misdemeanor if the child suffers substantial or great bodily harm because of the lack of medical care
- Is guilty of a felony if the child dies because of the lack of medical care, and may be subject to one or both of the following:
  o Imprisonment for not more than 2 years
  o A fine of not more than $4,000

The law providing that a parent, guardian, or caregiver may, in good faith, select and depend on spiritual means or prayer for treatment or care of a child does not exempt a parent, guardian, or caregiver from the duty to report under this provision.

False Reporting
Ann. Stat. § 626.556, Subd. 5

Any person who knowingly or recklessly makes a false report under the reporting laws shall be liable in a civil suit for any actual damages suffered by the person(s) so reported and for any punitive damages set by the court or jury, plus costs and reasonable attorney fees.

Mississippi

Failure to Report
Ann. Code. § 43-21-353(7)

Anyone who willfully violates any provision of this section shall be, upon being found guilty, punished by a fine not to exceed $5,000, by imprisonment in jail not to exceed 1 year, or both.

False Reporting

This issue is not addressed in the statutes reviewed.

Missouri

Failure to Report
Ann. Stat. § 210.165(1)

Any person violating any provision of the reporting laws is guilty of a Class A misdemeanor.

False Reporting
Ann. Stat. § 210.165(2)-(3)

Any person who intentionally files a false report of child abuse or neglect shall be guilty of a Class A misdemeanor.

Every person who has been previously convicted of making a false report to the Division of Family Services and who is subsequently convicted of making a false report is guilty of a Class D felony and shall be punished as provided by law.

Montana

Failure to Report Ann. Code § 41-3-207

Any mandatory reporter who fails to report known or suspected child abuse or neglect or who prevents another person from reasonably doing so is civilly liable for the damages proximately caused by such failure or prevention.

Any mandatory reporter who purposely or knowingly fails to report when required or purposely or knowingly prevents another person from doing so is guilty of a misdemeanor.

False Reporting
Ann. Code § 41-3-203(1)

Anyone reporting any incident of child abuse or neglect as required by law is immune from any liability, civil or criminal, that might otherwise be incurred or imposed unless the person was grossly negligent, acted in bad faith or with malicious purpose, or provided information knowing the information to be false.

Nebraska
Failure to Report Rev. Stat. § 28-717
Any person who willfully fails to make any report of child abuse or neglect required by § 28-711 shall be guilty of a Class III misdemeanor.
False Reporting Rev. Stat. § 28-716
Any person participating in an investigation, making a report of child abuse or neglect, or participating in a judicial proceeding resulting from a report shall be immune from any liability, civil or criminal, that might otherwise be incurred or imposed, except for maliciously false statements.

Nevada
Failure to Report Rev. Stat. § 432B.240
Any person who knowingly and willfully violates the provisions of the reporting laws is guilty of a misdemeanor.
False Reporting
This issue is not addressed in the statutes reviewed.

New Hampshire
Failure to Report Rev. Stat. § 169-C:39
Anyone who knowingly violates any provision of the reporting laws shall be guilty of a misdemeanor.
False Reporting
This issue is not addressed in the statutes reviewed.

New Jersey
Failure to Report Ann. Stat. § 9:6-8.14
Any person knowingly violating the reporting laws, including the failure to report an act of child abuse having reasonable cause to believe that an act of child abuse has been committed, is a disorderly person.
False Reporting
This issue is not addressed in the statutes reviewed.

New Mexico
Failure to Report
Ann. Stat. § 32A-4-3(F)
Any person who violates the provisions of this section pertaining to the duty to report is guilty of a misdemeanor and shall be sentenced pursuant to § 31-19-1.

Upon conviction, the person shall be imprisoned in the county jail for a definite term that is less than 1 year, be fined not more than $1,000, or both at the discretion of the judge.
False Reporting
This issue is not addressed in the statutes reviewed.

New York

Failure to Report Soc. Serv. Law § 420

Any mandatory reporter who willfully fails to report as required shall be guilty of a Class A misdemeanor.

Any mandatory reporter who knowingly and willfully fails to report as required shall be civilly liable for the damages proximately caused by such failure.

False Reporting
Penal Law § 240.50(4)

A person is guilty of falsely reporting an incident in the third degree when, knowing the information reported, conveyed, or circulated to be false or baseless, he or she reports, by word or action, an alleged occurrence or condition of child abuse or maltreatment that did not in fact occur or exist to:

- The statewide central register of child abuse and maltreatment
- Any person required to report cases of suspected child abuse or maltreatment, knowing that the person is required to report such cases, and with the intent that such an alleged occurrence be reported to the statewide central register

Falsely reporting an incident in the third degree is a Class A misdemeanor.

North Carolina

Failure to Report Gen. Stat. § 7B-310

No privilege shall be grounds for any person or institution failing to report that a juvenile may have been abused, neglected, or dependent, even if the knowledge or suspicion is acquired in an official professional capacity, except when the knowledge or suspicion is gained by an attorney from that attorney's client during representation only in the abuse, neglect, or dependency case.

False Reporting

This issue is not addressed in the statutes reviewed.

North Dakota

Failure to Report
Cent. Code § 50-25.1-13

Any person required by this chapter to report or to supply information concerning a case of known or suspected child abuse, neglect, or death resulting from abuse or neglect who willfully fails to do so is guilty of a Class B misdemeanor.

False Reporting
Cent. Code § 50-25.1-13

Any person who willfully makes a false report, or provides false information that causes a report to be made, is guilty of a Class B misdemeanor unless the false report is made to a law enforcement official, in which case the person who causes the report to be made is guilty of a Class A misdemeanor.

A person who willfully makes a false report, or willfully provides false information that causes a report to be made, also is liable in a civil action for all damages suffered by the person reported, including exemplary damages.

Northern Mariana Islands

Failure to Report

Commonwealth Code Tit. 6, § 5315

Knowing or willful failure of any person to make a report pursuant to § 5313 shall, upon conviction, be punished by one or both of the following:

- Imprisonment for up to 1 year
- A fine of not more than $1,000

False Reporting

This issue is not addressed in the statutes reviewed.

Ohio

Failure to Report Rev. Code § 2151.99

Any person who fails to report suspected child abuse or neglect, as required by § 2151.421, is guilty of a misdemeanor of the fourth degree.

Any person, required to report by § 2151.421(A)(4) [requiring reports by clergy], who fails to report when knowing that a child has been abused or neglected and knowing that the person who committed the abuse or neglect was a cleric or another person other than a volunteer, designated by a church, religious society, or faith to act as a leader, official, or delegate on behalf of the church, religious society, or faith, is guilty of a misdemeanor of the first degree if the person who has failed to report and the person who committed the abuse or neglect belong to the same church, religious society, or faith.

The person who fails to report is guilty of a misdemeanor of the first degree if the child suffers or faces the threat of suffering the physical or mental wound, injury, disability, or condition that would be the basis of the required report when the child is under the direct care or supervision of another person over whom the offender has supervisory control.

False Reporting

Rev. Code § 2921.14

No person shall knowingly make or cause another person to make a false report alleging that any person has committed an act or omission that resulted in a child being abused or neglected.

Whoever violates this section is guilty of making or causing a false report of child abuse or child neglect, a misdemeanor of the first degree.

Oklahoma

Failure to Report

Ann. Stat. Tit. 10A, § 1-2-101(C)

Any person who knowingly and willfully fails to promptly report suspected child abuse or neglect or who interferes with the prompt reporting of suspected child abuse or neglect may be reported to local law enforcement for criminal investigation and, upon conviction thereof, shall be guilty of a misdemeanor.

False Reporting

Ann. Stat. Tit. 10A, § 1-2-101(D)

Any person who knowingly and willfully makes a false report pursuant to the provisions of this section or a report that the person knows lacks factual foundation may be reported to local law enforcement for criminal investigation and, upon conviction thereof, shall be guilty of a misdemeanor.

If a court determines that an accusation of child abuse or neglect made during a child custody proceeding is false and the person making the accusation knew it to be false at the time the accusation was made, the court may impose a fine, not to exceed $5,000 and reasonable attorney fees incurred in recovering the sanctions, against the person making the accusation. The remedy provided by this paragraph is in addition to the first paragraph above or to any other remedy provided by law.

Oregon
Failure to Report
Rev. Stat. § 419B.010(3)
A person who violates the reporting laws commits a Class A violation. Prosecution under this law shall be commenced at any time within 18 months after the commission of the offense.
False Reporting
This issue is not addressed in the statutes reviewed.

Pennsylvania
Failure to Report
Cons. Stat. Ch. 23, § 6319
A mandatory reporter who willfully fails to report as required commits a misdemeanor of the third degree for the first violation and a misdemeanor of the second degree for a second or subsequent violation.
False Reporting
This issue is not addressed in the statutes reviewed.

Puerto Rico
Failure to Report
This issue is not addressed in the statutes reviewed.
False Reporting
This issue is not addressed in the statutes reviewed.

Rhode Island
Failure to Report Gen. Laws § 40-11-6.1
Any mandatory reporter who knowingly fails to report as required or who knowingly prevents any person acting reasonably from doing so, shall be guilty of a misdemeanor and upon conviction shall be subject to a fine of not more than $500, imprisonment for not more than 1 year, or both.

In addition, any mandatory reporter who knowingly fails to perform any act required by the reporting laws or who knowingly prevents another person from performing a required act shall be civilly liable for the damages proximately caused by that failure.

False Reporting

Gen. Laws § 40-11-3.2

Any person who knowingly and willingly makes or causes to be made to the department a false report of child abuse or neglect shall be guilty of a misdemeanor and, upon conviction thereof, shall be fined not more than $1,000 or imprisoned for not more than 1 year, or both.

South Carolina

Failure to Report Ann. Code § 63-7-410

Any mandatory reporter or any person required to perform any other function under the reporting laws, who knowingly fails to do so, or a person who threatens or attempts to intimidate a witness, is guilty of a misdemeanor and, upon conviction, must be fined not more than $500, be imprisoned for not more than 6 months, or both.

False Reporting

Ann. Code § 63-7-440

It is unlawful to knowingly make a false report of abuse or neglect. A person who violates this section is guilty of a misdemeanor and, upon conviction, must be fined not more than $5,000, imprisoned for not more than 90 days, or both.

South Dakota

Failure to Report

Ann. Stat. §§ 26-8A-3; 26-8A-4; 26-8A-6; 26-8A-7

Any mandatory reporter who knowingly and intentionally fails to make the required report is guilty of a Class 1 misdemeanor. This provision includes:

- Reports that must be made to the coroner when the reporter suspects that a child has died as a result of abuse or neglect
- Reports required of hospital staff
- Reports that are required of staff of public or private schools

False Reporting

This issue is not addressed in the statutes reviewed.

Tennessee

Failure to Report Ann. Code § 37-1-412

Any person who knowingly fails to make a report required by § 37-1-403 commits a Class A misdemeanor.

A person believed to have violated this section shall be brought before the court. If the defendant pleads not guilty, the juvenile court judge shall bind the defendant over to the grand jury. If the defendant pleads guilty, the juvenile court judge shall sentence the defendant under this section with a fine not to exceed $2,500.

False Reporting

Ann. Code Ann. § 37-1-413

Any person who either verbally or by written or printed communication knowingly and maliciously reports or causes, encourages, aids, counsels, or procures another to report a false accusation of child sexual abuse, or false accusation that a child has sustained any wound, injury, disability, or physical or mental condition caused by brutality, abuse, or neglect, commits a Class E felony.

Texas

Failure to Report Family Code § 261.109

A person commits an offense if the person has cause to believe that a child's physical or mental health or welfare has been or may be adversely affected by abuse or neglect and knowingly fails to report in accordance with the reporting laws.

An offense under this section is a Class A misdemeanor, except that the offense is a State jail felony if it is shown on the trial of the offense that the child was a person with mental retardation who resided in a State-supported living center, the medical assistance program for persons with mental retardation (ICF-MR) component of the Rio Grande State Center, or a facility licensed under Chapter 252, Health and Safety Code, and the actor knew that the child had suffered serious bodily injury as a result of the abuse or neglect.

False Reporting
Family Code § 261.107

A person commits an offense if, with the intent to deceive, he or she knowingly makes a report of child abuse or neglect that is false. An offense under this subsection is:

- A State jail felony
- A felony of the third degree if the person has previously been convicted under this section

A person who is convicted of an offense under this section shall:

- Pay any reasonable attorney's fees incurred by the person who was falsely accused of abuse or neglect
- Be liable to the State for a civil penalty of $1,000

Utah

Failure to Report
Ann. Code § 62A-4a-411

Any person, official, or institution required to report a case of suspected child abuse, child sexual abuse, neglect, fetal alcohol syndrome, or fetal drug dependency who willfully fails to do so is guilty of a Class B misdemeanor.

Action for failure to report must be commenced within 4 years from the date of knowledge of the offense and the willful failure to report.

False Reporting

This issue is not addressed in the statutes reviewed.

Vermont

Failure to Report
Ann. Stat. Tit. 33, § 4913(f)

A person who violates the law requiring mandated reporters to report suspected child abuse or neglect shall be fined not more than $500.

A person who violates the reporting laws with the intent to conceal abuse or neglect of a child shall be imprisoned not more than 6 months, fined for not more than $1,000, or both.

False Reporting

This issue is not addressed in the statutes reviewed.

Virgin Islands

Failure to Report
Ann. Code Tit. 5, § 2539

Any person, official, or institution required by this subchapter to report a case of alleged child abuse, sexual abuse, or neglect, or to perform any other act, who knowingly fails to do so, shall be guilty of a misdemeanor and shall be fined not more than $500, imprisoned for not more than 1 year, or both.

False Reporting
Ann. Code Tit. 14, §§ 2146(c); 2144(a)

A person is guilty of falsely reporting an incident in the second degree when, knowing the information reported, conveyed, or circulated to be false or baseless, he or she reports, by word or action, to the Department of Human Services or Department of Health, an alleged occurrence of child abuse or maltreatment that did not, in fact, occur or exist. A person who is found guilty of reporting an incident in the second degree shall be:

*   Fined $5,000
*   Imprisoned for not less than 5 years

Virginia

Failure to Report
Ann. Code § 63.2-1509(D)

Any person required to report pursuant to this section who fails to do so within 72 hours of his or her first suspicion of child abuse or neglect shall be fined:

*   Not more than $500 for the first failure
*   Not less than $100 nor more than $1,000 for any subsequent failures

False Reporting
Ann. Code § 63.2-1513(A)

Any person age 14 or older who makes or causes to be made a report of child abuse or neglect that he or she knows to be false shall be guilty of a Class 1 misdemeanor.

Any person age 14 or older who has been previously convicted under this subsection and who is subsequently convicted of making a false report of child abuse or neglect shall be guilty of a Class 6 felony.

Washington

Failure to Report
Rev. Code §§ 26.44.080; 9A.20.021

Every person who is required to make a report pursuant to the reporting laws and who knowingly fails to make such a report, shall be guilty of a gross misdemeanor.

Every person convicted of a gross misdemeanor shall be punished by imprisonment in the county jail for not more than 1 year, a fine of not more than $5,000, or both.

False Reporting
Rev. Code §§ 26.44.060(4); 9A.20.021

A person who intentionally and in bad faith knowingly makes a false report of alleged abuse or neglect shall be guilty of a misdemeanor.

Every person convicted of a misdemeanor shall be punished by imprisonment in the county jail for not more than 90 days, a fine of not more than $1,000, or both.

West Virginia
Failure to Report Ann. Code § 49-6A-8
Any mandated reporter who knowingly fails to report as required, or knowingly prevents another person acting reasonably from doing so, shall be guilty of a misdemeanor, and upon conviction shall be subject to confinement in the county jail for not more than 10 days, a fine of not more than $100, or both.
False Reporting
This issue is not addressed in the statutes reviewed.

Wisconsin
Failure to Report Ann. Stat. § 48.981(6)
Whoever intentionally violates the reporting laws by failure to report as required may be **fined not more than $1,000, imprisoned for not more than 6 months, or both.**
False Reporting
This issue is not addressed in the statutes reviewed.

Wyoming
Failure to Report
This issue is not addressed in the statutes reviewed.
False Reporting
Ann. Stat. § 14-3-205(d)
Any person who knowingly and intentionally makes a false report of child abuse or neglect, or who encourages or coerces another person to make a false report, is guilty of a misdemeanor that is punishable by imprisonment for not more than 6 months, a fine of not more than $750, or both.

End Notes

[1] See Child Welfare Information Gateway's *Mandatory Reporters of Child Abuse and Neglect* at www.child welfare policies/statutes/manda.cfm.

[2] The word *approximately* is used to stress the fact that the States frequently amend their laws. This information is current through December 2009. Maryland, North Carolina, Wyoming, and Puerto Rico currently do not have statutes imposing penalties for failure to report.

[3] The States that do not use the misdemeanor classification for failure to report include Connecticut, Delaware, Massachusetts, Mississippi, New Jersey, Vermont, Virginia, and Wisconsin.

[4] Alabama, California, Connecticut, Delaware, Florida, Louisiana, Maine, Massachusetts, Michigan, Minnesota, Mississippi, New Mexico, Rhode Island, South Carolina, Tennessee, Vermont, Virginia, Washington, West Virginia, and Wisconsin.

[5] Arkansas, Colorado, Iowa, Michigan, Montana, New York, and Rhode Island.

[6] Arizona, Arkansas, California, Colorado, Connecticut, Florida, Idaho, Illinois, Indiana, Iowa, Kansas, Kentucky, Louisiana, Maine, Massachusetts, Michigan, Minnesota, Missouri, Montana, Nebraska, Oklahoma, Rhode Island, South Carolina, Tennessee, Texas, Virginia, Washington, and Wyoming.

[7] Arizona, Arkansas, Colorado, Illinois (disorderly conduct), Indiana, Iowa, Kansas, Kentucky, Louisiana, Michigan, Missouri, New York, North Dakota, Ohio, Oklahoma, Rhode Island, South Carolina, Virginia, Washington, and Wyoming.

[8] Connecticut, Florida, Louisiana, Massachusetts, Michigan, Oklahoma, Rhode Island, South Carolina, Texas, Washington, and Wyoming.

[9] California, Colorado, Idaho, Indiana, Minnesota, and North Dakota.

In: Reporting Child Abuse and Neglect
Editor: Henry J. Pervall

ISBN: 978-1-62100-157-7
© 2012 Nova Science Publishers, Inc.

Chapter 6

IMMUNITY FOR REPORTERS OF CHILD ABUSE AND NEGLECT: SUMMARY AND STATE LAWS[*][1]

United States Department of Health and Human Services

To be eligible to receive Federal grants under the Child Abuse Prevention and Treatment Act (CAPTA), States are required to establish provisions for immunity from liability for individuals making good faith reports of suspected or known instances of child abuse or neglect.[1]

IMMUNITY FOR MAKING REPORTS

All States, the District of Columbia, Puerto Rico, American Samoa, Guam, the Northern Mariana Islands, and the U.S. Virgin Islands provide some form of immunity from liability for persons who in good faith report suspected instances of child abuse or neglect under the reporting laws. Immunity statutes protect reporters from civil or criminal liability that they might otherwise incur. This protection is extended to both mandatory and voluntary reporters.[2]

The term "good faith" refers to the assumption that the reporter, to the best of his or her knowledge, had reason to believe that the child in question was being subjected to abuse or neglect. Even if the allegations made in the report cannot be fully substantiated, the reporter is still provided with immunity. There is a "presumption of good faith" in approximately 17 States, the District of Columbia, American Samoa, and Guam, which means that the good faith of the reporter is assumed unless it can be proven to the contrary.[3]

---

[*] This is an edited, reformatted and augmented version of the United States Department of Health and Human Services publication, dated December 2008.

[1] This material may be freely reproduced and distributed. However, when doing so, please credit Child Welfare Information Gateway.

ADDITIONAL PROVISION OF IMMUNITY

States may provide immunity not only for the initial report of abuse or neglect, but also for many of the actions that a reporter may take following the filing of a report. For example, approximately 36 States, the District of Columbia, American Samoa, and Guam provide immunity to a reporter who participates in any judicial proceedings that may arise.[4] Approximately 26 States provide immunity to a reporter for assisting with or participating in an investigation of allegations of maltreatment.[5]

Many States also provide immunity for actions taken by medical practitioners in connection with making a report of suspected child maltreatment. These actions may include:

- Taking any necessary photographs or x-rays [6]
- Taking a child into emergency protective custody [7]
- Disclosing medical records or other information pertinent to a case[8]
- Performing a medical exam on the child [9]
- Performing medically relevant tests [10]

LIMITATIONS TO IMMUNITY

In many States, immunity from civil or criminal liability is specifically not provided in cases in which it can be shown that the person making a report acted with malice or in "bad faith" or knowingly made a false report.[11] Minnesota and North Dakota specifically deny immunity from any civil or criminal penalties for mandated reporters who fail to make required reports. Alaska provides no immunity for persons who knowingly make an "untimely report." Persons who are the alleged perpetrators of the suspected abuse or neglect are specifically not provided immunity from prosecution in 16 States.[12]

This publication is a product of the State Statutes Series prepared by Child Welfare Information Gateway. While every attempt has been made to be as complete as possible, additional information on these topics may be in other sections of a State's code as well as agency regulations, case law, and informal practices and procedures.

Alabama
Ala. Code § 26-14-9 (LexisNexis through 2008 1st Spec. Sess.)

Any person, firm, corporation or official, including members of a multidisciplinary child protection team, quality assurance team, child death review team, or other authorized case review team or panel, by whatever designation, participating in making a good faith report in an investigation or case review authorized under this chapter or other law or department practice or in the removal of a child pursuant to this chapter or participating in a judicial proceeding resulting therefrom, shall, in so doing, be immune from any liability, civil or criminal, that might otherwise be incurred or imposed.

Alaska

Alaska Stat. § 47.17.050 (LexisNexis through 2008 Reg. Sess.)

Except as provided below, a person who, in good faith, makes a report under the reporting laws, permits an interview, or participates in judicial proceedings related to submission of reports is immune from civil or criminal liability that might otherwise be incurred or imposed for making the report or permitting the interview, except that a person who knowingly makes an untimely report is not immune from civil or criminal liability based on the delay in making the report.

A person accused of committing the child abuse or neglect is not immune from civil or criminal liability for the child abuse or neglect as a result of reporting the child abuse or neglect.

American Samoa

A.S. Code § 45.2012 (A.S. Bar 2003)

Any person participating in good faith in the preparation of a report or in a judicial proceeding held under this chapter, and any person responsible for taking photographs or x-rays or placing temporary protective custody of a child under this chapter, is immune from any liability, civil or criminal, that otherwise might result by reason of the reporting. For the purpose of any proceedings, civil or criminal, any person reporting child abuse; any person taking, or causing to be taken, photographs or x-rays; or any person who has legal authority to place a child in protective custody is presumed to have acted in good faith.

Arizona

Ariz. Rev. Stat. Ann. § 13-3620(J) (LexisNexis through 2008 2nd Reg. Sess.)

A person who furnishes a report, information, or records required or authorized under this section or a person who participates in a judicial or administrative proceeding or investigation resulting from a report, information, or records required or authorized under this section, is immune from any civil or criminal liability by reason of that action unless the person acted with malice or unless the person has been charged with or is suspected of abusing or neglecting the child or children in question.

Ariz. Rev. Stat. Ann. § 8-805(A) (LexisNexis through 2008 2nd Reg. Sess.)

Any person making a complaint, providing information, or otherwise participating in the program authorized by this article shall be immune from any civil or criminal liability by reason of such action, unless such person acted with malice or unless such person has been charged with or is suspected of abusing, abandoning, or neglecting the child or children in question.

Arkansas

Ark. Code Ann. § 12-12-517 (LexisNexis through 2008 1st Ex. Sess.)

Any person or agency required to participate and acting in good faith in making notification, taking photographs or radiological tests, or removing a child while exercising protective services, shall be immune to suit and to liability, both civil and criminal.

If acting in good faith, all other persons making notification shall be immune from liability.

Any publicly supported school, facility, or institution acting in good faith pursuant to § 12-12-510(a)(1)(2) shall be immune from liability.

California
Cal. Penal Code § 11172(a), (b) (LexisNexis through 2008 Ch. 765)

No mandated reporter shall be civilly or criminally liable for any report required or authorized by this article, and this immunity shall apply even if the mandated reporter acquired the knowledge or reasonable suspicion of child abuse or neglect outside of his or her professional capacity or outside the scope of his or her employment.

Any other person reporting a known or suspected instance of child abuse or neglect shall not incur civil or criminal liability as a result of any report authorized by law unless it can be proven that a false report was made and the person knew that the report was false or was made with reckless disregard of the truth or falsity of the report, and any person who makes a report of child abuse or neglect known to be false or with reckless disregard of the truth or falsity of the report is liable for any damages caused.

No mandatory reporter, nor any person taking photographs at his or her direction, shall incur any civil or criminal liability for taking photographs of a suspected victim of child abuse or neglect, or causing photographs to be taken of a suspected victim of child abuse or neglect, without parental consent, or for disseminating the photographs with the reports required by law. However, this section does not grant immunity from liability with respect to any other use of the photographs.

Any person who, pursuant to a request from a government agency investigating a report of suspected child abuse or neglect, provides the requesting agency with access to the victim of known or suspected instance of child abuse or neglect shall not incur civil or criminal liability as a result of providing that access.

Colorado
Colo. Rev. Stat. Ann. § 19-3-309 (LexisNexis through 2008 Supp.)

Any person, other than the perpetrator, complicitor, coconspirator, or accessory, who participates in good faith in making a report pursuant to the reporting laws, the facilitation of the investigation of such a report or a judicial proceeding resulting therefrom, the taking of photographs or x-rays, the placing in temporary protective custody of a child, or otherwise performing his or her duties or acting pursuant to law, shall be immune from any civil or criminal liability or termination of employment that otherwise might result by reason of such acts of participation, unless a court of competent jurisdiction determines that such person's behavior was willful, wanton, and malicious.

For the purpose of any proceedings, civil or criminal, the good faith of any such person reporting child abuse, any such person taking photographs or x-rays, and any such person who has legal authority to place a child in protective custody shall be presumed.

Connecticut
Conn. Gen. Stat. Ann. § 17a-101e(b) (LexisNexis through 2008 Supp.)

Any person, institution, or agency that in good faith makes, or in good faith does not make, a report shall be immune from any liability, civil or criminal, that might otherwise be incurred or imposed and shall have the same immunity with respect to any judicial proceeding that results from such report provided such person did not perpetrate or cause such abuse or neglect.

Delaware
Del. Code Ann. Tit. 16, § 908(a) (LexisNexis through 8-8-08)

Anyone participating in good faith in making a report or notifying police officers; performing a medical examination without the consent of those responsible for the care, custody, and control of the child; or exercising emergency protective custody in compliance with provisions of this chapter, shall have immunity from any liability, civil or criminal, that might otherwise exist, and such immunity shall extend to participation in any judicial proceedings resulting from the above actions taken in good faith.

This section shall not limit the liability of any health-care provider for personal injury claims due to medical negligence that occurs as a result of any examination performed pursuant to statute.

District of Columbia
D.C. Code Ann. § 4-1321.04 (LexisNexis through 10-22-08)

Any person, hospital, or institution participating in good faith in making a report pursuant to the reporting laws shall have immunity from liability, civil or criminal, that might otherwise be incurred or imposed with respect to making the report. Any such participation shall have the same immunity with respect to participation in any judicial proceeding involving the report.

In all civil or criminal proceedings concerning the child or resulting from the report, good faith shall be presumed unless rebutted.

Florida
Fla. Stat. Ann. § 39.203(1) (LexisNexis through 2008 Reg. Sess.)

Any person, official, or institution participating in good faith in any act authorized or required by the reporting laws or reporting in good faith any instance of child abuse, abandonment, or neglect to the department or any law enforcement agency shall be immune from any civil or criminal liability that might otherwise result by reason of such action.

Nothing contained in the reporting laws shall be deemed to grant immunity, civil or criminal, to any person suspected of having abused, abandoned, or neglected a child, or committed any illegal act upon or against a child.

Georgia

Ga. Code Ann. § 19-7-5(f) (LexisNexis through 2008 Reg. Sess.)

Any person or persons, partnership, firm, corporation, association, hospital, or other entity participating in making a report, or causing a report to be made, to a child welfare agency providing protective services or to an appropriate police authority pursuant to the reporting laws or any other law or participating in any judicial proceeding or any other proceeding resulting therefrom, shall, in so doing, be immune from any civil or criminal liability that might otherwise be incurred or imposed, provided such participation is made in good faith.

Any person making a report, whether required by reporting laws or not, shall be immune from liability.

Guam

Guam Code Ann. Tit. 19, § 13206 (LexisNexis through 5-18-07)

Any person, hospital, institution, school, facility, or agency participating in good faith in making a report or testifying in any proceeding arising out of an instance of suspected child abuse or neglect, the taking of photographs, or the removal or keeping of a child pursuant to § 13302 of the Child Protective Act shall have immunity from any liability, civil or criminal, that might otherwise result by reason of such actions.

For the purpose of any proceeding, civil or criminal, the good faith of any person required to report cases of child abuse or neglect pursuant to law shall be presumed.

Hawaii

Haw. Rev. Stat. § 350-3 (LexisNexis through 2008 Spec. Sess.)

Anyone participating in good faith in making a report pursuant to the reporting laws shall have immunity from any civil or criminal liability that might otherwise be incurred, imposed by, or resulting from making the report. Any such participant shall have the same immunity with respect to participation in any judicial proceeding resulting from such report.

Any individual who assumes a duty or responsibility pursuant to statute shall have immunity from civil liability for acts or omissions performed within the scope of the individual's duty or responsibility.

Idaho

Idaho Code § 16-1606 (LexisNexis through 2008 Reg. Sess.)

Any person who has reason to believe that a child has been abused, abandoned, or neglected and, acting upon that belief, makes a report of abuse, abandonment, or neglect as required by the reporting laws, shall have immunity from any liability, civil or criminal, that might otherwise be incurred or imposed. Any such participant shall have the same immunity with respect to participation in any judicial proceeding resulting from such report.

Any person who reports in bad faith or with malice shall not be protected by this section.

Illinois
Ill. Comp. Stat. Ann. Ch. 325, § 5/9 (LexisNexis through 9-12-08)

Any person, institution, or agency that, under the reporting laws, participates in good faith in making a report or referral; the investigation of such a report or referral; taking photographs and x-rays; retaining a child in temporary protective custody; or making a disclosure of information concerning reports of child abuse and neglect in compliance with chapter 325, sections 5/4, 5/4.2, or 5/11.1, as it relates to disclosure by school personnel--and except in cases of willful or wanton misconduct--shall have immunity from any liability, civil or criminal, that otherwise might result by reason of such actions.

For the purpose of any proceedings, civil or criminal, the good faith of any persons required to report or refer, or who are permitted to report, cases of suspected child abuse or neglect...shall be presumed.

Indiana
Ind. Code Ann. § 31-33-6-1 (LexisNexis through 2008 Reg. Sess.)

Except as provided in § 31-33-6-2, a person, other than a person accused of child abuse or neglect, who makes or causes to be made a report of a child who may be a victim of child abuse or neglect; is a health-care provider and detains a child for purposes of causing photographs, x-rays, or a physical medical examination to be made; makes any other report of a child who may be a victim of child abuse or neglect; or participates in any judicial or other proceeding resulting from a report that a child may be a victim of child abuse or neglect or relating to the subject matter of the report, is immune from any civil or criminal liability that might otherwise be imposed because of such actions.

Ind. Code Ann. § 31-33-6-3 (LexisNexis through 2008 Reg. Sess.)

A person who makes a report that a child may be a victim of child abuse or neglect or assists in any requirement of the reporting laws is presumed to have acted in good faith.

Ind. Code Ann. § 31-33-6-2 (LexisNexis through 2008 Reg. Sess.)

Immunity does not attach for a person who has acted maliciously or in bad faith.

Iowa
Iowa Code Ann. § 232.73 (LexisNexis through 2007 Supp.)

A person participating in good faith in making a report, photographs or x-rays; the performance of a medically relevant test pursuant to the reporting laws; or aiding and assisting in an investigation of a child abuse report pursuant to the reporting laws, shall have immunity from any civil or criminal liability that might otherwise be incurred or imposed. The person shall have the same immunity with respect to participation in good faith in any judicial proceeding resulting from the report or relating to the subject matter of the report.

''Medically relevant test'' means a test that produces reliable results of exposure to cocaine, heroin, amphetamine, methamphetamine, or other illegal drugs or combinations or derivatives of the illegal drugs, including a drug urine screen test.

Kansas
Kan. Stat. Ann. § 38-2223(f) (LexisNexis through 2007 Supp.)

Anyone who, without malice, participates in making a report to the secretary [of Social and Rehabilitation Services] or a law enforcement agency that relates to a suspicion a child may be a child in need of care, or who participates in any activity or investigation relating to the report, or who participates in any judicial proceeding resulting from the report, shall have immunity from any civil liability that might otherwise be incurred or imposed.

Kentucky
Ky. Rev. Stat. Ann. § 620.050(1) (LexisNexis through 2008 1st Ex. Sess.)

Anyone acting upon reasonable cause in making a report or acting in good faith shall have immunity from any liability, civil or criminal, that might otherwise be incurred or imposed. Any such participant shall have the same immunity with respect to participation in any judicial proceeding resulting from such report or action.

Louisiana
La. Children's Code art. 611 (LexisNexis through 2008 Reg. Sess.)

No cause of action shall exist against any:

- Person who in good faith makes a report, cooperates in any investigation arising as a result of such report, or participates in judicial proceedings authorized under the provisions of this chapter
- Caseworker who in good faith conducts an investigation, makes an investigative judgment or disposition, or releases or uses information contained in the central registry for the purpose of protecting a child

Such individuals shall have immunity from civil or criminal liability that otherwise might be incurred or imposed. This immunity shall not be extended to:

- Any alleged principal, conspirator, or accessory to an offense involving the abuse or neglect of the child
- Any person who makes a report known to be false or with reckless disregard for the truth of the report

Maine
Me. Rev. Stat. Ann. Tit. 22, § 4014 (LexisNexis through 5-1-08)

A person, including an agent of the department, participating in good faith in reporting under the reporting laws or participating in a related child protection investigation or proceeding, including, but not limited to, a multidisciplinary team, out-of-home abuse investigating team, or other investigating or treatment team, is immune from any criminal or civil liability for the act of reporting or participating in the investigation or proceeding.

Good faith does not include instances when a false report is made and the person knows the report is false. Nothing in this section may be construed to bar criminal or civil action regarding perjury or regarding the abuse or neglect that led to a report, investigation, or proceeding.

A person participating in good faith in taking photographs or x-rays pursuant to the reporting laws is immune from civil liability for invasion of privacy that might otherwise result from these actions.

In a proceeding regarding immunity from liability, there shall be a rebuttable presumption of good faith.

Maryland

Md. Code Ann. Fam. Law § 5-708 (LexisNexis through 2008 Reg. Sess.)

Any person who makes or participates in making a report of abuse or neglect under §§ 5-704, 5-705, or 5-705.1 or participates in an investigation or a resulting judicial proceeding, shall have immunity from civil liability or criminal penalty.

Massachusetts

Mass. Gen. Laws Ann. ch. 119, § 51A(g) (LexisNexis through 2008 Sess.)

No mandated reporter shall be liable in any civil or criminal action for filing a report under this section or for contacting local law enforcement authorities or the child advocate, if the report or contact was made in good faith, was not frivolous, and the reporter did not cause the abuse or neglect. No other person filing a report under this section shall be liable in any civil or criminal action by reason of the report if it was made in good faith and if that person did not perpetrate or inflict the reported abuse or cause the reported neglect. Any person filing a report under this section may be liable in a civil or criminal action if the department or a district attorney determines that the person filing the report may have perpetrated or inflicted the abuse or caused the neglect.

Michigan

Mich. Comp. Laws Ann. § 722.625 (LexisNexis through 11-21-08)

A person acting in good faith who makes a report, cooperates in an investigation, or assists in any other requirement pursuant to the reporting laws is immune from civil or criminal liability that might otherwise be incurred by that action.

A person making a report or assisting in any other requirement of the reporting laws is presumed to have acted in good faith.

This immunity from civil or criminal liability extends only to acts done according to this act and does not extend to a negligent act that causes personal injury or death or to the malpractice of a physician that results in personal injury or death.

Minnesota

Minn. Stat. Ann. § 626.556, Subd. 4 (LexisNexis through Minn. 2008 Legis. Serv., Ch. 361)

The following persons are immune from any civil or criminal liability that otherwise might result from their actions, if they are acting in good faith:

Any person making a voluntary or mandated report under the reporting laws or assisting in an assessment

Any person with responsibility for performing duties under this section; a supervisor employed by a local welfare agency; or the commissioner of an agency responsible for operating or supervising a licensed or unlicensed day care facility, residential facility, agency, hospital, sanitarium, or other facility or institution required to be licensed, a school, or a nonlicensed personal care provider organization

A representative or employee of any public or private school or facility who permits access by a local welfare agency, the Department of Education, or local law enforcement agency and assists in an investigation or assessment

A person who is a supervisor or person with responsibility for performing duties under this section employed by a local welfare agency, the commissioner of human services, or the commissioner of education complying with the reporting laws or any related rule or provision of law is immune from any civil or criminal liability that might otherwise result from the person's actions if the person is (1) acting in good faith and exercising due care, or (2) acting in good faith and following the information collection procedures established by law.

This subdivision does not provide immunity to any person for failure to make a required report or for committing neglect, physical abuse, or sexual abuse of a child.

Mississippi

Miss. Code Ann. § 43-21-355 (LexisNexis through 2008 1st Ex. Sess.)

Any attorney, physician, dentist, intern, resident, nurse, psychologist, social worker, family protection worker, family protection specialist, child care giver, minister, law enforcement officer, school attendance officer, public school district employee, nonpublic school employee, licensed professional counselor, or any other person participating in making a required report pursuant to the reporting laws or participating in a judicial proceeding resulting therefrom shall be presumed to be acting in good faith.

Any person or institution reporting in good faith shall be immune from any civil or criminal liability that might otherwise be incurred or imposed.

Missouri

Mo. Stat. Ann. § 210.135 (LexisNexis through 9-2-08)

Any person, official, or institution complying with the provisions of the reporting laws in making a report; taking color photographs and/or making radiologic examinations...; removing or retaining a child pursuant to statute; or cooperating with the division or any other law enforcement agency, juvenile office, court, or child-protective service agency of this or any other State; in any activities pursuant to statute or any other allegation of child abuse, neglect, or assault shall have immunity from any liability, civil or criminal, that otherwise might result by reason of such actions.

However, any person, official, or institution intentionally filing a false report, or acting in bad faith or with ill intent, shall not have immunity from any liability, civil or criminal.

Any such person, official, or institution shall have the same immunity with respect to participation in any judicial proceeding resulting from the report.

Montana

Mont. Code Ann. § 41-3-203(1) (LexisNexis through 11-7-08)

Anyone investigating or reporting any incident of child abuse or neglect, participating in resulting judicial proceedings, or furnishing hospital or medical records pursuant to the reporting laws, is immune from any civil or criminal liability that might otherwise be incurred or imposed, unless the person was grossly negligent, acted in bad faith or with malicious purpose, or provided information knowing the information to be false.

Nebraska
Neb. Rev. Stat. Ann. § 28-716 (LexisNexis through 2008 Spec. Sess.)

Any person participating in an investigation or making a report of child abuse or neglect required by § 28-711 or participating in a judicial proceeding resulting therefrom shall be immune from any civil or criminal liability that might otherwise be incurred or imposed, except for maliciously false statements.

Nevada
Nev. Rev. Stat. Ann. § 432B.160 (LexisNexis through 2008 Spec. Sess.)

Except as otherwise provided below, immunity from civil or criminal liability extends to every person who in good faith:

- Makes a report pursuant to the reporting laws
- Conducts an interview or allows an interview to be taken
- Allows or takes photographs or x-rays
- Causes a medical test to be performed
- Provides a record, or a copy thereof, of a medical test to an agency that provides child welfare services to the child, a law enforcement agency that participated in the investigation of the report made pursuant to § 432B. 220, or the prosecuting attorney's office
- Holds a child pursuant to § 432B.400 [pertaining to the temporary detention of a child by a physician], takes possession of a child pursuant to § 432B.630 [pertaining to the delivery of a newborn child to a provider of emergency services], or places a child in protective custody
- Performs any act pursuant to § 432B.630(2)
- Refers a case or recommends the fling of a petition pursuant to § 432B.380 [pertaining to the referral of a case to a district attorney for criminal prosecution]
- Participates in a judicial proceeding resulting from a referral or recommendation

The provisions above do not confer any immunity from liability for the negligent performance of any act pursuant to § 432B.630.

In any proceeding to impose liability against a person for making a report pursuant to the reporting laws or performing any of the actions listed above, there is a presumption that a person acted in good faith.

New Hampshire
N.H. Rev. Stat. Ann. § 169-C:31 (LexisNexis through 2008 Spec. Sess.)

Anyone participating in good faith in making a report pursuant to the reporting laws is immune from any civil or criminal liability that might otherwise be incurred or imposed. Any such participant has the same immunity with respect to participation in any investigation by the Division for Children, Youth, and Families or judicial proceeding resulting from such report.

New Jersey
N.J. Stat. Ann. § 9:6-8.13 (LexisNexis through 11-10-08)

Anyone acting pursuant to the reporting laws in making a report under the reporting laws shall have immunity from any civil or criminal liability that might otherwise be incurred or imposed. Any such person shall have the same immunity with respect to testimony given in any judicial proceeding resulting from such report.

New Mexico
N.M. Stat. Ann. § 32A-4-5(B) (LexisNexis through 2008 2nd Spec. Sess.)

Anyone reporting an instance of alleged child neglect or abuse, or participating in a judicial proceeding brought as a result of a report required by the reporting laws, is presumed to be acting in good faith and shall be immune from liability, civil or criminal, that might otherwise be incurred or imposed by the law, unless the person acted in bad faith or with malicious purpose.

New York
N.Y. Soc. Serv. Law § 419 (LexisNexis through 10-7-08)

Any person, official, or institution participating in good faith in making a report or the taking of photographs, the removal or keeping of a child pursuant to this title, or the disclosure of Child Protective Services information in compliance with child reporting laws, shall have immunity from any civil or criminal liability that might otherwise result by reason of such actions.

For the purpose of any civil or criminal proceeding, the good faith of any such person, official, or institution required to report cases of child abuse or maltreatment or providing a reporting procedure service shall be presumed-provided that person, official, or institution was acting in the discharge of their duties and within the scope of their employment, and that such liability did not result from the willful misconduct or gross negligence of such person, official, or institution.

North Carolina
N.C. Gen. Stat. § 7B-309 (LexisNexis through 2008 Reg. Sess.)

Anyone who makes a report pursuant to the reporting laws, cooperates with the county Department of Social Services in a protective services assessment, testifies in any judicial proceeding resulting from a protective services report or assessment, or otherwise participates in the program authorized by law is immune from any civil or criminal liability that might otherwise be incurred or imposed for such action, provided that the person was acting in good faith.

In any proceeding involving liability, good faith is presumed.

North Dakota
N.D. Cent. Code § 50-25.1-09 (LexisNexis through 2007 Supp.)

Any person, other than the alleged violator, participating in good faith in making a report, assisting in an investigation or assessment, furnishing information, in providing protective services, or who is a member of the child fatality review panel, is immune from any civil or criminal liability--except for criminal liability as provided for under penalties for failure to report and false reporting--that otherwise might result from reporting the alleged case of abuse, neglect, or death resulting from child abuse or neglect.

For the purpose of any civil or criminal proceeding, the good faith of any person who is required to report cases of child abuse, neglect, or death must be presumed.

Northern Mariana Islands
CNMI Code Tit. 6, § 5314 (1999)

Any person making a good faith report shall be immune from civil or criminal liability that might otherwise arise from such action.

Ohio
Ohio Rev. Code Ann. § 2151.421(G)(1)(a) & (2)(b) (LexisNexis through 9-1-08)

Except as provided in the law regarding false reports, anyone or any hospital, institution, school, health department, or agency participating in the making of reports under § 2151.421(A); anyone or any hospital, institution, school, health department, or agency participating in good faith in making reports under § 2151.421(B); and anyone participating in good faith in a judicial proceeding resulting from the reports shall be immune from any civil or criminal liability for injury, death, or loss to person or property that otherwise might be incurred or imposed as a result of making the reports or the participating in the judicial proceeding.

In any civil or criminal action or proceeding in which it is alleged and proved that participation in making a report under this section was not in good faith, or that participation in a judicial proceeding resulting from a report made under this section was not in good faith, the court shall award the prevailing party reasonable attorney's fees and costs, and if a civil action or proceeding is voluntarily dismissed, the court may award reasonable attorney's fees and costs to the party against whom the civil action or proceeding is brought.

Oklahoma
Okla. Stat. Ann. Tit. 10, § 7105 (LexisNexis through 9-1-08)

Any person, in good faith and exercising due care, participating in making a report pursuant to reporting laws or allowing access to a child by persons authorized to investigate a report concerning the child, shall have immunity from any civil or criminal liability that might otherwise be incurred or imposed. Any such participant shall have the same immunity with respect to participation in any judicial proceeding resulting from such report.

The good faith of any physician, surgeon, osteopathic physician, resident, intern, physician's assistant, registered nurse, or any other health-care professional in making a report pursuant to the reporting laws shall be presumed.

A child advocacy center that is accredited by the National Children's Alliance and its employees, who are acting in good faith and exercising due care, shall have immunity from civil liability that be incurred or imposed through participation in the investigation process and any judicial proceeding resulting from the investigation process.

Oregon
Or. Rev. Stat. Ann. § 419B.025 (LexisNexis through 2007 Reg. Sess.)

Anyone participating in good faith in making a report of child abuse and who has reasonable grounds for the making thereof shall have immunity from any civil or criminal liability that might otherwise be incurred or imposed with respect to the making or content of such report. Any such participant shall have the same immunity with respect to participating in any judicial proceeding resulting from such report.

Pennsylvania
Pa. Cons. Stat. Ann. Ch. 23, § 6318 (LexisNexis through 7-11-08)

A person, hospital, institution, school, facility, agency or agency employee that participates in good faith in making a report--whether required or not--cooperating with an investigation, testifying in a proceeding arising out of an instance of suspected child abuse, the taking of photographs or the removal or keeping of a child pursuant to § 6315 (relating to taking child into protective custody), and any official or employee of a county agency who refers a report of suspected abuse to law enforcement authorities or provides services under this chapter, shall have immunity from civil and criminal liability that might otherwise result by reason of those actions.

For the purpose of any civil or criminal proceeding, the good faith of a person required to report pursuant to § 6311 (relating to persons required to report suspected child abuse) and of any person required to make a referral to law enforcement officers under this chapter shall be presumed.

Puerto Rico
P.R. Laws Ann. Tit. 8, § 446(c) (LexisNexis through December 2006)

Information provided in good faith by any persons, officials, or institutions bound to report situations of abuse, institutional abuse, neglect, and/or institutional neglect of minors, as set forth in this chapter, may not be used against them in any civil or criminal procedure that may be initiated as a result of said action. Nor may the information so reported by school and hospital employees and by law enforcement officers, who are obliged to allow the department's intervention pursuant to the provisions of this section, be used against them.

Rhode Island

R.I. Gen. Laws § 40-11-4 (LexisNexis through 8-5-08)

Any person participating in good faith in making a report pursuant to the reporting laws shall have immunity from any civil or criminal liability that might otherwise be incurred or imposed. Any such participant shall have the same immunity with respect to participation in any judicial proceeding resulting from the report.

South Carolina

S.C. Code Ann. § 63-7-390 (LexisNexis through S.C. 2008 Legis. Serv., Act 361)
Effective June 28, 2008

A person required or permitted to report pursuant to the reporting laws or who participates in an investigation or judicial proceedings resulting from the report, acting in good faith, is immune from civil and criminal liability that might otherwise result by reason of these actions. In all such civil or criminal proceedings, good faith is rebuttably presumed.

Immunity extends to full disclosure by the person of facts that gave the person reason to believe that the child's physical or mental health or welfare had been or might be affected adversely by abuse or neglect.

South Dakota

S.D. Codif ed Laws § 26-8A-14 (LexisNexis through 2008 Sess.)

Any person or party participating in good faith in making a report or submitting copies of medical examination, treatment, or hospitalization records pursuant to the reporting laws is immune from any liability, civil or criminal, that might otherwise be incurred or imposed and has the same immunity for participation in any judicial proceeding resulting from the report.

Immunity also extends in the same manner to persons requesting the taking of photographs and x-rays pursuant to the reporting laws, to persons taking the photographs and x-rays, to child protection teams established by the Secretary of Social Services, to public officials or employees involved in the investigation and treatment of child abuse or neglect or making a temporary placement of the child pursuant to this chapter, or to any person who in good faith cooperates with a child protection team or the Department of Social Services in an investigation, placement, or treatment plan.

The provisions of this section or any other section granting or allowing the grant of immunity do not extend to any person alleged to have committed an act or acts of child abuse or neglect.

Tennessee

Tenn. Code Ann. § 37-1-410(a)(1), (4),(5)(A) (LexisNexis through 2008 Reg. Sess.)

If a health-care provider makes a report of harm, as required by § 37-1-403, and if the report arises from an examination of the child performed by the health-care provider in the course of rendering professional care or treatment of the child or if the health-care provider who is highly qualified by experience in the field of child abuse and neglect, as evidenced by special training or credentialing, renders a second opinion at the request of the department or any law enforcement agency, whether or not the health-care provider has examined the child, rendered care or treatment, or made the report of harm, then the health-care provider shall not be liable in any civil or criminal action that is based solely upon:

- The health-care provider's decision to report what the provider believed to be harm
- The health-care provider's belief that reporting the harm was required by law
- The fact that a report of harm was made
- The fact that the second opinion was requested and provided

Nothing in this subsection shall be construed to confer any immunity upon a health-care provider for a criminal or civil action arising out of the treatment of the child about whom the report of harm was made.

If absolute immunity is not conferred upon a person pursuant to the subdivision above, and if, acting in good faith, the person makes a report of harm, as required by § 37-1-403, then the person shall not be liable in any civil or criminal action that is based solely upon:

- The person's decision to report what the person believed to be harm
- The person's belief that reporting the harm was required by law
- The fact that a report of harm was made

Tenn. Code Ann. § 37-1-410(a)(5)(B), (6)-(8) (LexisNexis through 2008 Reg. Sess.)

Because of the overriding public policy to encourage all persons to report the neglect of or harm or abuse to children, any person upon whom good faith immunity is conferred shall be presumed to have acted in good faith in making a report of harm.

No immunity conferred pursuant to this subsection shall attach if the person reporting the harm perpetrated or inflicted the abuse or caused the neglect.

A person furnishing a report, information, or records as required, requested, or authorized under this part shall have the same immunity and the same scope of immunity with respect to testimony that person may be required to give or may give in any judicial or administrative proceeding or in any communications with the department or any law enforcement official as is otherwise conferred by this subsection upon the person for making the report of harm.

If the person furnishing a report, information, or records during the normal course of the person's duties as required or authorized or requested under this part is different from the person originally reporting the harm, then the person furnishing the report, information, or records shall have the same immunity and the same scope of immunity with respect to testimony the person may be required to give or may give in any judicial or administrative proceeding or in any communications with the department or any law enforcement official as is otherwise conferred by this subsection upon the person who made the original report of harm.

Texas

Tex. Family Code Ann. § 261.106 (LexisNexis through 2007 Reg. Sess.)

A person acting in good faith who reports or assists in the investigation of a report of alleged child abuse or neglect, or who testifies or otherwise participates in a judicial proceeding arising from a report, petition, or investigation of alleged child abuse or neglect, is immune from civil or criminal liability that might otherwise be incurred or imposed.

Immunity from civil and criminal liability extends to an authorized volunteer of the Department of Human Services or a law enforcement officer who participates at the request of the department in an investigation of alleged or suspected abuse or neglect or in an action arising from an investigation if the person was acting in good faith and in the scope of the person's responsibilities.

A person who reports the person's own abuse or neglect of a child or who acts in bad faith or with malicious purpose in reporting alleged child abuse or neglect is not immune from civil or criminal liability.

Utah
Utah Code Ann. § 62A-4a-410(1)-(3) (LexisNexis through 2008 2nd Spec. Sess.)

Except as provided below, any person, official, or institution participating in good faith in making a report, taking photographs or x-rays, assisting an investigator from the division, serving as a member of a child protection team, or taking a child into protective custody pursuant to this part, is immune from any liability, civil or criminal, that otherwise might result by reason of those actions.

This section does not provide immunity with respect to acts or omissions of a governmental employee except as provided in Title 63G, Chapter 7, Governmental Immunity Act of Utah.

The immunity described above does not apply if the person, official, or institution:

- Acted or failed to act through fraud or willful misconduct
- Intentionally or knowingly gave, upon a lawful oath or in any form allowed by law as a substitute for an oath, false testimony material to the issue or matter of inquiry in a judicial or administrative proceeding
- Intentionally or knowingly fabricated evidence or, except as provided in § 62A-4a-410(4), with a conscious disregard for the rights of others, failed to disclose evidence that:
  - Was known to the person, official, or institution
  - Was known by the person, official, or institution to be relevant to a material issue or matter of inquiry in a pending judicial or administrative proceeding if the person, official, or institution knew of the pending judicial or administrative proceeding
  - Was known by the person, official, or institution to be relevant to a material issue or matter of inquiry in a judicial or administrative proceeding, if disclosure of the evidence was requested of the employee by a party to the proceeding or counsel for a party to the proceeding

Utah Code Ann. § 62A-4a-410(4) (LexisNexis through 2008 2nd Spec. Sess.)
Immunity is not lost under § 62A-4a-410 if the person, official, or institution:

- Failed to disclose evidence because the person, official, or institution is prohibited by law from disclosing the evidence
- Pursuant to the provisions of 45 Code of Federal Regulation 164.502(g)(5) [pertaining to the disclosure of protected health information], refused to disclose evidence to a person who requested the evidence

- After refusing to disclose the evidence described above, complied with or responded to a valid court order or valid subpoena received by the person, official, or institution to disclose the evidence

Vermont
Vt. Stat. Ann. Tit. 33, § 4913(d)(1) (LexisNexis through Vt. 2008 Legis. Serv., Act 168)

Any person, other than a person suspected of child abuse, who in good faith makes a report to the department, shall be immune from any civil or criminal liability that might otherwise be incurred or imposed as a result of making a report.

Virgin Islands
V.I. Code Ann. Tit. 5, § 2537 (LexisNexis through 2008 Reg. Sess.)

Any person, official, or institution participating in good faith in any act permitted or required by this subchapter shall be immune from any civil or criminal liability that otherwise might result by reason of such actions.

Virginia
Va. Code Ann. § 63.2-1512 (LexisNexis through End of 2008 2nd Spec. Sess.)

Any person who makes a report or complaint pursuant to the reporting laws, takes a child into custody pursuant to law, or participates in a judicial proceeding resulting therefrom shall be immune from any civil or criminal liability in connection therewith, unless it is proven that such person acted in bad faith or with malicious intent.

Washington
Wash. Rev. Code Ann. § 26.44.060(1)-(2), (5) (LexisNexis through 6-30-08)

Any person participating in good faith in making a report pursuant to the reporting laws or testifying as to alleged child abuse or neglect in a judicial proceeding shall be immune from any liability arising out of such reporting or testifying.

A person convicted of knowingly making a false report shall not be immune from liability under this subsection.

An administrator of a hospital or similar institution or any licensed physician taking a child into custody pursuant to § 26.44.056 shall not be subject to criminal or civil liability for such taking into custody.

A person who, in good faith and without gross negligence, cooperates in an investigation arising as a result of a report made pursuant to this chapter shall not be subject to civil liability arising out of his or her cooperation. This subsection does not apply to a person who caused or allowed the child abuse or neglect to occur.

West Virginia
W. Va. Code Ann. § 49-6A-6 (LexisNexis through 8-18-08)

Any person, official, or institution participating in good faith in any act permitted or required by the reporting laws shall be immune from any civil or criminal liability that otherwise might result by reason of such actions.

Wisconsin
Wis. Stat. Ann. § 48.981(4) (LexisNexis through 11-6-08)

Any person or institution participating in good faith in making a report, conducting an investigation, ordering or taking photographs, or ordering or performing medical examinations of a child or an expectant mother pursuant to this section shall have immunity from any liability, civil or criminal, that results by reason of the action.

For the purpose of any civil or criminal proceeding, the good faith of any person reporting under this section shall be presumed.

The immunity provided herein does not apply to liability for abusing or neglecting a child or for abusing an unborn child.

Wyoming
Wyo. Stat. Ann. § 14-3-209 (LexisNexis through 9-1-08)

Any person, official, institution, or agency participating in good faith in any act required or permitted by the reporting laws is immune from any civil or criminal liability that might otherwise result by reason of the action.

For the purpose of any civil or criminal proceeding, the good faith of any person, official, or institution participating in any act permitted or required by the reporting laws shall be presumed.

End Notes

[1] 42 U.S.C.A. § 5106a(b)(2)(A)(iv).

[2] Mandatory reporters are persons who are required to report; voluntary reporters are not required to report but may choose to report. For a State-by-State summary of mandatory reporting laws, see Information Gateway's *Mandatory Reporters of Child Abuse and Neglect*:
www.childwelfare.gov/systemwide/laws. pdf

[3] The word *approximately* is used to stress the fact that the States frequently amend their laws; this information is current through December 2008. The States that provide for an assumption of "good faith" include Colorado, Illinois, Indiana, Maine, Michigan, Mississippi, Nevada, New Mexico, New York, North Carolina, North Dakota, Oklahoma, Pennsylvania, South Carolina, Tennessee, Wisconsin, and Wyoming.

[4] The States that do NOT provide this immunity are: Arkansas, California, Florida, Illinois, Massachusetts, Michigan, Minnesota, New York, North Dakota, Utah, Vermont, West Virginia, Wisconsin, and Wyoming.

[5] Alabama, Arizona, Colorado, Illinois, Iowa, Kansas, Louisiana, Maine, Maryland, Michigan, Missouri, Montana, Nebraska, Nevada, New Hampshire, North Carolina, North Dakota, Oklahoma, Pennsylvania, South Carolina, South Dakota, Tennessee, Texas, Utah, Washington, and Wisconsin.

[6] In 14 States (Arkansas, California, Colorado, Illinois, Indiana, Iowa, Maine, Missouri, Nevada, New York, Pennsylvania, South Dakota, Utah, Wisconsin), American Samoa, and Guam.

[7] In 12 States (Alabama, Arkansas, Colorado, Delaware, Illinois, Missouri, Nevada, New York, Pennsylvania, Utah, Virginia, Washington), American Samoa, and Guam.

[8] In 11 States (Arizona, Illinois, Louisiana, Montana, Nevada, New York, North Dakota, South Carolina, South Dakota, Tennessee, and Utah) and Puerto Rico.

[9] In 3 States: Delaware, Indiana, and Wisconsin.

[10] In 2 States: Iowa and Nevada.

[11] Immunity is denied for acting with malice or in bad faith in 10 States: Arizona, Colorado, Idaho, Indiana, Missouri, Montana, New Mexico, Ohio, Texas, and Virginia. Immunity is denied for knowingly making a false report in 10 States: California, Louisiana, Maine, Missouri, Montana, Nebraska, North Dakota, Ohio, Utah, and Washington.

[12] Alaska, Arizona, Colorado, Connecticut, Florida, Indiana, Louisiana, Massachusetts, Minnesota, North Dakota, South Dakota, Tennessee, Texas, Vermont, Washington, and Wisconsin.

INDEX

Q

R